HAND-BOOK
OF
CHINESE BUDDHISM
BEING
A SANSKRIT-CHINESE DICTIONARY
WITH
VOCABULARIES OF BUDDHIST TERMS

HAND-BOOK
OF
CHINESE BUDDHISM
BEING
A SANSKRIT-CHINESE DICTIONARY
WITH
VOCABULARIES OF BUDDHIST TERMS

In Pali, Singhalese, Siamese, Burmese, Tibetan, Mongolian and Japanesa

BY

ERNEST J. EITEL, M.A., PH, D. (TUBING)

Inspector of Schools, Hongkong

WITH

A CHINESE INDEX

BY

K. TAKAKUWA

SECOND EDITION

REVISED AND ENLARGED

GYAN

Published by

GYAN

Gyan Publishing House
5, Ansari Road
Daryaganj, New Delhi-110002
Phone: 011-47034999, 9811692060
E-mail: books@gyanbooks.com

Distribution Network
gyanbooks.com
India, USA, Canada, UK, Australia, France

ISBN : 978-81-212-3461-0 (PB)

First Published, 1904

2nd Impression 2020

Printed at: Gyan Press, Delhi.

Hand-Book of Chinese Buddhism
Author: Ernest J. Eitel

HAND-BOOK

OF

CHINESE BUDDHISM

BEING

A SANSKRIT-CHINESE DICTIONARY

WITH

VOCABULARIES OF BUDDHIST TERMS

in Pali, Singhalese, Siamese, Burmese, Tibetan, Mongolian and Japanese.

BY

ERNEST J. EITEL, M. A., PH. D. (TUBING)
Inspector of Schools, Hongkong

WITH

A CHINESE INDEX

BY

K. TAKAKUWA.

SECOND EDITION

REVISED AND ENLARGED

TOKYO,
SANSHUSHA.
1904

PREFACE TO THE FIRST EDITION.

No apology is needed for the appearance of this little book, though it is the first attempt of its kind. The student of Chinese religious literature finds himself at almost every step hampered by the continual recurrence of Sanskrit and other foreign terms embedded in the text, generally without a word of explanation. These form a series of vexatious riddles for a clue to which one has to go beyond the range of a Chinese library. This is especially the case with Buddhist works, many of which are simply translations from Sanskrit or Pâli or Tibetan originals. Hence arises the need of a Dictionary like the present which aims at smoothing the pathway to an understanding of Buddhism and of native religions influenced by it. That this is a real want is proved by the cordial response with which the announcement of this publication has been received.

No doubt the present volume has many defects and omissions, but the author feels confident that it will enable any one who has acquired an ordinary acquaintance with the Chinese language, to read and understand all the popular Buddhist classics, from the study of which Missionaries and others have been deterred by the inability of Chinese Pundits to give any assistance in that direction.

The author has not confined himself to the results of his own investigations, but has freely drawn upon all books within his reach from which information upon these topics could be gleaned. It is consequently his pleasant duty to acknowledge the help thus derived. He begs, in the first instance, to give the most cordial thanks to the venerable Nestor of Chinese

Sanskrit studies, STANISLAS JULIEN, whose most valuable works have been—with the exception of Chinese texts—the principal source of reference and freely resorted to on all occasions. The author is similarly indebted to the works of the lamented E. BURNOUF, whose premature death has been a great loss to the students of Buddhism. To these names he must add that of C. F. KOEPPEN, whose masterly exposition of the whole system of Buddhism has greatly assisted the present writer to understand many intricate details of its Chinese development.

The running title "Sanskrit Chinese Dictionary" is to be nderstood *cum grano salis.* A comparatively small number of other terms—chiefly referring to topographical subjects—have been inserted in the same list, because they occur in Chinese texts mixed up with Sanskrit terms, but are not sufficiently numerous to justify a separate alphabetical list.

As regards the Sanskrit and Pâli terms given in the book, the author has in almost every instance the excellent authority of Julien and Burnouf to fall back upon. The orthography employed in the transliteration of Sanskrit and Pâli is not that generally adopted by English scholars, but the French orthography of Julien and Burnouf is retained, because it is to the works of these two Savants that every student of Chinese Buddhism will constantly refer. Theirs are works which cannot be dispensed with and will not easily be superseded. On the other hand, he has not slavishly followed their spelling, but has substituted s' for the peculiarly French ç and likewise u for ou. No pronunciation is given for the Chinese renderings of Indian terms, as any such attempt, besides unduly swelling the bulk of the book, would have been comparatively useless; for the modorn systems of pronunciation—dialectically different in the different parts of China—deviate considerably from the mode of pronuniation which was in vogue when the respective Chinese equivalents for Sanskrit and Pâli terms were invented. To the language then spoken in China no modern Chinese dialect comes nearer in sound than the very Sanskrit or Pâli forms themselves.

PREFACE TO THE SECOND EDITION.

After an interval of more than fifteen years, the publishers called for a new edition to satisfy a small continuous demand.

The whole of the 1547 articles contained in the first edition have accordingly been re-written with a view to condense as well as to correct the subject matter of the book, in order to admit of an addition of 577 new articles without materially increasing the bulk of the volume or omitting any point of interest. The literature, the biography, and the philosophy of Chinese and Tibetan Buddhism have been specially laid under contribution to extend the usefulness of this Handbook, whilst the substitution of a Japanese Vocabulary in place of the former Chinese Index now makes the book a guide to the understanding of Japanese as well as Chinese Buddhism.

The author has freely used whatever recent works of reference were at his command, but he desires specially to acknowledge the help derived from Bunyiu Nanjio's Catalogue of the Buddhist Tripitaka (Oxford, 1883) and the courteous assistance of the Rev. J. L. Gordon, M. D. who furnished the materials to the above mentioned Japanese Vocabulary.

Hongkong, March, 1888.

E. J. E.

In translating the Chinese explanations of Sanskrit phrases, the author has aimed at verbal exactitude. Where the Chinese explanation is ambiguous, he did not substitute a clearer form of expression, considering it important to preserve the exact manner in which Chinese Buddhists, more than a thousand years before European Scholars had discovered Sanskrit, understood and explained Sanskrit phraseology.

When speaking of the founder of Buddhism, the term S'âkyamuni has been employed in accordance with Chinese usage, which prefers this title to that of Gautama. As the famous Chinese travellers Fah-hien and Hiuen-tsang had to be referred to very frequently, the Chinese symbols 法顯 and 玄奘 (see Mahâyâna dêva and Mokchadêva) for their names have been omitted for the sake of brevity.

With regard to the frequently recurring measures of distance, it ought to be understood that the value of a Chinese *li* has been differently computed in different periods of time, but it will be safe to count one Chinese *li* as equal to 329 French metres or about one-sixth of an English mile.

Hongkong, February 1st, 1870.

E. J. EITEL.

PART I.

A SANSKRIT-CHINESE DICTIONARY.

A

ABABA or HAHAVA 阿波波 The fourth of the eight cold hells peculiar to Northern Buddhism. The beings imprisoned there cannot produce any articulate sound but this one, Ababa, their tongues being frozen.

ABHÂSVARA (Pâli. Abhassara) lit. all brightness (â-bhâsvara) 阿婆嚩羅 explained by 光音 lit. light and sound (âbhâ-svara) or by 極光淨 lit. extreme light and purity. The sixth of the eighteen celestial worlds called Brahmalôkas.

ABHÂSVARAS (Pâli. Abhassaras. Tib. Od-gsal) lit. those whose nature is brightness, â-bhâsvaras, 阿婆嚩囉庶 or 阿會亘修天 or 阿陂亘羞天 explained by 光音天 lit. dêvas of light and sound (âbhâ-svara). The inhabitants of the third of the three celestial regions which from the second Dhyâna.

ABHAYA 無畏 lit. fearless, an epithet given to every Buddha.

ABHAYAGIRI 無畏山 lit. mount Fearless. A mountain on Ceylon with an ancient monastery in which Fa-hien (A. D. 400) found 5,000 priests.

ABHAYAGIRI VÂSINAH 阿跋邪祇釐住部 explained by 無畏山住部 lit. school of dwellers on mount Fearless, or by 菂山部 lit. school of the wooded mount, or by 蜜林部 lit. school of the secret forest. A schismatic philosophical School, a branch of the Sthâvirâh School. The adherents of this School called themselves disciples of Kâtyâyana and studied the doctrines of both the small and great conveyance (v. Triyâna).

ABHAYAM̃DADA 施無畏者 lit. he who procures removal of fear. A standing epithet of Kwan-yin (v. Avalokitês'vara.)

ABHIDHARMA (Pâli. Abhidhana. Singh. Abhidhamma. Tib. Tchos non pa) 阿毗達磨 or 阿鼻達磨 or 阿毗

曇 explained by 傳 lit. tradition, or by 勝法 lit. overcoming the law or conquering law, or by 無比法 lit. peerless law. Buddhaghôsa defines Abhidharma as that law (dharma) which goes beyond (abhi) the law, i.e. by-law.

ABHIDHARMA PIṬAKA 論藏 lit. the collection of discourses. One of the three divisions of the Buddhist canon (v. Tripiṭaka) comprehending all philosophical works. Its first compilation is ascribed to Mahâkas'yapa, but it does not as a whole belong to the primitive period of Buddhism. This section of the Chinese canon is subdivided into 1. 大乘論 or the Abhibharma of the Mahâyana School, 2. 小乘論 or the Abhidharma of the Hinâyâna School, and 3. 宋元續入藏諸論 or the discourses included in the canon during the Sung and Yuen dynasties (A.D. 960-1368).

ABHIDHARMA DHARMA SKANDHA PÂDA S'ÂSTRA 阿毗達磨法蘊足論 A philosophical work by Maudgalyâyana.

ABHIDHARMA DJÑÂNA PRASTHÂNA S'ÂSTRA 阿毗達磨法智論 or 阿毗曇八犍度論 A philosophical work ascribed to Kâtyâyana.

ABHIDHARMA HṚIDAYA S'ÂSTRA 阿毗曇磨心論 A philosophical work by Upadjita.

ABHIDHARMA KÔCHA KARAKÂ S'ÂSTRA 阿毗達磨俱舍論 or 俱舍雹論 A work by Saṁghabhadra.

ABHIDHARMA KÔCHA S'ÂSTRA 阿毗達磨俱舍論 A tract by Vasubandhu refuting the doctrines of the Vibhâchâ School.

ABHIDHARMÂMRITA S'ÂSTRA 阿毗達磨甘露味論 A philosophical work by Ghosha.

ABHIDHARMA PRAKARAṆA PÂDA S'ÂSTRA 衆事分阿毗達磨論 A philosophical treatise by Vasumitra.

ABHIDHARMA PRAKARAṆA S'ASANA S'ÂSTRA 顯宗論 A philosophical treatise by Sanghabhadra.

ABHIDHARMA PRAKÂS'A SÂDHANA S'ÂSTRA 阿毗達磨明證論 A philosophical work, attributed to Is'vara.

ABHIDHARMA S'ÂSTRA 對法論 A philosophical work by Vasubandhu.

ABHIDHARMÂVATARA S'ÂSTRA 入阿毗達磨論 A philosophical work by Ârya

Skandharatna.

ABHIDHARMA MAHÂVIBHÂCHÂ S'ÂSTRA 阿毗達磨毗婆沙論 A work consisting of 100,000 stanzas, the compilation of which is ascribed to the five hundred Arhats supposed to have formed the synod convoked by king Kanichka.

ABHIDHARMA VIDJÑÂNA KAYA PÂDA S'ÂSTRA 阿毗達磨識身足論 A dialectical treatise, denying the existence of both *ego* and *non-ego*, by Dêvas'arma.

ABHIDJÑA or CHADABHIDJÑÂS (Pâli. Âbhinna. Singh. Abhignyawa) 六通 or 六神通 Six supernatural talents, which S'âkyamuni acquired in the night before he became Buddha, and which every Arhat takes possession of by means of the fourth degree of Dhyâna. Most Chinese texts reckon six such talents, while the Singhalese know only five. Sometimes however only five are mentioned. Particulars see under Divyatchakchus, Divyas'rôtra, Riddhisâkchâtkriyâ, Purvânivasânusmriti djñâna, Paratchittadjñâna and As'ravakchaya.

ABHIRATI 歡喜國 lit. kingdom of joy. A fabulous realm situated East of our universe, the sphere of two Buddhas, Akchôbhya and Mêrukûta.

ABHISHEKAIR 啞撇釋該而 An exclamation ('consecrate me by sprinkling') addressed in prayers to Tathâgatas.

ABHYUTGATA RÂDJA 大高王 lit. the great august monarch. Name of the Kalpa in the course of which Subha vyûha is to be reborn as a Buddha.

ABÎDA v. AMITÂBHA.

ABRAHMA TCHARIYÂ VERAMANÎ 不婬慾 lit. no debauchery. The third of the ten rules for novices (v. S'ikchâpada), enjoining abstinence from violation of the vow of chastity with the following clause, 'lay-men ought to abstain at least from fornication, ecclesiastics from all sexual intercourse.'

ACHṬÂU VIMÔKCHAS. See under Vimôkcha.

ÂCHÂḌHA 頞沙荼 The first month of summer, corresponding to the time from the 16th day of the 4th Chinese moon to the 15th day of the 5th moon.

ACHṬA BUDDHAKA NÂMA MAHÂYÂNA SÛTRA 佛說八部佛名經 Title of a book.

ACHṬA DAS'Â KÂS'A S'ÂSTRA 十八空論 Title of a book by Nâgârdjuna, introduced in China by Paramârtha, A. D. 557-689.

ACHṬA DAS'A NIKÂYA S'ÂSTRA 八十陪論 Title of a book.

ACHṬADAS'A NÂRAKA SÛTRA 佛說十八泥犂經 Title of a book.

ACHṬA MAṆḌALAKA SÛTRA 大乘八大曼拏羅經 Title of a book.

ACHṬA SÂHASRIKÂ PRADJÑÂ PARAMITÂ SÛTRA 聖八千頌般若波羅蜜多一百八名眞實 Title of a book.

ADBHUTA DHARMA 阿浮達摩 explained by 未曾有 lit. what never took place before, i.e. marvels. A section of Buddhist literature comprising books on miraculous events.

ADHIMÂTRA KÂRUṆIKA 大悲 lit. great mercy. One of the Mahâbrahmânas who appeared from the South East to worship Mahâbhidjña djñânâ bhibhû.

ADHIMUKTI (Pâli. Adhimutti. Tib. Mos-pa) lit. attention, 阿提目多 or 阿地目帝 or 阿提目多伽 explained by 善思惟 lit pious thoughtfulness; as an example of which is mentioned the lighting of a lamp fed with the oil of three flowers (Sandal, Sôma and Tchampaka) and the placing this lamp before the images of the Triratna. According to Singhalese and Tibetan sources, the meaning of adhimukti is inclination of the will. In the Lalitavistara (q. v.) its meaning seems to be 'intelligence.' Burnouf translates it sometimes by 'confidence.'

ADHYÂTMA VIDYÂ 內明 lit. the esoteric luminary. One of the 五明 Pantcha Vidyâ S'astras (q. v.)

ADINNÂDÂNÂ VÊRAMANÎ 不偷盜 lit. abstinence from theft and robbery. See Sikchpâda.

ADJÂTAS'ATRU (Pâli. Adjâtasattu. Singh. Aja'sat. Tib. MassKjessdGra) or Kchemadars'in 阿闍多設咄路 or 阿闍世王 explained by 未生怨 lit. an enemy before he was born, or no enmity in the heart, or (as the Tibetans explain it) 'not creating himself any enemies.' A king of Magadha, son of king Bimbisâra, originally one of S'âkyamuni's most formidable opponents. Converted to Buddhism, he became famous for his liberality in almsgiving. He died 24 years after S'âkyamuni (about 519 B. Ch.) His son and successor was Udâyi. There is a daughter of Adjâtas'atru mentioned under the name 阿術達 Asuddharda According to a

Tibetan legend, an infant son of Adjâtas'atru was kidnapped, exposed at the roadside and finally made king of Tibet under the name Njakritsanpo (研乞嘌贊普). The Mongols call the latter Sseger Ssandalitu or Küsühu schiretu.

ADJÂTAS'ATRU KAUKṚITTYA VINODANA MAHÂYÂNA SÛTRA 佛說阿闍世王經 Title of a book.

ADJITA (Pâli. Adjita, Singh. Ajita) 阿逸多 or 阿耆多 or 阿底多 or 阿制多 explained by 無能勝 lit. invincible. A title which S'âkyamuni gave to Mâitrêya, and which is now the standing epithet of the latter.

ADJITA KÊS'A KAMBALA (Pali. Adjita Kesa Kambali. Singh. Ajitá Kása Kambala) lit. the invincible one, who wears his hair for a covering 阿耆多舍欽婆羅 One of the six Tirthyas, the head of a brahminical ascetic sect, whose favourite dogma was the impermanency, the continuous self-destruction and consequent unreality of all things.

ÂDJÑÂTA KÂUṆḌINYA or ÂDJÑÂNA KÂUṆḌINYA (Tib Koun ches Kâuṇḍinya) 阿若憍陳如 explained as an automat (阿若 Adjñâna) of the Kâuṇḍinya (憍陳如) family. A famous disciple of S'âkyamuni, more commonly quoted as Kauṇḍinya (q.v.).

ADJITAVATÎ v. HIRANYAVATI.

ADYÂCHAYASANTCHODA SÛTRA 發覺淨心經 Title of a book.

ÂGAMA 阿伽摩 or 阿笈摩 explained by 無比法 lit. peerless law, or by 教法 lit. system of teaching. A section of Buddhist literature unknown to Nepaulese Buddhism. Like the Singhalese, the Chinese Buddhists divide the Sûtras of the small conveyance-school (v. Hinayâna) into the following four classes (四含). (1). Dîrghâgamas (Singh. digha nikayo or dik sangi) 長阿含 long âgamas; compilations treating on cosmogony. (2) Madhyamâgamas (Singh. majjhima nikayo or medun sangi) 中阿含 lit. middling âgamas; works on metaphysics. (3.) Samyuktâgamas (Singh. sanyutta nikayo or sanyut sangi) 雜阿含 lit. mixed âgamas; treatises on ecstatic contemplation. (4.) Ekôttarâgamas (Singh. anguttara nikayo or angotra sangi) 增一阿含

lit. numerical âgamas; general compilations, the subject matter being arranged numerically.

AGNI or AKNI 阿耆尼 Name of a kingdom in Central Asia, situated to the North of lake Lop.

AGNI DHÂTU SAMÂDHI 火界定 the contemplation of the world on fire, a degree of ecstatic contemplation (v. Samâdhi.)

AGNIVÂS'AYANA (Pâli. Aggivessâyana). v. DÎRGHA-NAKHA.

AGRA PRADÎPA DHÂRAṆÎ 東方最勝燈王神咒經 Title of a book.

AGURU (Beng. Agur. Arab. Ayalugi. Pers. Ayalur chee or Oud Hindee. Tib. Akaru) literally not heavy 惡揭嚕 explained by 沉水香 lit. perfume immersed in water. Agallochum or lignum Aloes, the decayed root of the Aquilaria agallocha. The Ahalim or Ahaloth of the Hebrews.

AGURU SÛTRA 阿鳩留經 Title of a book.

AHAHA or HAHAVA 嘔侯侯 The fifth of the eight cold hells (unknown to Southern Buddhism), so called because the cold is there so intense that the damned spirits cannot stir nor speak, whilst the cold air, passing through their throats, produces a sound like Ahaha.

ÂHARA ÂHARA MAMÂYUH SANTÂRAṆI 啞曷囉啞曷囉馬麻藹由而傘塔囉尼 An exclamation ('give me, give me, old age, oh protector') addressed in prayers to Tathâgatas.

AHIKCHÊTRA or AHIKHATRÂ 阿醯掣怛羅 An ancient city and kingdom in Central India, on the northern bank of the Kâlînadî, north of Pañtchâla (the present Duab).

AHÔRÂTRA 一日一夜 lit. one day and one night. A division of time.

AIS'VARIKAS 阿說羅部 A theistic School of Nepaul, which set up Adi Buddha as a supreme divinity. It never found any followers in China.

AKANICHṬHA (Pâli. Akanistaka. Tib. Og min) 阿迦尼瑟吒 or 阿迦尼吒 explained by 究色竟 lit. the final limits of the world of desire. The last of the eighteen Brahmalôkas, called Akanis'ta *i. e,* the highest. Originally only sixteen Brahmalôkas were known. Northern Buddhism added two, which are called 福生 happy birth and 福愛 happy love. Singhalese Buddhists count only sixteen.

AKANICHṬHAS 色究竟天 The dêvas inhabiting the final limits of the world of desire. The inhabitants of the ninth and last region of the fourth Dhyâna, appropriately called 'the highest ones.'

ÂKÂS'AGARBHA SÛTRA 虛空孕菩薩經 Title of a book, translated by Djñânagupta, A. D. 587.

ÂKÂS'AGARBHA BODHISATTVA DHÂRÂṆI SÛTRA 虛空藏菩薩神咒經 Title of a book, translated by Dharmamitra, A. D. 420—479.

ÂKÂS'A PRATICHṬHITA 虛空住 lit. dwelling in empty space. A fabulous Buddha living somewhere to the South of our universe. He was at a former time the fifth son of Mahâbhidjña djñânâ bhibhû.

AKCHARAMATI NIRDÊS'A NÂMA MAHÂYANA SÛTRA 阿差末菩薩經 Title of a book.

AKCHAYAMATI 無盡意菩薩 lit the Bodhisattva of exhaustless meaning. A fictitious being to whom S'âkyamuni addressed a series of remarks about Avalokitês'vara.

AKCHAYAMATI PARIPṚITCHTCH'Â 無盡意菩薩會 Title of a book, translated by Bodhirutchi, A.D. 618—907.,

AKCHÔBHYA (Tib. Hkhrougs pa) 阿芻鞞耶 or 阿閦婆 or 阿閦 explained by 無動 lit. motionless. 1. A numeral term equal to 1 followed by 17 ciphers. 2. A fabulous Buddha mentioned as a contemporary of S'âkyamuni and said to reside in a realm called Abhirati. See also under Djñânâkara.

AKCHÔBHYASYA TATHÂGATASYA MAHÂYÂNA SÛTRA 阿閦佛國經 Title of a book.

AKINTCHAVYÂYATANA 無所有處定 lit. contemplation of a state of having absolutely nothing. A degree of ecstatic meditation (定). See Samâdhi.

AKLÊS'A (Tib. Non mongs med) 無濁 lit. without corruption. A cognomen of Asita.

ALNI or ARNI 阿利尼 Name of a kingdom, which formed part of ancient Tokharâ, situated near to the sources of the Oxus, to the North of Munkan.

ÂMALAKA or ÂMALAKARKA 阿摩落果 or 阿摩落伽果 explained by 寶瓶 lit. precious vase. The fruit of the Phyllanthus emblica or the Mirobolana emblica, used as a medicine.

AMITÂBHA (variations of the same name are Amita, Abida,

Amitâya, Amitâyus, Amitarus'i. Tib. Od dPag med or Hopamé) 阿彌陀婆耶 or 阿彌陀 or 彌陀 or 大彌陀 explained by 無量壽 lit. boundless age. This explanation rests on a misconception of the original meaning of Amitâbha *i.e.* boundless light, but the latter idea is preserved in one of the many titles of this fabulous Buddha 無量光明 lit. boundless light. Other titles are 放大光明 lit. diffusing great light, 西天教主 lit. sovereign teacher of the Western Heaven, 西方接引 lit. guide to the West, 大慈大悲 lit. great mercy and sympathy, 本師和尙 lit. original teacher Upâdhyâya, 法界藏身 lit. embodiment of the sphere of the law. As the derivation of the term itself suggests, Amita was originally conceived of as impersonal, as the ideal of boundless light. Considering also the mention made of his name in a list of one thousand fictitious Buddhas which reminds one of the thousand Zarathustras of the Persians, and which was propagated by the Mahâyâna-school (about 300 A.D.), it is but natural, in the absence of authentic information as to the origin of this dogma, to suppose that it may have been originated by Persian or Manichaean ideas influencing the Buddhism of Cashmere and Nepaul. For it must have been from one of these countries that the dogma of Amita reached China, when a priest from Tokhara brought (147 A. D.) the first Amitâbha Sûtra to China It is remarkable that the Chinese travellers Fahien and Hiuen-tsang omit all mention of it. Southern Buddhism knows no Amita, neither are there any traces of a Brahminical or Vêdic origin of this doctrine. The most ancient Sûtras brought to China make no mention of it, and the first that alludes to Amita, the Amitâyus Sûtra, translated A. D. 148—170, was, like others of the same class, already lost when the well-known catalogue K'ai-yuenlu was compiled, A.D. 730. When the so-called Lotus-school or Pure-land-school 蓮花宗 or 淨土宗 began to flourish, and the peculiarly poetic tenets of this school, referring to a paradise in the West, began to influence the common people, Amita became the favourite of Chinese Buddhists. He is now by far the most popular Buddha in China.

There are some confused traditions as regards the antecedents of Amita. One account describes him as an incarnation of the ninth son of Mahâbhidjña djñânâbhibhu (q.v.), whilst another account alleges that he was the second son of a Tchakravarti of the lunar race and, like his father, called 憍尸迦 (Kaus'ika). It is further alleged that he was converted by a Buddha called 世自在王 (Sahês'vararâdja), that he embraced the religious life, made certain vows and was reborn as a Buddha in Sukhâvatî (q.v.), where Avalôkitês'vara and Mahâsthânaprapta joined him.

According to the teaching of the Mahâyâna School, Amita is looked upon as the celestial reflex of S'âkyamuni, and as having, by dint of contemplation (dhyâna), produced a spiritual son, viz., Padmapâni (i. e. Avalôkitês'vara). The Nepaulese doctrine, of a primordial Buddha (Âdi-Buddha) having procreated Amita, has not been adopted by Chinese Buddhism.

The doctrine of Amitâbha and his paradise in the West (v. Sukhâvatî) is, strictly speaking, no contradiction of the theory of Nirvâṇa, for it does not interrupt the circle of transmigration, though it offers to the devotee of Amitâbha aeons of rest. But the popular mind does, indeed, understand his paradise to be the practical equivalent of Nirvâṇa, the haven of final redemption from the eddies of transmigration.

AMITÂBHA VYÛHA SÛTRA 佛說阿彌陀經 Title of a translation, made A.D. 222—280.

AMITÂYUR VYÛHA SÛTRA 佛說大乘無量壽莊嚴經 Title of a translation by Fahien, A.D. 982—1,001.

AMITÂYUSHA VYÛHA 無量壽如來會 Title of a translation by Bodhirutchi, A.D. 618—907.

ÂMLA or **ÂMLIKA** 菴弭羅 The Tamarindus indica.

AMOGHA or **AMOGHAVADJRA** 阿目佉跋折羅 explained by 不空金剛 lit. the vadjra which is not hollow. A S'ramaṇa of northern India, a follower of the mystic teachings attributed to Samantabhadra. He followed his teacher, Vadjrabodhi, to China (A.D. 719) and eventually succeeded him in the leadership of the Yogâtchârya School (A.D. 732). From a journey through India and Ceylon (A.D. 741—746), he brought to China more than 500 Sûtras and S'âstras previously unknown in China. He introduced a new alphabet for the transliteration of Sanskrit and published 108 works, mostly translations. He introduced the All-souls-festival (v. Ullambana), so universally popular in China to the present day. He is the chief representative of Buddhist mysticism in China, which he succeeded in spreading widely through the patronage of three successive emperors, viz. Hiuen-tsung (A.D. 713—756), who prohibited his retiring to India (A.D. 749), Sutsung (A. D. 756—763), who gave him the title Tripiṭaka Bhadanta (大廣智三藏), and Taitsung (A.D. 763—780), who gave him, when he died (A.D. 774), the rank of a Minister of State and a posthumous title. He is commonly referred to as 不空 (Amogha).

AMOGHA PÂS'ARDDHIMANTRA HṚIDAYA SÛTRA 不空羂索神咒心經 Title of a translation, by Hiuentsang, A.D. 659.

AMOGHAPÂS'A DHÂRAṆÎ SÛTRA 不空羂索陀羅尼經 Title of a translation, A.D. 618—907.

AMOGHA PÂS'A HṚIDAYA MANTRA RÂDJA SÛTRA 不空羂索心咒王經 Title of a translation by Ratnatchinta, A.D. 693.

AMOGHAPÂS'A HṚIDAYA SÛTRA 不空羂索咒心經 Title of a translation by Bodhirutchi, A.D. 618—907.

AMOGHA PÂS'A KALPARÂDJA 不空羂索神變眞言經 Title of a translation by Bodhirutchi, A. D. 707—709.

AMOGHA PÂS'A MANTRA SÛTRA 佛說不空羂索咒經 Title of a translation by Djñânagupta and others, A.D. 587.

ÂMRA or ÂMRAKA or ÂMALÂ 菴羅 or 菴摩羅 or 阿末羅 A tree, the fruit of which is described as a cross between a plum and a pear. The mango tree, which is also called Mahâpala (大婆羅), from the Malay rendering of which the word mango is derived.

ÂMRADÂRIKÂ or ÂMRAPÂLÎ or ÂMBAPÂLÎ (lit. the guardian of the Âmra tree) 菴婆羅女 or 菴摩羅女 lit. the Âmra girl. A female devotee who presented to S'âkyamuni the Âmravana garden (柰園 lit. plum garden). Legends affirm that she was born of an Âmra tree. See also Djîvaka.

ÂMRADÂRIKÂ SÛTRA 柰女經 Title of a book.

AMRITA (Tib. Bdoud rtsi) 啞密哩達 or 啞瞇哩打 explained by 甘露 lit. sweet dew. The ambrosian food of the immortals. In Hindoostani the guava fruit is now called amrut.

AMRITÔDANA RÂDJA (Tib. Bdoud rtsi zas Pali. Amitôdana) 甘露飯王 lit. the king who feasted on ambrosia. A prince of Magadha, father of Anuruddha and Bhadrika, uncle of S'âkyamuni.

ANABHRAKA (Tib. Sprin med) lit. cloudless 福愛 lit. happy love. The second region of the fourth Dhyâna (q. v.), inhabited by dêvas called Anabhrakas. The eleventh Brahmalôka.

ANÂGÂMIN (Singh. Anágámi. Tib. Phyir mi hong ba) 阿那含 explained by 不還 lit. not returning, or by 不來 lit. not coming i. e. not to be reborn into the world of desire. The third degree of saintship, the third class of Âryas, embracing all those who are no more liable to be reborn as men, though they are to be born once more as dêvas, when they will forthwith become Arhats and enter Nirvâna.

ANAKCHARA GRANTHAKA ROTCHANA GARBHA SÛTRA. Title of three translations, viz. 大乘離文字普光明藏經 by Divâkara, A.D. 683; 大乘徧照光明藏經 by Divâkara, A. D. 618—907; 無字寶篋經 by Bodhirutchi, A.D. 386—534.

ÂNANDA (Tib. Kun dgah bo) 阿難陀 or 阿難 explained by 歡喜 lit. joy. A son of Drônôdana, called Ânanda (joy), because he was born at the moment when S'âkyamuni attained to Buddhaship. Under the teaching of the latter, Ânanda became an Arhat, famed especially for his memory or experience (多聞). The compilation and edition of the earliest Sûtras is attributed to him. Before his death (B.C. 866 or 463), he appointed S'ânavâsika as his successor and dispatched his second disciple, Madhyântika, to convert Cashmere. Ânanda is to re-appear on earth as Buddha Sâgara varadhara buddhi vikriditâbhidjña.

ÂNANDAPURA 阿難陀補羅 A kingdom and city in western India, N.E. of Gujerat; the present Bârnagar, near Kurree. It was one of the strongholds of the Jain sect.

ANANTAMATI 無量意 lit. boundless meaning. The third son of Tchandra sûrya pradîpa.

ANANTAMUKHA SÂDHAKA DHÂRAṆÎ. Title of eight translations, viz. 佛說無量門微密持經 A. D. 222—

280; 佛說出生無量門持經 by Buddhabhadra, A.D. 317—420; 阿難陀佉尼訶離陀隣尼經 by Buddhas'ânta A.D. 286—534; 佛說無量門破魔陀羅尼經 A. D. 420—479; 阿難陀目佉尼訶離陀經 by Guṇabhadra, A.D. 420—479; 舍利佛陀羅尼經 by Saṁghapâla, A.D. 502—557; 佛說一向出生菩薩經 by Djñânagupta. A.D. 585; 出生無邊門陀羅尼經 A.D. 618—907.

ANANTAMUKHA VINIS'ODHANA NIRDÊS'A 無邊莊嚴會 Title of a translation by Bodhirutchi, A.D. 618—907.

ANANTA TCHÂRITRA 無邊行 lit. unlimited action. A fictitious Bodhisattva who rose out of the earth.

ANÂTHA PINDIKA or ANÂTHA PIṆḌADA (Pâli. Anepida. Tib. Mgon med zas sbyin (lit. one who gives away his own without keeping (anâtha) a mouth full (pinda) for himself, 阿那他擯茶揭利訶跋底給 (anâtha piṇḍada grihapati), explained by 獨孤善 lit. supporter of destitutes and orphans, or by 善施 lit. a pious donor. A wealthy householder (v. Grihapati) of S'râvastî, famous for his liberality. See also Sudatta and Vâis'âkha.

ANÂTMÂ or ANÂTMAKA (Tib. stong pa nyid) 無我 lit. no ego. A metaphysical term designating self-inanition, vacuity, impersonality, as the aim and end of philosophic speculation.

ANAVADATA v. Anavatapta.

ANAVANATÂMITA VÂIDJYAYANTA 常立勝幡 lit. maintaining aloft the victorious banner. Name of the realm in which Ânanda is to re-appear as Buddha.

ANAVATAPTA or ANAVADATA (Pâli. Anâtattha. Singh. Anótatta. Siam. Anôdatasa. Tib. Ma dros pa. Mong. Mapam dalai) 阿那婆達多 or 阿那婆答多 or 阿耨達 or 阿耨 or 阿那達 explained by 無熱惱池 lit. the lake without heat or trouble. A lake on a high plateau, N. of the Himâlaya. It is said to be square, measuring 50 yôdjanas in circumference, and sending forth from each side a large river, viz. in the East the S'itâ, in the South the Gangâ, in the West the Sindhu and in the North the Vakchu. What is meant, is perhaps the Manaṣarovana lake (Lat.

31° N. Long. 81° 3.), which at certain seasons overflows and forms one lake with lake Roodh (ten miles distant), which latter sends forth one river, the S'atadru. The sources of three other rivers, vix. Bhramaputra, Ganges and Oxus lie within a short radius around those two lakes. Hiuentsang (incorrectly) identifies the Anavatapta lake with lake Sirikol (Lat. 38°20 N.) on the plateau of Pamir.

ANAVATAPTA NÂGARÂDJA PARIPRITCHTCH'Â SÛTRA 三昧弘道廣顯定意經 Title of a translation by Dharmarakcha, A.D. 308.

ANDHRA 案達羅 A kingdom in southern India, situated between the Krishnâ and Godavarî, with the capital Viñgila (q. v.).

AÑGÂRAKA (Tib. Mig dmár) 鴦哦囉迦 explained by 火星 lit. fire star. The planet Mars.

AÑGIRASA 鴦儗囉 An ancient Richi, an ancestor of S'âkyamuni.

ANGULIMÂLÎIA (Singh. Angulimála) 盎窶利魔羅 or 鴦掘魔 explained by 指鬘 lit. rosary of fingerbones. A S'ivaitic sect of fanatics who practised assassination as a religious act. One of them was converted by S'âkyamuni.

AÑGULIMÂLÎYA SÛTRA 鴦掘魔羅經 Title of a translation by Guṇabhadra, A.D. 420—479.

AÑGULIPARVA 指節 lit. finger-joint. A measure, the 24th part of a fore arm (Hasta).

ANILAMBHA SAMÂDHI 無緣三昧 lit. the cause-less samâdḥi. A degree of Samâdhi (q. v.).

ANIRUDDHA (Tib. Mah bgags pa) 阿魋樓馱 or 阿尼律陀 or 阿尼盧 or 阿那律 explained by 無貧 lit. not poor, and by 無滅 lit. not extinguished. Name of a disciple of S'âkyamuni, who being himself 'not poor', supported, during a famine, many Pratyêka Buddhas, which charitable act caused among the dêvas a joy which is, to the present day, 'not extinguished.' He is to reappear on earth as Buddha Samantaprabhâsa. See also Anuruddha.

ANITYA v. Trîvidyâ.

ANS'UVARMMA 鴦輸伐摩 explained by 光胄 lit. bright helmet. A King of ancient Nepaul, descendant of the Litchhavis (q. v.), author of the S'abdavidyâ S'âstra.

ANTÂRABHAVA SÛTRA 中陰經 Title of a translation. A.D. 384—417.

ANTARAVÂSAKA 安陁會 explained by 裙 lit. skirt. A sort of waistcoat, worn by priests instead of a shirt.

ANTIMA DÊHA DHÂRIṆO 住是最後身 lit. dwelling for the last time in a body. The last stage in the process of transmigration, preceding Nirvâṇa.

AṆU 阿耨 or 細塵 lit. fine dust. A division of a yôdjana (q.v.), equal to 7 atoms of dust.

ANUPADHIS'ÊCHA 無餘 lit. without remnants. Immateriality, as an attribute of those who have entered Nirvâṇa.

ANUPAPÂDAKA or AUPAPÂDUKA (Pâli. Opapâtika. Singh. Aupapâtika. Tib. Brdzus te skyes pa) 生化 lit. birth by transformation. One of the Tchatur yôni (q. v.), viz. supernatural birth (from a lotusflower, etc.) in full maturity, such as is ascribed to Buddhas and Bodhisattvas, the latter coming, from Tuchita, by this birth into the world.

ANURUDDHA 耨樓陀阿 explained by 如意 lit. conformity, and by 無貧 lit. not poor. The latter explanation properly refers to Aniruddha (q. v.) with whom Aniruddha is identified in Chinese texts. The former explanation is based on a derivation of the term from anu (lit. conformity). Anuruddha was a son of Amritôdana and therefore cousin german to S'âkyamuni, at whose death he was present.

ANUTTARA BODHI 無上等覺 lit. unrivalled intelligence.

ANUTTARA DHARMA 無上法 lit. peerless law.

ANUTTARA SAMYAK SAM̃BODHI lit. unexcelled perfect intelligence 阿耨多羅三藐三菩提 explained by 無上 unexcelled (anuttara) 正偏 correct equality (samyak) and 正道 correct intelligence (sam̃bodhi). An epithet of every Buddha, otherwise explained as signifying untarnished (a—) and unparalleled (nuttara) correct view (sam) and complete wisdom (myak) with complete possession of the highest sentiments (sambodhi).

APALÂLA 阿波邏羅 The nâga (guardian spirit) of the source of the S'ubhavastu (q. v.), converted by S'âkyamuni shortly before the latter's death.

APARADJITA DHÂRAṆÎ. Title of three translations, viz. 佛說無能勝旛王陀羅尼經 (see also Dhvadjâgrakeyûradhâraṇî), 無能勝大明心陀羅尼經 and 無能勝大明陀羅尼經.

APARAGODÂNA or GHÔDHANYA (Siam. Amarakô Jana Thavib. Tib. Noub Kyi va lang spyod 啞呢囉孤答尼耶 or 阿鉢唎瞿陀尼 or 瞿陀尼 or 瞿耶尼 or 俱耶尼 explained in Chinese texts as 'the continent in the West (apara) where the people use cattle (go) in place of money(dâna)'. One of the four continents of every universe, situated W. of Sumêru (q.v.), circular in shape, the faces of the inhabitants being also circular.

APARIMITÂYUS SÛTRA 佛說無量壽經 A book concerning Amitâbha, translated by Saṁghavarman, A.D. 252.

APARIMITÂYUS SÛTRA S'ÂSTRA 無量壽經優波提舍 A treatise by Vasubandhu (q.v.) on the doctrine of Amitâbha, translated by Bodhirutchi, A.D. 529.

APARÎVARTYA v. Avaivartya, and Avivartita.

APASMÂRAKA 阿跋摩羅 A class of demons hostile to men.

APKRITSNA SAMÂDHI v. Asakrit Samâdhi.

APRAMÂṆÂBHA (Pâli. Apramana) 無量光 lit. unlimited light. The fifth of the sixteen Brahmalôkas.

APRÂṆÂBHAS (Tib. Tshad med od) 無量光 lit. unlimited. The second region of the second Dhyâna, inhabited by dêvas.

APRAMÂṆAS'UBHA 無量淨 lit. unlimited purity. The second region of the third Dhyânas, inhabited by dêvas.

APSARAS (Tib. Lhahi bou mo) 天女 lit. female dêvas. Attendants on the regents of sun and moon, wives of Gandharvas, and other female dêvas.

ÂPTANÊTRAVANA 得眼林 lit. the forest of the recovered eyes.

ARADJAVARTAN 白象 lit. a white elephant. The form in which S'âkyamuni entered the womb of Mahâmâya. The immaculate path i.e. the immaculate conception (of Buddha).

ÂRAṆYA v. Dharmarakcha.

ÂRAṆYAKAḤ (Pâli. Âraññakangga. Tib. Dgon pa pa) 阿練若 explained by 寂靜處 lit. living in retirement and stillness; or 阿蘭陀 or 阿蘭攘 or 練若 explained by 無諍聲 lit. no sound of strife.. General designation of ascetics and especially hermits, of whom three classes are distinguished, v. Dharma Araṇyakaḥ, Mâtanga Âraṇyakah and Dânataka Âraṇyakaḥ.

ÂRATA (or Arâḍa) KALÂMA (Tib. Sgyou rtsal ches kyi bou ring hphour 阿藍迦蘭 or 阿藍迦 One of the first teachers of S'âkyamuni.

ARBUDA 頞浮陀 The first of the eight cold hells, where the cold chaps (arbuda) the skin of the culprits.

ARHÂN or ARHAT (Singh. and Burm. Rahat or Rahân. Siam. Arahāng. Tib. Dgra btshom pa. Mong. Daini daruksan or Chutuktu) 阿羅漢 or 羅漢 explained by 佛果 lit. fruit of Buddha (v. Buddhaphalam). The original meaning of Arhat (worthy) is overlooked by Chinese commentators, who prefer the derivation ari-hat (destroyer of the enemy). The following two explanations are most common, viz., 殺賊 destroying the thief i.e. conquering all passions, and 不生 exempt from birth i.e. from transmigration. A third, less common, explanation is perhaps based on the original meaning of Arhat, viz, 應供 lit. deserving worship. The Arhat is the perfected Ârya, and the state of Arhat can accordingly be attained only by passing through the different degrees of saintship (v. Ârya). Arhatship implies, strictly speaking, possession of supernatural powers and successive promotion to Buddhaship and Nirvâṇa. But in popular parlance the term Arhat simply means an advanced disciple of S'âkyamuni. The Chinese text of the Saddharma pundarîka employs, accordingly, the term Arhat occasionally as a synonyme of S'ravaka (q. v.) and constantly includes under it the largest circle of 1200 disciples of S'âkyamuni as well as the smaller ones of 500 and of 18 disciples. At present, the term Arhân or Lo-hân (羅漢) is used as a designation of all famous disciples of S'âkyamuni, but denotes more especially those 500 Arhats who are to reappear on earth as Buddhas, each assuming then the title Samantha prabhâsa.

There are some attributes of every Buddhist saint which are often used as synonymes for the term Arhat, viz., 殺賊 destroying the thief (Kchinas'rava) and 不學 exempt from study (As'âikcha opp. 學者 one who studies, S'âikcha).

ARITÎ v. Hâritî.

ARTHAS'IDDHI v. Sarvârtthasiddha.

ARTHAVINIS'TCHAYA DHARMAPARIYÂYA 佛說法乘義決定經 Title of a translation by Suvarṇa Dhâraṇî, about A.D. 1113.

ARUṆA 阿路猱 or 阿盧那 A mountain (said to increase and decrease periodically), S. of Sphîtavaras (q.v.) in the Punjab.

ARÛPADHATU or ARÛPAVATCHARA (Tib. Gzugs med pai khams) 無色界 lit. the world without form (desire). The third of the three worlds (v. Trâilôkya), towering above the Mêru. That world in which there is neither form nor sensation, comprising four heavens and forming the antechamber of Nirvâṇa.

ÂRYA (Pâli. Ariya. Singh. Arya. Tib. Hphags pa. Mong. Chutuktu). 阿畧 or 阿犁耶 or 阿利耶 or 阿羅訶 explained by 聖 lit. holy or by 尊者 lit. the Reverend. A title given to those who have mastered the Âryani satyâni (q.v.) and thereby entered the Ârya imârga i. e. the Ârya's path to Nirvâṇa. This path, having four stations, is called 四道 the fourfold path. Those four stations, being accessible only through personal growth in holiness, are called 四果 the four fruits. Corresponding with this distinction of four stations or four fruits, and identic with it in meaning, is a distinction of 四有 four beings or 四部 four classes of Âryas. For particulars regarding this distinction, see under S'rotâpanna, Sakridâgâmin, Anâgâmin and Arhat. The title Ârya is also an epithet of every patriarch.

ÂRYA DÂSA 阿梨耶馱娑 or 聖使 lit. holy apostle. A famous representative of the Mahâsaṃghikaḥ School.

ÂRYA DJAMBHALA DJALENDRA YATHÂLABDA KALPA SÛTRA 聖寶藏神儀軌經 Title of a translation by Dharmadêva, A. D. 960-1127.

ÂRYAGAGANA GANDJA PARIPRITCHTCH'Â 百千頌大集經地藏菩薩請問法身讚 Title of a book (abstract).

ÂRYA NÂGÂRDJUNA BODHISATTVA SUHṚILLEKA. Title of three translations, viz. 龍樹菩薩爲禪陀迦法要偈 by Guṇavarman, A.D. 431; 勸發諸王要偈

by Saṁghavarman, A.D. 434; and 龍樹菩薩誡王頌, A.D. 700-712.

ÂRYA PÂRS'VIKA v. Pârs'va.

ÂRYASATYÂNI or ÂRYÂNI-SATYANI or TCHATURSATYA 四諦 lit. four dogmas. Four truths, the mastering of which constitutes an Ârya (q.v.). They are, (1.) Dukḥa 苦諦 lit. the dogma of misery, viz., that misery is a necessary concomitant of sentient existence; (2.) Samudaya 聚諦 lit. the dogma of accumulation, viz., that misery is intensified by the passions; (3.) Nirôdha 滅諦 lit. the dogma of extinction, viz., that the extinction of passion (and existence) is practicable; (4.) Mârga 道諦 lit. the dogma of the path, viz., that there is a path (v. Arya) leading to the extinction of passion (and existence).

ÂRYASÊNA 阿稚耶斯那 or 聖軍 lit. holy army. One of the principal representatives of the Mahâsaṁghikaḥ School (about A.D. 600).

ÂRYASIṀHA 師子尊者 or 師子比丘 lit. the lion-Bhikchu. The 24th patriarch, a Brahman by birth, a native of Central India. He died a martyr's death in Cashmere (A.D. 259).

ÂRYAS'ÛRA 聖勇 lit. Ârya the brave, or 大勇 lit. the great Brave. An Indian Buddhist, author of several works.

ÂRYATÂRÂ or SRAGDHARÂ 阿唎耶多羅 A female divinity of the Tantra School.

ÂRYA TÂRABHADRA NAMÂ ACHṬAS'ATAKAM. Title of three books viz., (1.) 聖多羅菩薩一百八名陀羅尼經 (2.) 佛說聖多羅菩薩經 (3.) 聖多羅菩薩梵讚.

ÂRYAVARMMA 阿梨耶伐摩 or 聖冑 lit. holy helmet. A priest of the Sarvástivâdâḥ School, author of a work on the Vâibhâchika philosophy.

ÂRYA VASUMITRA S'ÂSTRA 尊婆須蜜所集論 Title of a book.

AS'ÂIKCHA see under Arhat.

ASAKRIT SAMÂDHI (lit. repeated samâdhi) 不供三昧 lit. the samâdhi which is not collective (in one formula). A degree of ecstatic contemplation.

ASAṀGHA or ASAÑGHA or ÂRYASAṀGHA 阿僧伽 or 無著 lit. no contiguity. A native of Gândhâra, originally a follower of the

Mahîs'âsakaḥ School. He lived mostly in Ayôdhya (Oude). where he taught the principles of the Mahâyâna School and wrote many works in explanation of its doctrines. Strongly influenced by Brahmanism and S'ivaism, he became the founder of a new School, the Yogâtchârya or Tantra School, the tenets of which are expounded with dialectic subtilty in Asamgha's principal work, the Yogâtchârya bhûmi s'âstra (q. v.). His teachings received wide acceptation in consequence of the belief that Asamgha had been miraculously transported to the heaven Tuchita where Maitrêya taught him the principles of the Tantrasystem, and addressed to him the substance of the above mentioned S'âstra. He is said to have lived 1000 years after S'âkyamuni, i.e. about 550 A.D. and as no translation of any of his works appeared earlier than 590—616 A.D., this date is probably near the mark.

ASAMKHYÊA (Pâli. Asamkheyya. Singh. Asankya.) 阿僧企耶 or 阿僧祇 or 僧祇 explained by 無數 lit. countless. (1.) The highest sum for which a conventional term exists, according to Chinese calculations equal to 1 followed by 17 cyphers. Tibetan and Singhalese computations estimate one Asamkhyêa as equal to 1 followed by 97 cyphers, whence Burnouf concluded that Asamkhyêa is the highest conventional sum constituted by the highest odd units (7 and 9), suggesting also that the two numbers 7 and 9 have some mystic meaning. (2.) Name of a class of kalpas (q.v.). Every Mahâkalpa (q. v.) consists, in every universe, of 4 Asamkhyêa kalpas, viz., the period of destruction (壞刧); the period of continued destruction or emptiness (空刧); the period of reproduction or formation (成刧); and the period of continued reproduction or settlement (住刧). Each of these Asamkhyêa kalpas is subdivided into 20 small kalpas (小刧).

ASANDJNI SATTVA or ARANGI SATTVA (Pâli. Asanga satta. Singh. Assanja satthaya. Tib. Sems tchan hdon tches med) 無熱 lit. without heat. The 15th of the 18 Brahmalôkas. The 6th region of the 4th Dhyâna.

ÂS ÂLINÎ DHARMA S'ÂLÂ 奇特寺 lit. the odd monastery. A vihâra in Kharachar.

ASAT 妙無 lit. the incomprehensible nothing A philosophical term.

ASITA (Singh. Kala dewala. Tib. Nap po or Trang srong

tsien po) 阿私陁 or 阿氏多 or 阿私 or 阿夷 explained by 無比 lit. peerless. A richi (仙) whom S'âkyamuni, in a former life, served as a slave. On S'âkyamuni's subsequent re-birth, Asita pointed out the lakchaṇas (q.v.) on the child's body. One of the 18 Arhats (羅漢), worshipped in China, is called 'Asita, the Ârya of mount Ghridhrakûṭâ.' See also Aklês'a and Tapasvî.

AS'MAGBHA (Pâli. Vadjira. Tib. Rdohi snid po *i.e.* essence of stone) 阿輸摩竭婆 or 阿舍摩揭婆 or 阿濕摩揭婆 explained by 石藏 lit. stone deposit, and by 琥魄 lit. amber. One of the Saptaratna (q.v.), either amber (Rémusat), or coral (Julien), or diamond (Burnouf), or emerald (Wilson).

AS'MAKÛTA 積石山 lit. stone heap mountain. The eastern border of the desert of Gobi.

AS'ÔKA (Pâli. Asoka or Piadassi. Singh. Asoka. Tib. Mya gnan med pa. Mong. Chasalang oughei Nom un khaghan) 阿恕迦 or 阿輸迦 or 阿育 explained by 無憂 lit. sorrowless. (1.) A king, described by Chinese texts as 'a Tchakravartin, a grandson of Adjâtas'atru'. The latter remark refers to Kâlâs'ôka (453 B.C.) and not to Dharmâs'ôka who was the grandson of Tchandragupta (381 B.C.) and who reigned about 319 B.C. But the Chinese constantly confound these two. As'ôka, they say, gained the throne by assassination of his nearest relatives. Converted to Buddhism, through an Arhat whom he had boiled alive and who proved invulnerable, he became the Constantine of the Buddhist Church and distinguished himself by the number of vihâras and stûpas he erected. He is supposed to be identic with the Piyadasi whose edicts are found inscribed on pillars and rocks throughout India. His younger brother (correctly 'son') was Mahêndra. In the 17th and 18th years of his reign the third synod was held by Mahâmaudgalyâyana. (2.) Name of a tree (無憂樹 lit. sorrowless tree) under which Mahâmâyà (q.v.) was delivered without pain. The Jonesia asoka.

AS'ÔKADATTÂ VYÂKARAṆA. Title of two translations, viz., 無畏德菩薩會 by Buddhas'ânta, A.D. 539, and 佛說阿闍世王女阿術達菩薩經 by Dharmarakcha A.D. 317.

AS'ÔKA RÂDJA DJÂTAKA 阿育王傳 Title of a book.

AS'ÔKA RÂDJÂVADÂNA SÛTRA 阿育王譬喩經 Title of a translation, A. D. 317—420.

A'SÔKÂRÂMA 無憂伽藍 A vihâra in Pâṭaliputtra (q. v.), in which the third synod was held.

AS'ÔKA SÛTRA 阿育王經 Title of a translation by Saṁghapâla, A.D. 512.

ÂS'RAVAKCHAVA (Pali. Asavasaṁkhaya) lit. destruction of faults, 漏盡 or 盡漏 lit. finality of the stream. The Chinese explanation derives the term from the root s'ru (落 to drop) and supposes the word âs'rava to refer to 'the stream' of metempsychosis. Accordingly ás'ravakchaya, one of the 6 Abhidjñâs (q.v.), designates 'supernatural knowledge of the finality of the stream of life.'

ASURA (Singh. Asur. Tib. Lha ma yin or Lha min. Mong. Assuri) 阿脩羅 or or 阿素羅 or 阿須倫 explained by 非天 lit. those who are not dêvas. The 4th class of sentient beings, the mightiest of all demons, titanic enemies of the dêvas.

AS'VADJIT (Singh. Assaji. Tib. Rta thoul) 阿溼婆持 or 阿說示多 or 阿說示 or 阿奢輸 explained by 馬勝 lit. horse tamer. (1.) A military title (v. Upasêna). (2.) Name of one of the first five followers of S'âkyamuni.

AS'VAGHÔCHA (Singh. Assagutta) 阿溼縛窶沙 or 馬鳴 lit. a horse neighing. The 12th patriarch, a native of Benares, a noted antagonist of Brahmanism. He converted Kapimala, and is the author of a number of works. He is said to have died B.C. 327 (correct date about A. D. 100). His posthumons title is 切勝 lit. absolute conqueror. The earliest translation of any of his works was published in A.D. 405.

AS'VAGHÔCHA BODHISATTVA DJÂTAKA 馬鳴菩薩傳 Title of a book (abstract).

AS'VAKARṆA (Pâli. Assakanna. Singh. Aswakarnna. Siam. Assakan) 阿輸割那 or 頞溼縛羯拏 explained by 馬耳山 lit. horse ear mountain. The 5th of the 7 concentric circles of gold-hills (七金山), which surround Sumêru, 2,500 yôdjanas high and separated by oceans from the 4th and 6th circles. A Buddha, called 華光大帝 (lit. great ruler of glory and light, title of the Chinese god of fire), and mentioned in a list of 1,000 Buddha (of the last kalpa), is said to have lived on these mountains.

ÂS'VAYUDJA 頞溼縛庾闍 The first month of autumn.

AṬALI 阿吒利 A province of the kingdom of Malva.

ATAPAS (Pali. Atappa. Tib. Mi gdoung ba) 無煩 lit. without trouble. The 13th Brahmalôka The 5th region of the 4th Dhyâna.

AṬAṬA 阿吒吒 The 3rd of the 8 cold hells; where the culprits' lips are frozen, so that they can but utter this sound, Aṭaṭa.

ATCHALÂ 無厭足 lit. insatiable. Name of a Rakchasî.

ATCHÂRA 阿折羅 An Arhat of the kingdom of Andhra, founder of a vihâra.

ATCHÂRYA or ATCHÂRIN 阿遮利耶 or 阿闍黎 or 阿闍梨 or 阿祇利 or 闍黎 explained by 軌範師 lit. a teacher of morals, or by 能糾正弟子行 lit. able to elevate the conduct of one's disciples, or by 正行 lit. correct conduct. (1.) A title of honour given to those who have passed through the novitiate. (2.) A series of duties obligatory for the same.

ATCHINTYABUDDHAVICHAYA NIRDÊS'A. Title of two translations by Bodhirutchi, viz., 善德天子會, and 文殊師利所說不思議佛境界經 A.D. 693.

ATCHINTYAPRABHÂSA BODHISATTVA NIRDÊS'A SÛTRA 不思議光菩薩所說經 Title of a translation by Kumâradjiva, A.D. 384—417.

ATHARVA VÊDA or ATHARVAṆA 阿闥婆拏 explained by 呪術 lit. magic incantations, or by 術論 lit. a S'âstra on magic, or by 禳災 lit. averting calamity of prayer. The 4th portion by the Vêda, containing proverbs. incantations and magic formulas.

ATIGUPTA 阿地瞿多 explained by 無極高 lit. infinitely high. A native of Central India who (A.D. 630) introduced into China a Sûtra called 陀羅尼集經.

ÂTMA MADA 我慢 lit. selfish pride Spiritual selfishness.

ÂTMANÊPADA 阿答末遲 A conjugation, so called because the action is supposed to revert (pada) to oneself (âtmane). e. g. dâ (to give), thus conjugated, means 'to give to oneself, to take'.

ATYANVAKÊLA 阿點婆翅羅 An ancient kingdom, the country near Corachie (Lat. 24° 51 N. Long 67° 16E).

AVABHÂSA 光德國 lit. the kingdom of light and virtue. A fabulous realm in which Mahâkâs'yapa is to be reborn as Buddha.

AVADÂNA 阿波陀那 or 波陀 explained by 譬喩 lit. comparisons, or by 出曜 lit. illustrations. One of twelve classes of Sûtras, illustrating doctrinal points by the use of metaphors and parables, or stories.

AVADÂNA SÛTRA 出曜經 Title of a Sûtra by Dharmatrata, translated A. D. 399. See also Dharmapada.

AVÂIVARTIKA (Tib. Phyir miltog pa) 不退轉 lit. not turning back (i. e. going straight to Nirvâna). An epithet of every Buddha.

AVAIVARTYA SÛTRA or APARIVARTYA SÛTRA 阿惟越致遮經 Title of a translation by Dharmarakcha, A.D. 284. See also Avivartita.

AVAKAN v. Invakan.

AVALÔKITÊS'VARA (Tib. Spyan ras gzigs or Cenresig. Mong. Ergetu Khomsim. Chin. Kwanyin) or Âryávalôkitês'vara 阿唎耶婆盧羯帝爍鉢囉耶 or 亞略巴魯幾爹督勒呀 or 阿縛盧枳多伊溼伐羅 or 耶婆盧吉帝 correctly explained by 觀自在 lit. onlooking (avalôkita) sovereign (is'vara). (1.) An Indian male divinity, unknown to Southern Buddhism, perhaps an ancient local deity of Southern India, adopted by the followers of the Mahâyâna School in India (especially in Magadha) and highly revered, from the 3rd to the 7th centuries, in conjunction with Mañdjus'rî, as a Bodhisattva who, from of old, appeared on earth in a variety of places (but especially at Pôtala) and under numerous forms (but always as a male), saving for instance Simhala (q.v.) from shipwreck and generally acting as a sort of Saviour of the faithful, and bearing some similarities to Vishnu. (2.) The first male ancestor (Brasrinpo) of the Tibetan nation, the principal tutelary deity of Tibet, adopted by Tibetan Buddhism under the name Padmapâṇi (i.e. lotus bearer or lotus-born) as an incarnation of Avalôkitês'vara, and highly revered, in conjunction with Mandjus'rî (the representative of creative wisdom, corresponding with Brahmâ) and Vadjrapâṇi (the representative of divine power, corresponding with Indra), as the representative of compassionate Providence (corresponding partly with Shiva), the controller of metempsychosis and special head of the present Buddhist church. The six mystic syllables ôm maṇi padme hûm̃ (q.v.) are specially used to invoke this male deity, who is often represented with 11 heads (in 3 tiers) and 8 hands, and with the Shivaitic necklace of skulls. He is supposed to have appeared on earth in various incarnations as the spiritual mentor of all believers, and especially to have been incarnate in the King of Tibet called Srong-tsan-gam-bo and in every successive Dalai Lama. The Tantra School of Tibet declared this Tibetan deity to be the Dhyâni Bodhisattva (spiritual reflex in the world of forms, produced by contemplation) of Amitâbha Buddha. His special sanctuary is on mount Potala in Lhassa. (3.) A Chinese female deity, probably an ancient local goddess of mercy (and progeny), worshipped in China, before the advent of Buddhism, under the name Kwanyin and adopted by Buddhists as an incarnation of Avalôkitês'vara (or Padmapaṇi). According to Chinese accounts, Kwanyin was the third daughter of 妙莊王 (v. S'ubhavyûha), a ruler of a northern kingdom, supposed to be identic with 莊王 Chwang-wang of the Chow dynasty (B. C. 696). She was so determined, it is said, to become a nun, that she absolutely refused to be married, even when put (by her father's order) to degrading duties in the convent. Her father ordered her to be executed with the sword, but the sword was broken into 1,000 pieces without hurting her. Her father then ordered her to be stifled, when her soul left the body and went down to hell, but hell forthwith changed into paradise. To save his hell, Yama sent her back to life, whereupon she was miraculouly transported, on a lotus flower, to the island of P'ootoo (Potara), near Ningpo, where she lived for 9 years healing disease and saving mariners from shipwreck. Her father having fallen ill, she cut the flesh off her arms and made it into a medicine which saved his life. To show his gratitude, he ordered a statue to be erected in her honour, saying 全手全眼 'with completely formed (ts'uen), arms and eyes', but the sculptor misunderstood the order for 千手千眼 'with a thousand (ts'ien) arms and eyes,' whence it happened that a statue with a 1,000 eyes and 1,000 arms perpetuated her memory, and she was henceforth known and revered as 千手千眼大慈大悲觀音菩薩 'the Bodhisattva Kwanyin who has 1,000 arms and 1,000 eyes, great in mercy and great in compassion.' To identify Kwanyin as an incarnation of Avalôkitês'vara, her name Kwanyin 觀音 was explained as meaning avalôkita (觀 lit. looking on) svara (音 lit. sound i.e. of prayers). She is also styled 觀世音自在 lit. the sovereign (ishvara) who looks on or regards (avalôkita) the sounds or prayers (svara), and, by abbreviation, 觀世自在 lit. the sovereign (ishvara) who looks on the world (avalôkita). Other epithets are 光世音 lit. sound of the world of light, and 觀尹 lit. onlooking controller (Kwanyin), which two epithets may be modern corrupt forms or archaic relics of her ancient name. Kwanyin is also styled 高王 (v. Abhyutgata râdja) lit. the august monarch, and as such regarded as the patron of those who are under criminal prosecution. Another title is 白衣大士 lit. white robed great scholar, and as such she is represented with a baby on her arm and worshipped by people desiring progeny. She is also styled Bodhisattva (q. v.) and Abhayamdada (q.v.) Some Chinese texts confound Kwanyin with Maitrêya (q. v.), because the former is the predicted successor of Amitâbha, whilst Maitrêya is to be the next Buddha to appear in this world. If other texts increase the confusion by identifying Kwanyin both with Maitrêya and with Pûrṇa Mâitrâyaṇi puttra (q. v.), the explanation is likewise easy, for Kwanyin's title 大慈 (lit. great mercy) is likely to be confounded with that of Maitrêya viz. 慈氏 lit. family of mercy and with that of Pûrṇa viz. 滿慈子 lit. the son of full mercy. Some texts also assert that Kwanyin was 'the third son of the grihapati Anâtha piṇḍika of the bamboo garden Djêtavana near the Gridhrakûta mountain and was called Sudatta.' But as they add that this was but one of the many incarnations of Kwanyin, there is no contradiction in the statement, though it is based on a mistake, as Sudatta was the name of the father.

AVALÔKITÊS'VARA BODHISATTVA SAMANTAMUKHAPARIVARTA 妙法蓮華經觀世音菩薩普門品經 Title of a translation, of a chapter from the Suddharma puṇḍarîka, by Kumâradjîva (who translated the prose) A.D. 384—417, and by Djñânagupta (who translated the gáthâs), A.D. 557—589.

AVALÔKITÊS'VARAIKÂDAS'AMUKHA DHÂRAṆÎ. Title of two translations, viz. 佛說十一面觀世音神咒經 by Yas'ogupta, A.D. 557—581, and 十一面神咒心經 by Hiuen-tsang, A. D. 656.

AVALÔKITÊS'VARA MÂTRI DHÂRAṆÎ 觀自在菩薩母陀羅尼經 Title of a book.

AVALÔKITÊS'VARA PADMA DJÂLAMÛLA TANTBANÂMA DHÂRAṆÎ. Title of four books, viz. (1.) 千眼千臂陀羅尼神咒 2.) 千手千眼姥陀羅尼身經 (3.) 千手千眼廣大圓滿無礙大悲心經 (4.) 秘密藏神咒經.

AVAṆḌA 阿奮荼 An ancient kingdom, probably the modern district of Shekarpoor, Lat. 27° 36 N. Long. 69° 18 E.

ÂVANTIKHÂH (Tib. Srung pa vahi sde) 大不可棄子部 lit. the great School of the son who could not be abandoned. A subdivision of the Sammataḥ School, so called because its founder was, as a newborn babe, abandoned by his parents.

AVARAS'ÂILÂḤ (Singh. Seliyás) 阿伐羅塾羅 or 西山住部 lit. the School of the dwellers on the western mountain. A subdivision of the Mahâsaṁghikaḥ School.

AVARAS'ÂILÂ SAṀGHÂRÂMA 阿伐羅塾羅僧伽藍 explained by 西山寺 lit. the monastery of the western mountain. A vihâra in Dhanakatchêka, built 600 B.C., deserted A. D. 600.

AVATAMS'AKA SÛTRAS. 華嚴部 A subdivision of the Sûtra Piṭaka.

AVÂTÂRA 阿跋多羅 explained by 化生 lit. metamorphosis. The Brahminical idea of incarnation corresponding to anupâpadaka (q. v.)

ÂVÊNIKA DHARMA (Singh. Buddha dharmma) 十八不共法 lit. 18 detached characteristics. The distinctive marks of a Buddha who is 'detached' from the imperfections which mark ordinary mortals.

AVIDDHA KARṆA SAMGHARÂMA 阿避陀羯刺拏僧伽藍 or 不穿耳伽藍 lit.

the monastery of those whose ears are not pierced. An ancient vihâra near Yôdhapatipura.

AVIDYÂ (Singh. Awidya. Tib. Ma rig pa) 無明 lit. absence of perception. The last (or first) of the 12 Nidânas (q. v.), viz. ignorance which mistakes the illusory phenomena of this world for realities.

AVILÔMA 羊毛 lit. a sheep's hair. A subdivision of a yôdjana.

AVÎTCHI (Singh. and Siam. Awichi. Tib. Mnar med) 阿鼻旨 or 阿惟越致 or 阿毗至 or 阿鼻 or 阿毗 explained by 無間地獄 lit. uninterrupted hell. The last of the 8 hot hells, where the culprits die and are re-born without interruption (yet not without hope of final redemption).

AVIVARTITA (or APARIVARTYA) SÛTRA 不退轉法輪經 Title of a translation, A.D. 397—439. See also Vaipulya vyûhâvivartita dharmatchakra sûtra.

AVRIHA (Singh. Awiha. Tib. Mitchheba) lit. making no effort, 無想 lit. absence of thought. The 13th Brahmalôka. The 4th region of the 4th Dhyâna.

AYAMUKHA (or Hayamukha) 阿耶穆佉 An ancient kingdom, probably the region near Surajepoor, Lat. 26° 26 N. Long. 86° 16 E.

AYANA 行 lit. a march. A division of time, equal to 6 months.

AYATANA 阿也怛那 General term for the organs of sense. See Chaḍayatana and Vidjñana.

AYÔDHYÂ 阿踰陀 The capital of Kôs'ala, the head quarters of ancient Buddhism, the present Oude, Lat. 26° N. Long. 82° 4 E.

ÂYURVÊDA 阿由 explained by 命論 or 壽論 lit. the S'âstra of longevity. One of the Vêdas, a ritual to be used at sacrifices.

AYUTA (Tib. Ther hboum) 阿由多 or 那由他 explained by 百俱胝 lit. 100 kôṭi. A numeral, equal to 1,000,000,000.

B.

BADAKCHÂN 鉢鐸創那 or 巴達克山 A mountainous district of Tokhâra, the region near Gumbeer, Lat. 34° 45 N. Long. 70 E.

BAGHELÂN 縛伽浪 The country W. of the Bunghee river, between Koondooz and Ghoree, Lat 36° N. Long. 68°E.

BAHUDJANA 僕呼繕那 explained by 衆生 lit. all living beings.

BAKTRA 縛喝羅 or 縛喝 A city of Bactriana, once a nursery of Buddhism, A. D. 600 still famous for its sacred relics and monuments. The present Balkh, Lat. 36° 48 N. Long 67° 4 E.

BALA (Singh. Purnna) 婆羅 The sister of the girl Ananda (Singh. Sujata) who supplied S'âkyamuni with milk.

BALÂ or Pantchabalâni (Singh. Balayas) 五力 lit. five powers, with the note 'bala signifies 制止 lit. to limit, to stop.' One of the categories forming the 37 Bodhi pakchika dharma (q. v.), embracing (1.) the power of faith, v. S'raddhâbala, (2.) the power of energy, v. Vîryábala, (3.) the power of memory, v. Smritîbala, (4.) the power of meditation, v. Samâdhîbala, and (5.) the power of wisdom, v. Pradjñábala. See also under Indriya.

BÂLÂDITYA 婆羅阿迭多 explained by 幼日 lit. the early sun. A king of Magadha, protector of Buddhists, who if identic with Balihita, reigned A. D. 191.

BÂLAPATI 薄羅鉢底 Name of an ancient Kingdom of India.

BÂLAPRITHAGDJANA (Pâli. Balaputhudjdjana) 婆羅必利他伽闍那 or 婆羅必栗託仡那 explained by 小兒別生 lit. a little child born apart, or by 愚異生 lit. born a fool and differing (sc. from the saints). A designation of unbelievers.

BALI 婆稚 explained by 有縛 lit. one who has ties (sc. of relationship). Name of a king of Asuras.

BÂLUKÂ 跋祿迦 An ancient kingdom of eastern Turkestan, the present Aksu, Lat. 40°7 N. Long. 39°29 E.

BANDUPRABHA 親光 Author of the Buddhabhûmi Sûtra S'âstra.

BARUKATCHÊVA 跋祿羯呫婆 An ancient kingdom in Gujerat, S. of the Nerbudda, near Baroche, Lat. 21°44 N. Long. 72°56 E.

BÂS'PAH (Tib. Bhachbah or Phaggs pa lama) 八思巴 or 帕克斯巴 or 巴思巴 or 拔合思巴 or 拔思發 or 發思八 A S'ramaṇa of Tibet (土波), teacher and confidential adviser of Kublai Khan, who appointed him head of the Buddhist church of Tibet (A. D. 1,260). He is the author of a manual of Buddhist terminology (彰所知論) and translated another work into Chinese. He constructed (A. D. 1,269) for the Mongol language an alphabet and syllabary borrowed from the Tibetan and known by the term Horyik, for which, however, the Lama Tsordjiosen subsequently (A. D. 1307—1311) substituted another alphabet, based on that of S'âkyapandita.

BAYANA 梵衍那 An ancient kingdom and city in Bokhara, famous for a statue of Buddha (entering Nirvâṇa), said to have been 1,000 feet long. The present Bamyân, Lat 34°50 N. Long. 67°40 E.

BHADANTA (Pâli. Bhanta) 婆檀陀 explained by 大德 lit. great virtue. A title of honour (like Reverend) given to priests (especially of the Hinâyana School).

BHADRA (Pâli. Bhaddha) 跋達羅 or 跋陀 explained by 善 lit. virtuous, or by 賢 lit a sage. (1.) An epithet of every Buddha. (2.) Name of tree. (3.) Name of the realm in which Yas'ôdharâ is to be reborn.

BHADRAKALPA (Pâli. Bhaddha Kappa. Siam. Phattakala) 賢刧 lit. the kalpa of the sages. A designation for the kalpa (q.v.) of stability, so called because 1,000 Buddhas (sages) appear in the course of it. Our present period is a Bhadrakalpa and 4 Buddhas have already appeared. It is to last 236 million years, but over 151 million years have already elapsed.

BHADRAKALPIKA SÛTRA 賢刧經 Title of a translation by Dharmarakcha, A.D. 300.

BHADRAKÂ RÂTRÎ 佛說善夜經 Title of a translation A.D. 701.

BHADRA KÂTCHANÂ v. Yas'ôdharâ.

BHADRA MÂYÂKÂRA PARIPRITCHTCH'A. Title of two translations, viz. 幻士仁賢經 by Dharmarakcha, A.D. 265—316, and 授幻師跋陀羅記會 by Bodhirutchi, A.D. 618—907.

BHÂDRAPADA 婆達羅鉢陀 Name of the last month of summer.

BHADRAPÂLA 跋陀婆羅 or 颰陀波羅 A Bodhisattva who, with 500 others, slighted S'âkyamuni in a former life, but was afterwards converted and became Buddha.

BHADRAPÂLA S'RECHṬHI

PARIPRITCHTCH'Â. Title of two translations, viz. 賢護長者會 by Djñânagupta, A. D. 596, and 大乘顯識經 by Divâkara and others, A. D. 680.

BHADRAPÂLA SÛTRA 拔陂菩薩經 Title of a translation by Lokalakcha.

BHADRA RUTCHI 跋陀羅樓支 explained by 賢愛 lit. good and loving. A priest of Parvata whose disputation with a Brahman was cut short by the latter sinking down into hell.

BHADRATCHARÎ PRAṆIDHÂNA 普賢菩薩行願讚 Title of a translation by Amoghavadjra, A.D. 746—771.

BHADRA VIHÂRA 跋達羅毗訶羅 explained by 賢寺 lit the monastery of sages. A vihâra in Kanyâkubdja.

BHADRAYÂNÎYÂḤ or Bhadraputtrîyâḥ 跋陀與尼與部 or 賢部 lit. the School of Bhadra, or 賢乘部 lit. the School of the conveyance of Bhadra, or 賢胄部 lit. the School of the descendants of Bhadra. A School founded by a famous ascetic called Bhadra.

BHADRIKA or Bhadraka (Pâli. Bhaddaji. Tib. Ngang zen or Ming zan) 跋提梨迦 or 跋提離 or 跋提 A son of Amritôdana, one of the first 5 disciples of S'âkyamuni.

BHAGAI 孛伽夷 A city S. of Khoten, famous for a statue exhibiting all the lakchaṇâni (q. v.).

BHGÂRÂMA (lit. the arâma, or dwelling, of the god-Bhaga) 瞿盧薩謗 Grosapam or Karsana (Ptolemy), the capital of Kapis'a, the modern Begrâm.

BHAGAVADDHARMA 伽梵達摩 or 尊法 lit. honourable law. A S'ramaṇa of western India who translated into Chinese a popular work in honour of Avalôkitês'vara.

BHAGAVAT or Bhagavan (Pâli. Bhagavâ. Singh. Bagawa. Siam. Phakhava. Tib. Btsham ldan das) 婆嚩誐帝 or 婆葛斡諦 or 薄伽梵 or 婆伽婆 An epithet, 'the man of virtue (or merits)', given to every Buddha.

BHAṆÎ 婆尼 or 婆尼 A minister of S'as'añka.

BHÂRYÂ 婆利耶 A wife.

BHASKARA VARMMA 婆塞羯摩伐羅 explained by 日胄 tit. armour of the sun. A king of Kâmarupa, a descendant of Narâyana Dêva.

BHAVA (Singh. Bhawa) 有 lit. existence. One of the 12 Nidânas, existence, as the moral agent that assigns every individual to one or other of the Trâilôkya (三有 lit. three modes of actual existence). The creative cause of Bhava is Upâdâna. Its consequence is Djâti.

BHAVASAÑGKRÂMITA SÛTRA. Title of 3 translations, viz. (1.) 大方等修多羅王經 by Bodhirutchi, A.D. 386—534; (2.) 佛說轉有經 by Buddhas'ânta, A. D. 539; (3.) 佛說大乘流轉諸有經 A.D. 618—907.

BHAVA VIVÊKA 婆毗吠伽 or 清辯 lit. clear argument. A disciple of Nâgârdjuna, who retired to a rock cavern to await the coming of Maitrêya. Author of the 大乘掌珍論 Mahâyânatâlaratna S'âstra, translated by Hiuentsang, A.D. 648.

BHÊCHADJYAGURU VAIḌÛRYAPRABHÂSA PÛRVAPRAṆIDHÂNA 藥師瑠璃光如來本願功德經 Title of a translation by Hiuentsang, A.D. 650. See also Saptatathâgata pûrvapraṇidhâna vis'êchavistara.

BHÊCHADJYAGURU PÛRVAPRAṆIDHANA 藥師如來本願經 Title of a translation by Dharmagupta, A.D. 615.

BHÊCHADJYA RÂDJA 藥王 lit. the medical king. A disciple of S'âkyamuni. See also Survasattvapriyadars'ana and Vimalagarbha.

BHÊCHADJYARÂDJA BHÊCHADJYASAMUDGATA SÛTRA 佛說觀藥王藥上二菩薩經 Title of a translation by Kâlayas'as, A. D. 424.

BHÊCHADJYA SAMUDGATA 藥上菩薩 lit. the superior medical Bodhisattva. A disciple of S'âkyamuni. See also Vimalanêtra.

BHICHMAGARDJITA GHÔCHASVARA RÂDJA 威音王 lit. the king of grave utterance. The name under which numberless Buddhas successively appeared, in Mahâsambhava, during the Vinirbhôga Kâlpa.

BHIKCHU (Pâli. Bhikkhu. Singh. Bhikchu. Tib. Dgeslong. Mong. Gelong) 比丘 or 苾芻 explained by 乞士 lit. mendicant scholars or by 釋種 lit. followers of S'âkya. (1.) A fragrant plant, emblem of the virtues of a religious mendicant. (2.) Two classes of S'ramaṇas (q.v.), viz. esoteric mendicants (內乞) who control their nature by the law, and exoteric mendicants (外乞) who control their nature by diet. Every true Bhikchu is supposed to work miracles.

BHIKCHUṆÎ Tib. Dge slong ma, or Ani. Mong. Tshibaganza) 比丘尼 or 苾芻尼 Female religious mendicants who observe the same rules as any Bhikchu.

BHIKCHUṆÎ PRATIMOKCHA SÛTRA 十誦律比丘尼戒經 Title of a compilation by Fa-hien.

BHIKCHUṆÎ SAÑGHIKA-VINAYA PRATIMOKCHA SÛTRA 比丘尼僧祇律波羅提木叉戒經 Title of a translation by Fa-hien and Bhuddhabhadra, A.D. 414.

BHÎMÂ 毗摩 or 媲摩 (1.) Name of S'iva's wife (the terrible). (2.) A city, W. of Khoten, possessing a statue (of Buddha) said to have transported itself thither from Udyâna.

BHÛROM 喑嚂 An exclamation, frequently occurring at the beginning of mantras (q. v.), probably in imitation of Bhramanic mantras which begin by invoking bhûr (earth), bhuvah (atmosphere) and svar (heaven). Perhaps a contraction of bhûr (earth) and om (q.v.)

BHÛTA 部多 explained by 自生 lit. spontaneous generation, or by 化生 lit. born by transformation.

BHÛTAS 鋪多 Heretics who besmeared their bodies with ashes. Probably a Shivaitic sect.

BIMBISÂRA or Bimbasâra or Vimbasâra (Singh. Bimsara. Tib. Srenika, or Gzugs tshan sningpo. Mong. Margisiri amogo langa ouile duktchi, or Tsoktsasun dshirüken) 頻毗娑羅 or 頻婆娑羅 or 蓱沙王 explained by 影堅 lit. a shadow (rendered) solid, or by 瓶沙 lit. the sand of a vase. A King of Magadha, residing at Râdjagriha, converted by S'âkyamuni, to whom he gave the Vêṇuvana park. He was murdered by his son Adjâtas'atru.

BIMBISÂRA RÂDJA SÛTRA. Title of 2 books, viz. (1.) 頻毗娑羅王詣佛供養經 and (2.) 蓱沙王口願經

BODHI or Sambodhi (Tib. Byang cûb) 菩提 explained by 道 lit. intelligence, or by 正覺 lit. (the act of keeping one's mind) truly awake, in contradistinction from Buddhi (the faculty of intelligence). That intelligence or knowledge by which one becomes a Buddha or a believer in Buddhism.

See also Bodhi pakchika dharma.

BODHIDHARMA 達摩大師 The 28th Indian (1st Chinese) patriarch, originally called Bodhitara (菩提多羅). He was a Kchattriya by birth, being the son of a king of southern India. His teacher Panyatara (般若多羅) gave him the name Bodhidharma to mark his understanding (bodhi) of the law (dharma) of Buddha. Bodhidharma brought the almsbowl of S'âkyamuni (v. pâtra) to China (9th moon, 21st day, A.D. 520), visited Canton, and then Lohyang, where he remained engaged in silent meditation for 9 years, being thenceforth known as 'the wall-gazing Brahman' (壁觀婆羅門). He is supposed to have died *circa* A.D. 529.

BODHIDRUMA or Bodhivrikcha 菩提樹 lit. bodhi-tree, or 道樹 lit. tree of intelligence, or 卑鉢羅 lit. pippala, or 賓撥梨力叉 lit. pippali vrikcha, or 阿濕喝咃波力叉 lit. asvas'tha vrikcha. The tree (Ficus religiosa) under which S'âkyamuni did 7 years' penance, and under which he became Buddha. This tree, originally 400 (Chinese) feet high, and 50 feet high when Hiuen-tsang saw it (A.D. 629—645), still exists, 2 miles S.E. of Gayâ, on the left bank of the Nâiranjana. Cuttings of this tree, which is considered to be a symbol of the spread and growth of Buddhism, are planted in China in front of monasteries and temples. Fah-hien (A.D. 399—414) mistook this tree for a palmtree (v. Patra), with which the Bodhi tree is now generally identified in China.

BODHILA 佛地羅 A native of Cashmere, author of the Tattva sañtchaya s'âstra (集眞論) belonging to the Mahâsaṁghikâḥ School.

BODHIMAṆḌA (Singh. Bodhimandala) 菩提道場 lit. the platform of bodhi, or 道場 lit. the platform of intelligence, or 金剛坐 lit. the diamond throne (vadjrâsana). The terrace, said to have raised itself out of the ground, surrounding the Bodhidruma, where all Bodhisattvas sit down when about to become Buddhas. This ground, said to be as solid as diamond, is believed to form the navel (centre) of the earth.

BODHIRUTCHI 菩提留支 or 菩提流支 or 流支 explained by 覺希 lit. understanding and hope, or by 道

希 lit. intelligence and hope. (1.) S'ramaṇa of northern India, who arrived in Loh-yang A. D. 508, and translated some 30 works. (2.) Cognomen of Dharmarutchi (q. v.)

BODHISATTVA (Pâli. Bodhisatto. Singh. Bodhisat. Siam. Phothisat. Tib. Byang cub sems dpa) lit. he whose essence (sattva) has become intelligence (bodhi) 菩提薩埵 or 𡨥膘薩督呀 or 扶薩 or 菩薩 explained by 覺有情 lit. knowledge in possession of one's affections or by 道心 lit. the mind of intelligence. The third class of saints who have to pass only once more through human life before becoming Buddhas, including also those Buddhas who are not yet perfected by entering Nirvâṇa (v. Mahâsattvas). One of the three means of conveyance to Nirvâna (v. Triyâna), compared with an elephant fording a river.

BODHISATTVA BODHIDRUMA SÛTRA 菩薩道樹經 Title of a book.

BODHISATTVA BUDDHÂNUSMṚÎTI SAMADHI 佛說菩薩念佛三昧經 Title of a translation, A.D. 462.

BODHISATTVA PIṬAKA 菩薩藏經 A section of the Tripiṭaka, sûtras treating on the state of a Bodhisattva.

BODHISATTVA PIṬAKA SADDHARMA SÛTRA 佛說大乘菩薩藏正法經 Title of a translation by Dharmarakcha, A. D. 1004—1058.

BODHISATTVA PIṬAKA SÛTRA 菩薩藏會 Title of atranslaticn by Hiuen-tsang, A.D. 645.

BODHISATTVA PIṬAKÂVATAM̃SAKA MAÑDJUS'BÎMULA GARBHA TANTRA 大方廣菩薩文殊師利根本儀軌經 Title of a translation, A.D. 980—1001.

BODHISATTVA TCHARYÂ NIRDÊS'A. Title of two translations, viz. 菩薩善戒經 by Guṇavarman, A. D. 431, and 菩薩地特經 by Dharmarakcka, A. D. 414—421.

BODHIVAKCHO MAÑDJUS'RI NIRDÊS'A SÛTRA 佛說大乘善見變化文殊師利問法經 Title of a translation, A.D. 980—1001.

BODHI VIHÂRA 菩提寺 lit. the temple of intelligence. A favourite name, given to many monasteries.

BODHIVRIKCHA v. Bodhidruma.

BODHYANGA (Pâli. Sam̃bodjhana. Singh. Bowdyânga) 七菩提分 or 七覺分 lit. seven divisions of bodhi, or 七覺支 lit. seven branches of understanding. One of the 37 categories of the Bodhi pakchika dharma, comprehending 7 degrees of intelligence, viz. (1.) memory v. Smriti; (2.) discrimination v. Dharma pravitchaya; (3.) energy v. Vîrya; (4.) joy v. Prîti; (5.) tranquillity v. Pras'rabdhi; (6.) ecstatic contemplation v. Samâdhi; (7.) indifference v. Upêkchâ.

BOLOR 鉢露兒 or 鉢露羅 A kingdom, N. of the Indus, S.E. of the Pamir, rich in minerals. The modern Balti, or Little Tibet (by the Dards called Palolo). It is to be distinguished from the city Bolor in Tukhâra.

BRAHMA (Siam. Phrom. Tib. Tshangs. Mong. Esrun tegri) 婆羅吸摩 or 婆羅賀磨 or 梵覽摩 or 梵天王 or 梵王 or 梵 explained by 一切衆生之父 lit. the father of all living beings. The first person of the Brahminical Trimurti, adopted by Buddhism, but placed in an inferior position, being looked upon, not as creator, but as a trasitory dêvata whom every saint, on obtaining bodhi, surpasses.

BRAHMA DJÂLA SÛTRA. Title of two translations, viz. 佛說梵網六十二見經 A.D. 222—280, and 梵網經 by Kumâradjîva, A.D. 406.

BRAHMADATTA 梵摩達 or 梵授 lit. gift of Brahma. (1.) A king of Kanyâkubdja. (2.) A king of Vârânas'î, father of Kâs'yapa. (3.) Same as Brahmânandita.

BRAHMADHVADJA 相梵 lit. Brahma's figure. A fabulous Buddha, whose domain is S. W. of our universe, an incarnation of the 8th son of Mahâbhidjña djñanâ bhibhû.

BRAHMAKALA 梵迦羅 Name of a mountain.

BRAHMAKÂYIKAS (Siam Phrom. Tib. Tshangs bkhor) 梵迦夷天 or 梵天 lit. the dêvas of Brahma. The retinue of Brahma.

BRAHMÂKCHARAS 梵字 or 梵書 lit. Brahma's writing. Pâli or Sanskrit, the former being considered by by Chinese writers the more ancient system, both as a written and spoken language.

BRAHMALÔKA 梵天 lit. the heavens of Brahma, or 世主天 lit. the heavens of the ruler of the world. Eighteen heavenly mansions constituting the world of form (v.

Rûpadhâta) and divided into 4 regions of contemplation (v. Dhyâna). Southern Buddhism knows only sixteen. Northern Buddhists added Puṇyaprasava and Anabhraka.

BRAHMAṆA (Tib. Bram ze) 跋濫摩 or 婆羅門 explained by 淨行 lit. pure walk. (1.) A term of social distinction (姓 lit. clan), the caste of Brahmans. (2.) A religious term, designating a man whose conduct is pure.

BRAHMÂNANDITA 梵豫 lit. Brahma's elephant. A king of Vâis'âli, who had 1000 sons, also called Brahmadatta.

BRAHMAṆAPURA 婆羅門邑 A city, N. E. of the capital of Mâlava.

BRÂHMAṆARACHTRA 婆羅門國 or 梵摩難國 lit. the kingdoms of the Brahmans. A general name for India.

BRÂHMAṆARACATRA RÂDJA SÛTRA 佛說梵摩難國王經 Title of a book.

BRAHMAPARICHADYÂḤ 梵衆 lit. the assembly of the Brahmas. The 1st Brahmalôka. The 1st region of the 1st Dhyâna.

BRAHMAPURA 婆羅吸摩補羅 explained by 女國 lit. the woman-kingdom. A kingdom of northern India, the dynastic title of which was entailed upon the female line exclusively. Its capital was situated near Sirenuggur, Lat. 30°10 N. Long 78° 46 E.

BRAHMA PURÔHITAS 梵輔 lit. the attendants of Brahma. The 2nd Brahmalôka. The 2nd region of the 1st Dhyâna.

BRAHMA SAHAM̃PATI or Mahabrahma sahâm̃pati 梵摩三鉢天 or 堪忍界王 lit. lord of the world of patient suffering. A title of Brahma, as ruler of the Sahalôkadhâtu.

BRAHMATCHÂRI 梵志 explained by 淨裔 lit. descendants of purity. (1.) A young Brahman. (2.) A Buddhist ascetic, irrespective of caste or descent.

BRAHMÂVADÂNA SÛTRA 佛說梵霓喻經 Title of a book.

BRAHMA VASTU 梵章 Title of a syllabary, in 12 parts.

BUDDHA (Siam. Phutthô. Tib. Sangs rgyas. Mong. Burchan) 浮圖 or 佛陀 or 勃塔 or 毋馱 or 沒馱 or 佛 explained by 覺 lit. awake (understanding). (1.) The first person of the Triratna. (2.) The highest degree of saintship, Buddhaship. (3.) Every intelligent person who has broken through the bondage of sense, perception and self, knows the utter unreality of all phenomena, and is ready to enter Nirvâṇa.

BUDDHABHADRA 佛陀跋多羅 or 佛駄跋陀羅 explained by 覺賢 lit. intelligent sage. (1.) A native of Kapilavastu, a descendant of Amritôdana Râdja, who came to China A. D. 406, introduced an alphabet of 42 characters and translated and composed many books. (2) A disciple of Dharmakôcha, whom Hiuen-tsang (A.D. 630—640) met in India.

BUDDHABHÛMI SÛTRA 佛說佛地經 Title of a translation by Hiuen-tsang, A. D. 645.

BUDDHABHÛMI SÛTRA S'ÂSTRA 佛地經論 A commentary on the preceding work, translated by Hiuen-tsang A.D. 649.

BUDDHADÂSA 佛陀駄索 explained by 覺使 lit. envoy of intelligence. A native of Ayamukha, author of the Mahâvhibhâcha s'âstra.

BUDDHADHARMA same as Avênikadharma.

BUDDHADJIVA 佛陀什 explained by 覺壽 lit. intelligence and longevity. A native of Cabul, who arrived in China A. D. 423 and translated 3 works.

BUDDHAGAYÂ v. Gayâ.

BUDDHAGUPTA 佛陀毱多 explained by 覺蜜 lit. honey of intelligence, and by 覺護 lit. protection of intelligence. A king of Magadha, son and successor of S'akrâditya.

BUDDHA HṚIDAYA DHÂRAṆÎ. Title of two translations, viz. 諸佛心陀羅尼經 by Hiuen-tsang A. D. 650, and 諸佛心印陀羅尼經 of later date.

BUDDHAKCHÊTRA (Singh. Buddhasêtra. Siam. Puthakhet. Tib. Sangs rgyas kyi zing) 紇差怛羅 or 差多羅 or 刹怛利耶 or 佛刹 explained by 佛土 lit. the land of Buddha, or by 佛國 lit. the kingdom of Buddha. The sphere of each Buddha's influence, said to be of fourfold nature, viz. (1.) the domain where good and evil are mixed 淨穢雜居土; (2.) the domain in which the ordinances (of religions) are not altogether ineffectual 方便有餘土, though impurity is banished and all beings reach the state of S'râvaka and Anâgâmin; (3.) the domain in which Buddhism is spontaneously accepted and carried into practice 自受用土, where its demands are fully responded to 實報土, and where even ordinary beings accept and carry them into practice 他受用土; (4.) the domain of spiritual nature 法性土, where all beings are in a permanent condition of stillness and light 常寂光土.

BUDDHAMITRA 伏馱密多 or 佛陀密多 The 9th Indian patriarch, a native of northern India, by birth a Vâis'ja, author of the 五門禪經要用法 Pañtchadvâra dhyâna sûtra mahârtha dharma, and therefore styled Mahâdhyânaguru (great teacher of contemplation). He died B.C. 487.

BUDDHANANDI 佛陀難提 The 8th Indian patriarch, a native of Kamarûpa and descendant of the Gautama family.

BUDDHAPÂLI 佛陀波利 explained by 覺護 lit. guarded by intelligence. (1.) A disciple of Nâgârdjuna and and founder of a subdivision of the Madhyamika School. (2.) A native of Cabul who translated (A. D. 676) a Dhâraṇî into Chinese.

BUDDHAPHALA 佛果 lit the fruit of Buddha. The fruition of Arhatship or Arahattvaphala.

BUDDHAPIṬAKA NIGRAHANÂMA MAHÂYÂNA SÛTRA 佛藏經 Title of a translation by Kumâradjîva, A.D. 405.

BUDDHASAMGHATI SÛTRA 諸佛要集經 Title of a translation by Dharmarakcha, A.D. 265—316.

BUDDHAS'ÂNTA 佛陀扇多 explained by 覺定 lit. fixed intelligence. A native of Central India, who translated some 10 works into Chinese, A.D. 524—550.

BUDDHASIMHA 佛陀僧訶 explained by 師子覺 lit. a lion's intelligence (i.e. supreme intelligence). (1.) A disciple of Asamgha. (2.) An epithet of Buddhochinga (q. v.).

BUDDHAS'RÎDJÑÂNA 覺吉祥 lit. the good omen of intelligence. A Bodhisattva, author of the 集大乘相論 Mahâyâna lakchaṇasamghîti s'âstra.

BUDDHATCHARITA KÂVYA SÛTRA 佛所行讚經 A narrative of the life of S'âkyamuni by As'vaghôcha, translated by Dharmarakcha A.D. 414—421.

BUDDHATCHARITRA 佛本行集經 Title of a history of Shâkyamuni, translated by Djñânagupta, A.D, 587.

BUDDHATCHHAYÂ 佛影 lit. the shadow of Buddha. The shadow of S'âkyamuni, exhibited in various places in India, but visible only to those 'whose mind is pure.'

BUDDHATRÂTA 佛陀多羅多 or 佛陀多羅 explained by 覺救 lit. intelligent saviour. (1.) Name of an Arhat, of the Sammatîya School. (2.) A native of Cabul, translator of the 大方廣圓覺修多羅了義經 Mahâvaipulya pûrṇabuddha sûtra prasannârtha sûtra (circa A.D. 650).

BUDDHAVANAGIRI 佛陀伐那山 A mountain near Râdjagriha. S'âkyamuni once lived in one of its rock caverns.

BUDDHAVARMAN 浮陀跋摩 or 佛陀跋摩 explained by 覺鎧 lit. cuirass of intelligence. A native of India, co-translator of the 阿毗曇毗婆沙論 Abhidharma vibhâchâ s'âstra, A.D. 437—439.

BUDDHÂVATAMSAKA MAHÂVAIPULYA SÛTRA 大方廣佛華嚴經 Title of a translation by Buddhabhadra and others, A.D. 418—420.

BUDDHAYAS'AS 佛陀耶舍 explained by 覺明 lit. intelligent and bright. A native of Cabul, translator of 4 works, A.D. 403—413.

BUDDHOCHINGA 佛圖澄 A native of India, also styled Buddhasiṁha, who propagated Buddhism in China (about 348 A. D.) with the aid of magic.

BUDDHÔCHṆÎCHA 佛頂骨 The skullbone of S'âkyamuni, an object of worship (v. Uchṇîcha).

BUKHARA 捕喝 or 捕揭 The present Bokhara, Lat, 39°47 N. Long. 64°25 E.

C.

CHAḌABHIDJÑÂS v. Abhidjñâ.

CHAḌAKCHARA VIDYÂ-MANTRA. Title of 3 translations, viz. (1.) 六字神咒經 by Bodhirutchi, A. D. 693, (2.) 六字咒王經 A.D. 317—420, and (3.) 六字神王經 A. D. 502—557.

CHAḌÂYATANA (Singh. Wêdanâkhand. Tib. Skye mtchhed) 六呵也怛那 or 六處 lit. 6 dwellings or 六入 lit. 6

entrances or 六塵 lit. six guṇas. One of the 12 Nidânas; sensation, the objects of sensation, the organs of sensation (eye, ear, nose, tongue, body, mind).

CHADPÂDÂBHIDHARMA 六足阿毗曇摩 Title of a philosophical work.

CHADUMÂN 忽露摩 A district of Tukhâra, on the upper Oxus.

CHAGHNÂN 尸棄尼 A district E. of Chadumân.

CHAṆṆAGARIKÂḤ 山拖那伽梨柯部 or 六城部 lit. the School of 6 cities. A philosophical School.

CHAṆMÛKA 商莫迦 A Bodhisattva, famous for filial piety.

CHANMUKHI DHÂRAṆÎ 佛說六門陀羅尼經 Title of a translation by Hiuen-tsang, A. D. 645.

CHARAKA 沙落迦 A monastery in Kapis'a.

D.

DÂGOBA v. Stûpa.

DAKCHIṆA (lit. the right, south) 達櫬拏 or 馱器尼 or 達嚫國 or 榰嚫 The Deccan, S. of Behar, often confounded with 大秦國 Syria.

DAKCHIṆÂYANA 南行 lit. course (of the sun) to the south. A period of 6 months.

DAKCHIṆAKÔSALA v. Kôsala.

DAMAMÛKL NIDÂNA SÛTRA (Mong. Dsanglun) 賢愚因緣經 Title of a translation (lit. the sûtra of the causes of wisdom and foolishness), A.D. 445.

DÂNA 檀那 or 柦那 explained by 布施 lit. exhibition of charity. The first of the 6 Pâramitâs, charity, as the motive of alms, sacrifices, self-mutilation snd self-immolation.

DÂNAPÂLA 施護 lit. donor of salvation. A native of Udyâna, who translated into Chinese some 111 works and received (A.D. 982) from the Emperor the title 顯教大師 lit. great scholar and expositor of the faith.

DÂNAPATI 檀越 lit. by charity crossing (the sea of misery) or 施主 lit. sovereign of charity. A title given to liberal patrons of Buddhism.

DÂNATAKA ÂRAṆYAKAḤ 檀那陁迦阿蘭若 Hermits living on the seashore or on half-tide rocks.

DANTAKÂCHṬHA 憚哆家瑟託 explained by 齒木 lit.

dental wood (restoring decayed teeth when chewed). A tree, said to have grown from a toothpick of S'âkyamuni.

DANTALÔKAGIRI 彈多落迦山 or 檀特山 A mountain (the *montes Daedali* of Justin) near Varucha, with a cavern (now called Kashmiri-Ghâr), where Sudâna lived.

DARADA 陀歷 The country of the ancient Dardae, now called Dardu, Lat. 35°11 N. Long. 73°54 E.

DAS'ABALA 十力 lit. ten powers. An epithet of every Buddha, as possessing 10 faculties, consisting of some of the 6 Abhidjñas and of some of the 8 Mârgas.

DAS'ABALA KÂS'YAPA v. Vâchpa.

DAS'ABHÛMI PRATICHṬHITE 荅攝蒲密卜羅牒瑟吒諦 An exclamation (lit. 'thou who art standing upon the ten regions') addressed to Tathâgatas in prayers.

DAS'ABHÛMIKA SÛTRA. Title of 2 translations, viz. (1.) 漸備一切智德經 by Dharmarakcha, A.D. 297, and (2.) 十住經 by Kumâradjîva and Buddhayas'as, A. D. 384-417.

DAS'ABHÛMIKA SÛTRA S'ÂSTRA 十地經 A compilation by Vasubandhu, translated by Bodhirutchi, A.D. 508—511.

DAS'ABHÛMIVIBHACHÂ S'ASTRA 十住毗婆沙論 Commentary, by Nâgârdjuna, on the two foregoing works, containing the earliest teaching regarding Amitâbha, translated by Kumâradjîva, circa A. D. 405.

DAS'ADHARMAKA. Title of two translations, viz. (1.) 大乘十法會 by Buddhas'anta, A.D. 539, and (2.) 佛說大乘十法經 by Saṁghapâla, A.D. 502—557.

DAS'ADIGANDHAKÂRA VIDHVAṀSANA SÛTRA 佛說滅十方冥經 Title of a translation by Dharmarakcha, A.D. 306.

DAS'ASÂHASRIKÂ PRADJÑÂPÂRAMITÂ. A section of the Mahâpradjñâpâramitâ sûtra (q. v.), identic with the Achṭasâhasrikâ pradjnâpâramitâ sûtra (q.v.), and separately translated under the following titles, viz. (1.) 道行般若波羅蜜經 by Lokarakcha, A. D. 179, (2.) 小品般若波羅蜜經 by Kumâradjîva, A. D. 408, (3.) 摩訶般若波羅蜜鈔經 (incomplete) by Dharmapriya, A. D. 382, (4.) 大

明度無極經 A. D. 222—280, (5.) 佛母出生三法藏般若波羅蜜多經 by Dânapâla, A.D. 980-1,000.

DAS'ATCHAKRA KCHITIGARBHA. Title of two translations, viz. (1.) 大乘大集地藏十輪經 A.D. 651, and (2.) 佛說大方廣十輪經 A.D. 397—439.

DELADÂ (Singh. Dalada) 佛齒 lit. Buddha's tooth. A sacred relic, the left canine tooth of S'âkyamuni.

DÊVA (Singh. Dewa. Tib. Lha. Mong. Tegri) 提婆 explained by 梵天人 lit. inhabitants of the Brahmalôkas, or by 天神 lit. spirits of heaven. (1.) General designation of the gods of Brahminism, and of all inhabitants of the Dêvalôkas who are subject to metempsychosis. (2.) Name of the 15th patriarch, a native of southern India, a disciple of Nágârdjuna, also called Dêvabodhisattva 提婆菩薩 and Ârya Dêva 聖天, and Nîlanêtra 靑目 (lit. azure eye) or 分別明 (lit. distinguishing brightness), author of 9 works, a famous antagonist of Brahminism.

DÊVADARS'ITA or Dêvadis'tha (Singh Dêvadaho) 天臂城 The residence of Suprabuddha.

DÊVADATTA (Singh. Dewadatta. Tib. Lhas byin or Hlan dshin. Mong. Tegri Oktigâ) 提婆達多 or 調達 explained by 天授 lit. gift of dêvas. The rival and enemy of S'âkyamuni, an incarnation of Asita, swallowed up by hell, worshipped as Buddha by a sect, up to 400 A.D., supposed to reappear as Buddha Dêvarâdja (天王) in an universe called Dêvasôppâna (天道).

DÊVÂLAYA (Singh. Dewala) 天祠 lit. shrine of a dêva. Name of all brahminical temples.

DÊVALÔKA (Singh. Dewaloka. Tib. Lha yul) 天 lit. heaven or 天宮 lit. mansion of dêvas. The 6 celestial worlds, situated above the Mêru, between the earth and the Brahmalôkas. See Tchatur mahârâdja kâyikas; Trayastriñs'as; Yama; Tuchita; Nirmanarati; Paranirmita.

DÊVANAGARI 天迦盧 explained by 西藏梵字 lit. Indian characters used in Tibet, or by 神字 lit. the writing of dêvas. See under

Sanskrita.

DÊVAPRADJÑA 提雲般若 or 提曇陀若那 explained by 天智 lit. wisdom of a dêva. A native of Kustana who translated 6 works into Chinese.

DÊVAS'ARMAN 提婆設摩 A Sthavira, author of two works (in which he denied the existence of both ego and non-ego), who died 100 years after S'âkyamuni.

DÊVASÊNA 提婆犀那 explained by 天軍 lit. army of dêvas. An Arhat who could transport himself and others into Tuchita.

DÊVATÂ SÛTRA 天請問經 Title of a translation by Hiuentsang, A.D. 648.

DÊVATIDÊVA 天中天 lit. the dêva among dêvas. The name given to Siddharta (v. S'âkyamuni), when, on his presentation in the temple of Mahês'vara (S'iva), the statues of all the gods prostrated themselves before him.

DEVÊNDRA SAMAYA 天主教法 lit. doctrinal method of the lord of dêvas. A work (on royalty), in the possession of a son of Râdja balêndrakêtu.

DÊVÎ (Singh. Dewi) 提鞞 explained by 天女 lit. a female dêva. Same as Apsaras.

DHANADA v. Vâis'ramaṇa.

DHANAHATCHÊKA 馱那羯磔迦 An ancient kingdom in the N.E. of modern Madras presidency.

DHANU 弓 lit. a bow. A measure of length, the 4000th part of a yôdjana.

DHARANA or Purâna. 陀那 explained by 銖 lit. the 24th part of a tael. An Indian weight, equal to 70 grains.

DHARAṆIM̃DHARA 持地 lit. grasping the earth. A fabulous Bodhisattva to whom Buddha revealed the future of Avalôkitês'vara.

DHÂRAṆÎ 陀羅尼 explained by 咒 lit. mantras. Mystic forms of prayer, often couched in Sanskrit, forming a portion of the Sûtra literature (Dhâraṇîpiṭaka) in China as early as the 3rd century, but made popular chiefly through the Yogâtchârya (q. v.) School. See also Vidyâdharapiṭaka; Mantra; Biddhi; Vidya mantra.

DHARMA (Pâli. Dhamma. Singh. Dharmma. Tib. Los krims) 達磨 or 答哩麻 or 達而麻耶 explained by 法 lit. law. (1.) The Buddhist law, principles, religion, canon, and objects of worship. (2.) The perception of character or kind, one of the Chaḍayatanas. (3.) One of the Triratna (q. v.)

DHARMA ÂRAṆYAKAḤ 達磨阿蘭若 or 法阿蘭若 Hermits and ascetics, holding that the principles(dharma) of human nature are originally calm and passive. Their favourite tree is the Bodhi tree.

DHARMABALA 竺法力 A S'ramaṇa of the West, translator (A.D. 419) of the Sukhâvatî vyûha.

DHARMABHADRA 法賢 or 安法賢 A S'ramaṇa of the West, translator of 2 sûtras. See also under Dharmadêva.

DHARMABODHI 達磨菩提 or 法覺 A S'ramaṇa, translator (A. D. 386-550) of the Nirvaṇa s'âstra.

DHARMADÊVA 法天 A S'ramaṇa of Nâlanda saṁghârâma, who translated (under this name) 46 works (A. D. 973-981), and under the name Dharmabhadra (法賢) 72 works (A.D. 982—1,001).

DHARMADHARA 曇摩持 or 持法 or 曇摩侍 or 法惠 or 法慧 (Dharmapradjña) or 法海 (1.) A S'ramaṇa of the West who translated (A. D. 367) several works on the Vinaya. (2.) A fabulous king of Kinnaras.

DHARMADHÂTU HṚIDDYA SAÑVṚITA NIRDÊS'A 法界體性無分別會 Title of a translation by Mandra, A. D. 502—557.

DHARMAJÂTAYAS'AS 曇摩伽陀耶舍 or 法生稱 A native of Central India, translator (A.D. 481) of the Amitharta sûtra (無量義經).

DHARMA GAHANÂBHYUDGATA 空王 A fictitious Buddha said to have taught 'absolute intelligence'.

DHARMAGUPTA or Dharmakoti (Pâli. Dhammagutta) 曇磨毱多 or 達摩笈多 or or 達瞿諦 or (incorrectly) 曇無德 or 法密 or 法藏 or 法護 (1.) An ascetic of Ceylon, founder (circa 400 A. D.) of the Dharmaguptaḥ (法密部 or 法藏部 or 法護部) School, a branch of the Sarvâstivâdâḥ (2.) A native of southern India who translated (A. D. 590—616) many works into Chinese.

DHARMAGUPTA BHIKCHU KARMAN 四分僧羯磨 Title of a compilation by a disciple of Hiuen-tsang.

DHARMAGUPTA BHIKCHUNÎ KARMAN 四分比丘尼羯磨法 Title of a translation by Guṇavarman, A.D. 431.

DHARMAGUPTA VINAYA 四分律藏 Title of a translation by Buddhayas'as (A. D. 405) and another.

DHARMAKALA 曇摩迦羅 or 曇柯迦羅 or 法時 A native of Central India, the first translator of a book on discipline (Pratimokcha of the Mahâsaṁghika vinaya) introduced in China (A.D. 250).

DHARMÂKARA 達摩羯羅 or 法性 lit. religious nature. (1.) A title of honour. (2.) A previous incarnation of Amitâbha, when a disciple of Lôkês'vararâdja. (3.) A native of Baktra, follower (A.D. 630 of the Hinâyâṇa School.

DHARMAKÂYA (Tib. Cos kyi sku) 法身 lit. the spiritual body. (1.) The first of the 3 qualities (v. Trikâya) belonging to the body of every Buddha, viz. luminous spirituality. (2) The 4th of the Buddhakchêtras.

DHARMAMATI 達摩摩提 or 法意 lit. mind of the law. (1.) The 8th son of Tchandra sûrya pradîpa. (2.) A S'ramaṇa of the West who translated (A. D. 430) two works.

DHARMAMITRA 曇摩密多 or 法秀 lit. flourishing of the law, or 連眉禪師 lit. the man with connected eyebrows, teacher of dhyâna. A S'ramana of Cabul who translated (A. D. 424—442) many works.

DHARMANANDÎ 曇摩難提 or 法喜 lit. joy of the law. A S'ramaṇa of Tukhâra who translated (A. D. 384—391) five works.

DHARMAPADA (Pâli. Dhammapada). Title of 4 versions of a work by Dharmatâata, viz. (1.) 法句經 or 曇鉢偈 Dharmapada gâthâ A.D. 224, (2.) 法句譬喻經 Dharmapadâvadâna sûtra A. D. 290—306, (3.) Avadâna sûtra (q.v.), (4.) 法集要頌經 Dharmasaṁgraha mahârtha gâthâ sûtra, A. D. 980—1001.

DHARMAPÂLA 達摩波羅 or 護法 lit. guardian of the law. A native of Kântchipura, who preferred the priesthood to the hand of a princess. He is famous as a dialectician, an opponent of Brahminism, and author of four works (translated into Chinese A.D. 650—710).

DHARMAPHALA 曇果 or S'âkya Dharmaphala 釋曇果 A S'ramana of the West who introduced in China (A.

D. 207) the 中本起經 Madhyama ityukta sûtra (a biography of S'âkyamuni).

DHARMAPRABHÂSA 法明 lit. brightness of the law. A Buddha who, in the Ratnâvabhâsa Kalpa, will appear in Suvis'uddha, when there will be no sexual difference, birth taking place through anupapâdaka.

DHARMAPRADJÑA v. Dharmadhara.

DHARMAPRAVITCHAYA (Pâli. Dhamma vitchaya) 擇 lit. discrimination or 擇覺 lit. the (second) bodhyanga (q. v.), viz. discrimination, i.e. the faculty of discerning truth and falsehood.

DHARMAPRYIA 達摩畢利 or 曇摩卑 or 曇摩蜱 or 法愛 lit. love of the law or 法善 lit. goodness of the law. (1.) A S'ramaṇa from India, translator of the Das'âsahasrikâ (A. D. 382) and of a work on the vinaya (A. D. 400). (2.) An adherent of the Hinayâna School from Baktra (A.D. 630).

DHARMARAKCHA. Name of five persons, viz. (1.) 竺法蘭 lit. Indu Dharma Âraṇya (Tib. Gobharaṇa or Bhâraṇa), translator (with Kás'yapa Mâtañga) of the sûtra of 42 sections (A.D. 67); (2.) 竺曇摩羅察 or 竺曇摩羅剎 or 竺法護 lit. Indu Dharmarakcha, a native of Tukhâra, who introduced the first alphabet in China and translated (A. D. 266—317) some 175 works; (3.) 竺曇無蘭 (Indu Dharma Âraṇya) or 法正 lit. correctness of the law, translator of seveal works (A. D. 381—395); (4.) 曇無讖 or 曇摩讖 or 曇謨讖 or 曇摩羅讖 or 法豐 lit. prosperity of the law, translator of 24 works (A.D. 414—421); (5.) 法護 lit. guardian of the law, translator of 12 works (A. D. 1,004—1,058).

DHARMARÂDJA 法王 lit. king of the law (religion). Epithet of every Buddha.

DHARMARATNA 法寶 lit. treasures of the law. Collective name for all sûtras.

DHARMARUTCHI 曇摩流支 or 法希 lit. hope of the law, or 法樂 lit. joy of the law. Name of three persons, viz. (1.) a S'ramana of southern India, translator of three works (A.D. 501—507); (2.) a S'ramana of southern India who changed his name (A.D. 684—705) to Bodhirutchi (q. v.), translator of 53 works (died A. D. 727); (3.) the subject of a legend, a fictitious contemporary of Kchêmaṁkara Buddha.

DHARMAS'ÂLÂ or Puṇyas'âlá 達摩舍羅 or 福舍 lit. dwelling of happiness, i. e. an asylum, or dispensary.

DHARMASAÑGÎTI SÛTRA 法集經 Title of a translation by Bodhirutchi (A. D. 515).

DHARMASAÑGRAHA SÛTRA 法集名數經 Title of a translation by Aânapála (A.D. 980—1,000).

DHARMAS'ARÎRA 法舍利 General term for all s'arîras (q. v.)

DHARMAS'ARÎRA SÛTRA 佛說法身經 Title of a book.

DHARMASATYA 曇諦 or 曇無諦 or 法實 lit. truth of the law. A S'ramaṇa from Parthia, who introduced in China (A.D. 254) the 羯磨 Karman of the Dharmagupta nikâya.

DHARMASIM̃HA 達摩僧伽 A famous dialectician in Kustana.

DHARMASMṚITY UPASTHÂNA (Pâli. Dhammânupassanâ) 念諸法從因緣生本無有我 lit. remember that the constituents (of human nature) originate according to the Nidânas and are originally not the self. The 4th mode of recollection (v. Smrityupasthâna). One of the 37 Bodhipakchika dharma.

DHARMÂS'ÔKA (Mong. Ghassalung ügei nomihu chan) 法阿育 The name given to As'ôka on his conversion.

DHARMAS'ÛRA or Dharmavikrama or S'âkyadharmas'ûra 釋法勇 or 曇無竭 or 法勇 lit. the brave of the law. A native of Chihli, of the surname Li 李, who visited India (A.D. 420—453) and brought to China the 觀世音菩薩得大勢菩薩受記經 Avalôkitês'vara mahâsthâmaprâptavyâkaraṇa sûtra.

DHARMATCHAKRA 法輪 lit. the wheel of the law. The emblem of Buddhism as a system of cycles of transmigration, the propagation of which is called 轉法輪 lit. turning the wheel of the law.

DHARMATCHAKRA PRAVARTANA SÛTRA. Title of two translations, viz. (1.) 轉法輪經 A.D. 25—220, and (2.) 佛說三轉法輪經 A. D. 710.

DHARMATRÂTA 達摩怛邏羅多 or 達磨多羅 or

法救 lit. saviour of the law. A native of Gândhâra, maternal uncle of Vasumitra, and author of 7 works (translated into Chinese A. D. 663—1001).

DHARMATRÂTA DHYÂNA SÛTRA 達磨多羅禪經 Title of a translation by Buddhabhadra (A. D. 398—421).

DHARMAVARTI v. Kâs'yapa Buddha.

DHARMAVIKRAMA v. Dharmas'ûra.

DHARMAVIVARDHANA 法益 lit. increase of the law. Official title of Kunâla.

DHARMAYAS'AS 曇摩耶舍 or 法稱 lit. fame of the law. (1.) A native of Cabul, translator (A. D. 407—415) of several works. (2.) A native of India, author of several works (translated into Chinese A. D. 973—1058).

DHARMÔTTARÂḤ 達謨多梨與部 or 達摩鬱多梨部 or 法上部 lit. the School of the superior of the law, or 勝法部 lit. the School of the conqueror of the law. A School founded by Dharmôttara, a famous expositor of the Vinaya.

DHÂTU 頭陀 or 馱都 explained by 堅實 lit. firm and real or 抖擻 lit. raised. Sacred relics, s. a s'arîra (q. v.)

DHÂTUGÔPA v. Stûpa.

DHATUKÂYAPÂDA S'ÂSTRA 阿毗達磨界身足論 Title of a work by Vasumitra (or Pûrṇa), translated by Hiuentsang, A. D. 663.

DHRIṬAKA (Tib. Dhitika) 提多迦 or 通眞量 lit. penetrating correct measures. The 5th Indian patriarch, born at Magadha. a disciple of Upagupta. He converted the heretic Mikkhaka and died (circa 286 B. C.) by ecstatic contemplation.

DHRITARÂCHṬRA (Siam. Thatarot. Tib. Yul bhkor srung. Mong. Ortchilong tetkuktchi) 第黎多曷羅殺吒羅 or 提頭賴吒 or 提多羅吒 or 持國者 lit. controller of the kingdom. The white guardian of the East, one of the Lôkapâlas, a king of Gandharvas and Pis'atchas.

DHRITIPARIPÛRṆA 堅滿菩薩 lit. the firm and complete Bodhisattva. A Buddha expected to appear as Padma vrichabha vikrâmin, attending on Padmaprabha.

DHRUVAPAṬU 杜魯婆跋吒 or 常叡 lit. constantly intelligent. A king of Vallabhi (A. D. 630), son-in-law of S'îladitya.

DHVADJÂGRAKÊYÛRA 妙幢相三昧 A degree of ecstatic meditation (v. Samâdhi).

DHVADJÂGRAKÊYÛRA DHÂRAṆÎ 佛說無能勝旛王如來莊嚴陀羅尼經 Title of a translation by Dânapâla, A.D. 980—1000.

DHYÂNA (Tib. Sgompa. Mong. Dyan) 第耶那 or 持訶那 or 禪那 or 禪 lit. abstraction, or 禪定 lit. fixed abstraction, or 觀 lit. contemplation, or 念修 lit. exercises in reflection. One of the 6 Pâramitâs, abstract contemplation, intended to destroy all attachment to existence in thought or wish. From the earliest times Buddhists taught four different degrees of abstract contemplation by which the mind should free itself from all subjective and objective trammels, until it reached a state of absolute indifference or self-annihilation of thought, perception and will. In after times, when the dogma of metempsychosis became the ruling idea and a desire arose to have certain localities corresponding to certain frames of mind where individuals might be reborn in strict accordance with their spiritual state, the 18 Brahmalôkas were divided into 4 regions of contemplation (四禪). The first region of Dhyâna (初禪), comprising the heavens called Brahma parichadya, Brahma purôhita and Mahâbrahma, was said to be as large as one whole universe The second Dhyâna (第二禪) was made to comprehend the heavens Parittâbha, Apramabha and Abhâsvara and to correspond in size to a small chiliocosmos (小千界). The next three Brahmalôkas, Parîttas'ubha, Apramânâs'ubha and S'ubhakritsna, were assigned to the third Dhyâna (第三禪) and described as resembling in size a middling chiliocosmos (中千界). The fourth Dhyâna (第四禪), equal in proportions to a large chiliocosmos (大千界), was formed by the remaining 9 Brahmalôkas, namely, Puṇyaprasava, Anabhraka, Vrihatphala, Asandjñisattva, Avriha, Atapa, Sudris'a, Sudars'ana and Akanichṭha. The first region, being of the size of 1 universe, was also considered to comprise, as every universe does, 1 sun and moon, 1 central mountain (Mêru), 4 large continents and 6 Dêvalôkas. Consequently the second region, being equal to a chiliocosmos, had to be counted as numbering 1 second Dhyâna with 1,000 first Dhyânas, 1,000 suns and moons, 1,000 Mêrus, 4,000 continents and 6,000 Dêvalôkas. Likewise the third region was now described as being formed by the third Dhyâna with 1,000 second Dhyânas, 10 millions, of first Dhyânas, 10 million suns and moons 10 million Mêrus, 40 million continents and 60 million Dêvalôkas. The fourth region was made up by the fourth Dhyâna with 1,000 third Dhyân as, 10 million second Dhyânas, 10,000 kôt'is of first Dhyânas, as many suns, moons and Mêrus, 40,000 kôṭis of continents and 60,000 koṭis of Dêvalôkas. But having once given to those 4 Dhyânas a place in cosmology, the Buddhist mind logically proceeded to make them participate in those changes to which every universe was believed to be subject by the rotation of kalpas (see under Asam̃kyêa). Consequently it was said that, in the course of every 'kalpa of destruction (壞刼) within a cycle of 64 kalpas, the first Dhyâna is destroyed 56 times (â 1 kalpa) by fire, the second Dhyâna 7 times by water, and the third Dhyâna once (during the 64th kalpa) by wind. The fourth Dhyâna, corresponding fo a state of absolute indifference, was declared to remain untouched by all the revolutions of the worlds. 'When fate (天命) comes to an end, then the fourth Dhyâna may come to an end too,' but not sooner.

DIGNÂGA or Mahâdignâga 大域龍 lit. the dragon of the great region or Mahâdignâgârdjuna 大域龍樹 lit. the dragon tree of the great region. Author of several works translated into Chinese A.D. 648—1,000.

DINABHA 提那婆 A deity worshipped by heretics in Persia.

DÎPAM̃KARA (Singh. Dipankara. Tib. Marmemzad) 提和竭羅 or 燃燈佛 or 定光佛 lit. the Buddha of fixed light. The 24th predecessor of S'âkyamuni (who foretold the coming of the latter), a disciple of Varaprabha.

DÎRGABHÂVANA SAM̃GHÂRÂMA 地迦婆縛那僧伽藍 A monastery, near Kustana, with a statue which had 'transported itself' thither from Kharachar.

DÎRGHÂGAMA v. Âgama.

DÎRGHÂGAMA SÛTRA 佛說長阿含經 Title of a compilation of 30—34 Sûtras, translated by Buddhayas'as A.D. 413.

DÎRGHANAKHA or Agnivais'-yâna (Pâli. Aggivêssâyana) 長爪 lit. long claws. An

Arhat, uncle of S'âriputtra.

DÎRGHANAKHA PARIVRÂDJAKA PARIPṚITCHTCHÂ 長爪梵志請問經 Title of a translation, A. D. 700.

DIVÂKARA 地婆訶羅 or 日照 lit. sunshine. A S'ramana of Central India, translator (A.D. 676—688) of 18 or 19 works author of a new alphabet.

DIVYAS'RÔTRA (Pâli. Dibbasôta) 天耳 lit. celestial ear. The 2nd Abhidjña, ability to understand any sound produced in any universe.

DIVYATCHAKCHUS (Páli. Dibbatchakkhu) 天眼 lit. celestial eye. The 1st Abhidjña, instantaneous view of any object in any universe.

DJALADHARA GARDJITA GHÔCHASUSVARA NAKCHATRA RÂDJA SAMKUSUMITÂBHIDJÑA 雲雷音宿王華智 lit. flowery wisdom of the ruler of the constellation of 'the sound of thunder clouds.' A fictitious Buddha of the Priyadars'ana kalpa.

DJALAGARBHA 水藏 lit. treasury of water. Second son of Djalavâhana, reborn as Gôpâ.

DJALÂMBARA 水滿 lit. fulness of water. Third son of Djalavâhana, reborn as Râhula.

DJÂLANDHARA 闍爛達羅 Ancient kingdom and city in the Punjaub, now Jalendher. Lat. 31°21 N., Long. 75° 38 E.

DJALAVÂHANA 流水 lit. flowing water. A physician, son of Djâtimdhara, reborn as S'âkyamuni.

DJAMBALÂ (Tib. Dzám bha la) 擔步羅 or 苫婆羅 Citrus acida.

DJAMBU (Singh. Damba. Tib. Dzám bu) 瞻部 or 剡浮 or 閻浮樹 A tree with triangular leaves, perhaps the Eugenia jambolana.

DJAMBUDVÎPA (Singh. Dampadiwa. Siam. Xom phuthavib. Tib. Djambugling or Djambudwip. Mong. Djambudip) 咱輔的發 or 閻浮 or 譫浮洲 or 瞻部洲 or 剡浮 One of the 4 continents of our universe, of triangular (v. Djambu) shape, situated S. of the Mêru, the southern continent, designation of the inhavited world known to Buddhists, ruled by Narapati (人王 lit. king of men) in the E., by Gadjapati (象王 lit. king of elephants) in the S., by Tchatrapati (寶王) lit. king of the parasol jewel) in the W., by As'vapati (馬王 lit. king of horses in the N., and including, grouped around the Anavatapta (lake) and the Himâlaya, (1.) the countries of the Huns, Uigurs, Turks, etc. in the N., (2.) China, Corea, Japan, and some islands in the E., (3.) northern India (27 kingdoms), eastern India (10 kingdoms), southern India (15 kingdoms) and central Indian (30 kingdoms) in the S., and (4.) 34 kingdoms in the W.

DJAÑGULÎ VIDYÂ 佛說穰麌梨童女經 Title of a translation by Amoghavadjra, A.D. 746—771.

DJARÂMAVANA 老死 lit. decrepitude and death. One of the 12 Nidânas, the primary truth of Buddhism, i.e. recognizing that decrepitude and death are the natural products of the maturity of the 5 Skandhas.

DJÂTAKA or Djâtakamâla 闍多伽 or 祇夜 or 本生事 lit. adventures of original (former) births. Books detailing previous incarnations of saints.

DJÂTAKAMÂLÂ S'ÂSTRA 菩薩本生鬘論 Title of a compilation of 14 Djâtakas of S'âkyamuni by Aryasûra, commented on by Djinadêva, translated A.D. 960—1127.

DJÂTAKA NIDÂNA 佛說生經 Title of a translation by Dharmarakcha, A.D. 285.

DJATARÛ PARADJATA PAṬIGGAHANÂ VÊRAMANÎ 不捉持生像金銀寶物 lit. refrain from acquiring or possessing uncoined or coined gold, silver or jewels. The 10th rule for novices (v. Sikkhâpadâni), enforcing strict poverty.

DJÂTI 生 lit. birth. One of the 12 Nidânas, birth, taking place according to the Tchatur Yôni (q. v.) and in each case placing a being in some one of the 6 Gâti.

DJÂTIKA 闍提 or 金錢 lit. gold-cash. An odoriferous flower.

DJÂTIM̃DHARA 持水 lit. holding water. A physician who adjusted prescriptions and diet to the seasons; reborn as S'uddhôdana.

DJAYAGUPTA 闍耶毱多 A teacher of Hiuen-tsang when in Srughna.

DJAYAPURA 闍耶補羅 A city in the Punjaub, now Hasaurah, 30 miles N.W. of Lahore.

DJAYASÊNA 闍耶犀那 or 勝軍 lit. conquering army. A Vedic scholar of Surâchṭra, disciple of S'ilabhadra.

DJAYÊNDRA VIHÂRA 闍耶因陀羅寺 A monastery of Pravarnasenapura (now Srinagar) in Cashmere.

DJÊTA 逝多 or 祇陀 or 祇陀大子 lit. Djêta Kumâra. Son of Prasênadjit, original owner of the park Djêtavana.

DJÊTAVANA VIHÂRA 逝多林 or 逝多苑 or 祇樹 or 祇洹 or 給園 lit. the garden that was given or 金田 or 金地 lit. gold fields, or 戰勝林 lit. the park of fight and victory (Djêtrivana), or 祇洹精舍 lit. the monastery of Djêta. A vihâra of seven storeys, in the park which Anâthapiṇḍaka bought of prince Djêta and gave to S'âkyamuni.

DJÊTAVANÎYÂH or Djêtîyas'âilâḥ 只底舸部 or 只底與世羅部 or 支提加部 or 支提山部 or 制多山部 or 住支提山部 lit. School of the dwellers on mount Djêta, or 勝林部 lit. School of Djêtrivana. A subdivision of the Stâvirâḥ School.

DJIHVÂ 舌 lit. tongue, taste. (1.) One of the 5 Indriyas, the organ of taste. (2.) One of the 6 Vidjñânas, the sense of taste.

DJINA 耆那 or 視那 or 最勝 lit. most victorious. (1.) An epithet given to every Bud. dha. (2.) 陳那 A native of Andhra, author of some 6 s'âstras, translated A. D. 557—711.

DJINABANDHU 辰那飯茶 or 最勝親 lit. most victorious and intimate. An adherent (A. D. 650) of the Mahâyâna School.

DJINAMITRA 勝友 lit. victorious friend. An eloquent priest of Nâlanda (A.D. 630), author of the 根本薩婆多部律攝 Sarvâstivâda vinaya saṁgraha, translated A. D. 700.

DJINAPUTRA 愼那弗呾羅 or 最勝子 lit. most victorious son. A native of Parvata, author of the 瑜伽師地論釋 Yogâtchâryabhûmi s'âstra kârikâ, translated by Hiuentsang, A.D. 654.

DJINATRÂTA 辰那多羅多 or 最勝救 lit. most victorious saviour. An adherent (A.D. 630) of the Mahâsaṁghikaḥ School.

DJÎVAKA 時縛迦 or (incorrectly) 耆城 or 能活 lit. able to revive. A physician, illegitimate son of Bimbisâra by Âmradârikâ, who resigned the succession in favour of Adjâtas'âtru.

DJÎVAKAHRADA 救命池

lit. life-saving pond. A tank near Mrigadâva.

DJÎVAÑDJÎVA (Tib. Chang chang chou) 命命 A singing bird, famous by the sweetness of its note.

DJÑÂNA 若那 or 智 lit. knowledge. Supernatural intuition, as the result of samâdhi.

DJÑANABHADRA 若那跋達羅 or 攘那跋陀羅 or 智賢 lit. wise and sage. (1.) A native of 波頭摩 (Padma?), translator (A. D. 558), with Djñanayas'as, of a s'âstra on the Pañtcha vidyâ. (2.) A native of 波陵 or 訶陵 in 南海 co-translator (with others) of the 大般涅槃經後分 latter part of the Mahâparinirvâṇa sûtra. A. D. 665.

DJÑANAGUPTA 闍那崛多 or 志德 lit. determined virtue. A native of Gandhâra, translator (A. D. 561—592) of 43 works.

DJÑÂNÂKARA 智積 lit. accumulation of knowledge. Eldest son of Mahâbhidjṇâdjnânabhibhu, reborn as Âkchôbhya.

DJÑÂNAMUDRA 智印三昧 lit. the samâdhi called 'the seal of knowledge.' A degree of ecstatic meditation.

DJÑÂNAPRABHA 智光 lit. light of knowledge. A disciple of S'îlabhadra, an opponent of Brahminism.

DJÑÂNAS'RÎ 智吉祥 lit. happy omen of knowledge. A S'ramaṇa of India, translator (about A. D. 1053) of two works.

DJÑÂNATCHANDRA (1.) 智月 lit. moon of knowledge. Name of a prince of Kharachar who entered the priesthood (A. D. 625.) (2.) 慧月 lit. moon of wisdom. Name of the (heretical) author of the 勝宗十句義論 Vais'èchika nikâya das'apadârtha s'âstra, translated by Hiuentsang, A. D. 648. Perhaps the two names refer to one and the same person.

DJÑÂNAYAS'AS 闍那耶舍 or 藏稱 lit. fame of the piṭaka, or 勝名 lit. name of the conqueror. A native of Magadha, teacher of Yas'ogupta and Djñâgupta, cotranslator (A.D. 564—572) of 6 works.

DJÑÂNÔLKÂ 慧炬三昧 lit. the samâdhi called 'the torch of wisdom.' A degree of ecstatic meditation.

DJÑÂNÔLKÂ DHÂRAṆÎ SARVADURGATI PARIS'ODHANÎ. Title of 2 translations, viz. 佛說智炬陀羅尼經 by Dêvapradjñ and others, A. D. 691, anad

佛說智光滅一切業障陀羅尼經 by Dânapâla A. D. 980—1000

DJÑANOTTARA BODHISATTVA PARIPRITCHTCHÂ. Title of 3 translations, viz. (1.) 慧上菩薩問大善權經 by Dharmarakcha, A. D. 285, (2) 大乘方便會 by Nandi, A.D. 420. (3.) 佛說大方廣善巧方便經 by Dânapâla, A.D. 980—1000.

DJÑÂTAKA 市演得迦 or Sadváhana 娑多婆漢那 A king of southern India, patron of Nâgârdjuna.

DJUḌINGAS 殊徵伽 Heretics, who wear rags and eat putrid food.

DJVALAPRAS'AMANI DHÂRAṆÎ Title of 2 translations, viz. (1.) 佛說救面然餓鬼陀羅尼神咒經 by S'ikchânanda about A. D. 695. (2.) 佛說救拔口燄餓鬼陀羅尼經 by Amoghavadjra, A.D. 746—771.

DJYÂICHṬHA 逝瑟吒 The last month in spring.

DJYÔTICHKA 殊底色迦 or 樹提伽 or 星曆 lit. sphere of the stars. A native of Râdjagriha (B. C. 525), who gave all his wealth to the poor.

DJYÛTICHPRAB'HA 光明大梵 lit. the great Brahmin called 'light and bright.' A fictitious Buddha connected with the Amitâbha legend.

DRÂVIḌA or Drávira 達羅毗茶 A kingdom between Madras and the Cauveri.

DRIḌHÂ 堅牢地神 A goddess of the earth.

DRÔṆA 斛 A picul (133⅓ pounds).

DRÔṆASTÛPA 瓶窣都波 stûpa containing a picul of relics of S'âkyamuni's body (stolen by a Bhramin).

DRÔṆÔDANA RÂDJA (Tib. Bhudh rtsizas. Mong. Rachiyan ideghetu) 途盧諾檀那 or 斛飯王 or 斛王 A prince of Magadha, father of Dêvadatta and Mahânâma, uncle of S'âkyamuni.

DRÛMA 法堅那羅王 A king of Kinnaras.

DÛCHASANA 突舍薩那寺 A monastery in Tchinapati.

DUḤKHA v. Âryani satyânt.

DUKÛLA 頭鳩羅 Fine silk.

DUNDUBHÎS'VARA RÂDJA (Tib. Rnga byangs ldan pa) 雲自在燈王 or 天鼓音 lit. sound of celestial drums. Name of each kôṭi of Buddas taught by Sadâparibhûta.

DURGÂ 突迦 or Bhîmâ or Marichi. The wife of Mahês'vara, to whom human flesh was offered once a year in autumn.

DUS'TCHARITRA (Pâli. Burm. Duzzaraik) 十惡 lit. ten wicked deeds, viz. (1.) three deeds of the body, i.e. taking life, theft, and adultery; (2.) four deeds of the mouth, i.e. lying, exaggeration, abuse and ambiguous talk; (3.) three deeds of the mind, i.e. coveting, malice and unbelief.

DVÂDAS'ABUDDHAKA SÛTRA. Title of 2 translations, viz. (1.) 十二佛名神咒校量功德除障滅罪經 by Djñânagupta, A. D. 587, and (2.) 佛說稱讚如來功德神咒經 A.D. 711.

DVADAS'ANIKÂYA S'ÂSTRA 十二門論 Title of a tract by Nâgârdjuna, translated by Kumâradjîva, A. D. 408.

DVÂDAS'AVIHARAṆA SÛTRA 十二遊經 The life of S'âkyamuni (to his 12th year), translated by Kâlodaka, A. D. 392.

DVÂRAPATI 墮羅鉢底 An ancient kingdom, on the upper Irawaddy.

DVÎPA (Siam. Thavib) 提鞞波 or 洲 lit. island. A continent; four such composing a universe.

E.

ÊKAS'RIÑGA RICHI 獨角仙人 lit. the unicorn-richi. An ascetic who, ensnared by a woman, lost his riddhi.

ÊKAUYAHÂRIKÂḤ (Singh. Ekabhyòhârikâs) 猗柯毗與婆訶梨柯部 or 一說部 or 執一說言部 lit. School of one language. A School which repeated the teachings of the Mahâsaṁghikâḥ.

EKÔTTARÂGAMAS or Ekôttarikâgama v. Âgama.

ÊLAPATRA 翳羅鉢呾羅 or 伊那跋羅 (1.) A Nâga who consulted S'âkyamuni about rebirth in a higher sphere. (2.) A palm tree. formerly destroyed by that Nâga.

F.

FERGHANA 怖捍 or 霍罕 Province and city in Turkestan, on the upper Jaxartes.

G.

GADGADASVARA 妙音 lit. wonderful sound. A fictitious Bodhisattva, master of 17 degrees of samâdhi, residing in Vâirotchana ras'mi pratimaṇḍita.

GADJAPATI v. Djambudvîpa.

GAHAN 喝捍 An ancient kingdom, W. of Samarkand, now a district of Bokhara.

GANDHA (Singh. Gandhan) 香 lit. fragrance. One of the Chaḍâyatana; the sense of smell.

GANDHAHASTÎ 香象 lit. incense elephant. The 72nd of 1,000 Buddhas of the Bhadrakalpa.

GANDHA MÂDANA 香山 lit. incense mountain. One of 10 fabulous mountains (known to Chinese Buddhism), the region of the Anavatapta lake.

GÂNDHÂRA 乾陀羅 or 犍陀衛 or 犍馱邏 An ancient kingdom in the North of the Punjab (about Dheri and Bajour), famous as a centre of Buddhism. S'âkyamuni, in a former life, lived there and tore out his eyes to benefit others. See also under Kuṇâla.

GANDHARVAS or Gandharva Kâyikas (Singh. Gandharwa. Siam. Thephakhon than) 乾闥婆 or 健達縛 or 揵達婆 or 彥達縛 or 犍陀羅 or 犍陀 explained by 嗅香 lit. smelling incense, or by 食香 lit. feeding on incense. Demons (superior to men), living on Gandha mâdana; the musicians of Indra; the retinue of Dhritarachtra and others.

GAṆÊNDRA 不可說佛 lit. the dumb Buddha. The 733rd of the 1,000 Buddhas of the Bhadra Kalpa.

GANÊS'A v. Vinâyaka.

GAÑGÂ (Siam. Khongka) 競伽 or 殑伽 or 强伽 or 恒伽 or 恒河 explained by 福水 lit. happy river (Mahâbhadrâ) or by 天堂來者 lit. that which came from heaven (sc. to earth, gâm-gâ). The Ganges, which drops from S'iva's ear inio the Anavatapta lake, thence passes out, through the mouth of the silver cow (gômukhi), and falls, after permeating eastern India, into the southern ocean, 'heretical superstition' ascribing to the water of the Ganges sin-cleansing power.

GAÑGADVÂRA 競伽河門 lit. the gate of the river Ganges. A famous dêvâlaya, the present Hurdwar.

GANGI 競祇 A sorcerer of the time of Kâs'yapa Buddha, a former incarnation of Apalâla.

GAÑGOTTAROPÂSIKÂ PARIPṚITCHTCH'Â 恒河上優婆夷會 Title of a translation by Bodhirutchi, A. D. 618—907.

GARBHA SÛTRA. Title of 4

translations, viz. (1.) 佛說胞胎經 by Dharmarakcha, A. D. 303, (2.) 菩薩處胎經 A.D. 384—417, (3.) 佛爲阿難說人處胎經 by Bodhirutchi, A. D. 618—907, and (4.) 佛說入胎藏會 A. D. 618—907.

GARUḌA (Singh. Garunda. Siam. Khrut. Tib. Mka Iding or Phreng thogs) 揭路茶 or 伽樓羅 or 迦樓羅 or 誐嚕拏 explained by 金翅鳥 lit. a bird with golden wings. Monstrous birds (superior to men), the enemies of Nâgas. The Garuḍa, king of birds, is, in Brahminism, the constant companion of Vishnu.

GATCHI 揭職 An ancient kingdom, the region of Rooee, between Balkh and Bamian.

GÂTHA 伽陀 or 伽他 or 偈 explained by 諷頌 lit. hymns and chants, or by 孤起頌 lit. singly raising a chant i. e. detached stanzas (to be distinguished from Gêya). Metrical narratives or hymns with a moral purport. Gâthâs of 32 works are called Âryâgîti.

GÂTI (Tib. Grobai rigs drug) 六道 or 六趣 lit. 6 paths. Six conditions of sentient existence, viz, dêvas, men, asûras, beings in hell, prêtas and animls. The latter three are called 'lower paths' (下三途).

GAUTAMA (Singh. Gautama. Siam. Samonokôdom or Phrakôdom. Tib. Geoutam. Mong. Goodam) 喬答摩 or 瞿曇 explained by 地最勝 lit. on earth (gâu) the most victorous (tama). (1.). The sacerdotal name of the S'âkya family. (2.) An ancient richi, member of that family. (3.) A name of S'âkyamuni.

GAUTAMA DHARMADJÑÂNA 瞿曇達磨闍那 or Dharmapradjña 達摩般若 or 達摩波若 or 曇法智 The eldest son of Gautama Pradjñarutchi; governor of Yangchuen, translator (A.D. 582) of a work on Karma.

GAUTAMA PRADJÑARUTCHI 瞿曇般若流支 or 智希 A Brâhmana of Vârâṇas'î, translator (A. D. 538—543) of some 18 works.

GAUTAMA SAṂGHADÊVL 瞿曇僧伽提婆 or 衆天 lit. the assembled dévas. A native of Cabul, translator (A.D. 383—398) of some 7 works.

GAUTAMÎ 憍曇彌 or 瞿夷 explained by 明女 lit. intelligent woman, or 尼衆主

lit. ruler of the assembled nuns. A title of Mahâpradjâpatî.

GAVÂM̃PATI 憍梵婆提 explained by 牛司 lit. ruminating like a cow. A man born with a mouth like a cow (in expiation of sins committed in a former life).

GAYÂ 伽邪 A city of Magadha (N. W. of present Gayah), where S'âkyamuni became Buddha (v. Bodhidruma).

GAYÂKÂS'YAPA (Singh. Gayakasyappa) 伽邪迦葉波 A brother of Mahâkâs'yapa, originally a fire worshipper, one of the 11 foremost disciples of S'âkyamuni. See also Samantaprabhâsa.

GAYÂS'ATA 伽邪舍多 A native of 摩提國 (Madra), descendant of Udra Râma; laboured, as the 18th Indian patriach, among the Tokhari Tartars, and died (B. C. 13) 'by the fire of ecstatic meditation'.

GAYÂS'ÎRCHA SÛTRA. Title of 4 translations viz. (1.) 文殊師利問菩提經 by Kumâradjîva, A. D. 384—417; (2.) 伽邪山頂經 by Bodhirutchi, A.D. 386—534; (3.) 佛說象頭精舍經 by Vinîtarutchi, A. D. 582; (4.) 大乘伽邪山頂經 by Bodhirutchi, A. D. 693.

GAYÂS'ÎBCHA SÛTRA ṬÎKÂ 文殊師利菩薩問菩提經論 Commentary (on the preceding work), by Vasubandhu, translated (A. D. 535) by Bodhirutchi.

GAYATA 闍夜多 A native of northern India, the 20th Indian patriarch, teacher of Vasubandhu; died A. D. 47.

GÊYA 祇夜 or 重頌 lit repetitional chants. (1.) Metrical interpolations, repeating the sense of preceding prose passages. (2.) Odes in honour of saints. See also Gâthâ.

GHANAVYÛHA SÛTRA 大乘密嚴經 Title of a translation by Divâkara, A. D. 618—907.

GHAṆṬÂ 揵稚 or 揵 A large gong or bell used in monasteries.

GHAṆṬISÛTRA 揵稚梵讚 A transliteration by Dharmadêva, A. D. 973—981.

GHAZNA v. Hosna.

GHÔCHA 瞿沙 or 妙音 lit. wonderful voice. An Arhat, author of the Abhidharmâmrita s'âstra, who restored the eyesight of Kuṇâla by washing his eyes with the tears of people moved by his eloquence.

GHÔCHAMATI 響意 lit. meaning of noise. The 7th son of Tchandra sûrya pradîpa.

CHÔCHIRA 具史羅 or 瞿史羅 or 劬師羅 A grihapati of Kâus'âmbî, who gave S'âkyamuni the Ghôchiravana (Singh. Gosika) park 瞿師羅 (the modern Gopsahasa, near Kosam).

GHRÂṆA (Pâli. Ghâna. Singh. Ghanan) 鼻 lit. the nose. One of the 6 Vidjñânas, the organ and sense of smell.

GHÛR or Ghôri 活國 An ancient kingdom and city between Koondooz and Cabul, near Khinjan.

GÎTAMITRA 祇多蜜 or 祇蜜多 or 謌友 lit. the singing friend. A S'ramaṇa of the West, translator (A.D. 317—420) of some 25 works.

GÔDHANYA v. Aparagodâna.

GÔKÂLÎ v. Kukâlî.

GÔKAṆTHA SAṂGHÂRÂMA 俱昏荼伽藍 A monastery in Sthânês'vara.

GÔLÔMA 牛毛 lit. a cow's hair. A subdivision of a yôdjana.

GÔMATI 瞿摩帝 (1.) The river Goomth, which rises in Rohilcund, and falls into the Ganges below Benares. (2.) A monastery (A. D. 400) in Kustana.

GÔPÂ (Tib. Satshoma. Mong. Bumiga) 瞿波 or 瞿夷 or 劬毗耶 explained by 守護地 lit. guardian of the ground. A title of Yas'odhara. See also Djalagarbha.

GÔPÂLA 瞿波羅 (1.) A nâga king of Pradîpa prâbhâpura, converted by S'âkyamuni. (2.) An Arhat of Vâisaka, famous as an author, who taught the existence of both ego and non-ego.

GÔPALÎ 瞿波利 A person, perhaps identic with Kukâlî.

GÔS'ÎRCHA TCHANDANA 牛首旃檀 Copperbrown sandalwood, such as found on the mountains of Uttarakuru, which continent is said to be shaped like 'the head of a cow.' The first image of S'âkyamuni was made of this wood.

GÔS'RIÑGA 瞿室餕伽 or 牛角 lit. cow's horn. A mountain, near Kustana.

GÔVIS'ANA 瞿毗霜那 An ancient kingdom, the region near Ghundowsee, S. of Moradabad, in Rohilcund.

GRAHAMÂTRIKÂ DHÂRAṆÎ 佛說聖母陀羅尼經 Title of a translation by Dharmadêva, A.D. 973—981.

GRÎCHMA 漸熱 lit. gradual heat. The months Djyâichtha and Âchâḍha (from the 16th day of the 1st, to the

15th day of the 3rd Chinese moon).

GHRIDHRAKÛTA (Pâli. Ghedjakabo) 耆闍崛山 or 姞栗陀羅矩吒 or 闍崛山 or 靈鷲山 or 鷲峰山 lit. vulture peak. A mountain (Giddore) near Râdjagriha, famous for its vultures and caverns inhabited by ascetics. where Pis'una, in the shape of a vulture, hindered the meditations of Ânanda.

GṚIHAPATI (Singh. Gihi) 揭利呵跋底 or 長者 lit. an elder. A wealthy householder; proprietor.

GRÔSAPAM v. Bhagârâma.

GUHYAGARBHARÂDJA SÛTRA 佛說秘密相經 Title of a translation (A.D. 980—1,000) by Dânapâla.

GUHYASAMAYAGARBHA RÂDJA SÛTRA 佛說秘密三昧大敎王經 Title of a translation (A.D. 980—1,000) by Dânapâla.

GUṆA 求那 or 塵 lit. atom, or 作者 lit. the active principle. Nature, looked upon as an active principle, operating in the Chaḍâyatanas. A term of the heretical Sañkhya philosophers, designating 3 stages of evolution, 3 worlds, 3 forces, the interaction of which is the cause of all variation in the forms of existence.

GUṆABHADRA 求那跋陀羅 or 德賢 lit. virtuous sage. (1.) A follower of the Mahîs'âsakâḥ in kapis'a (2.) A Brâhmana of Central India, translator (A.D. 435—443) of some 78 works.

GUṆADA 功德施 Author of 金剛般若波羅蜜經破取著不壞假名論 Vadjra pradjñâparamitâ sûtra s'âstra, translated (A. D. 683) by Divâkara.

GUṆAMATI 瞿那末底 or 德慧 lit. goodness and wisdom. A native of Parvata, who lived at Vallabhi, a noted antagonist of Brahminism, author of the 隨相論 Lakchaṇânusâra s'âstra, translated (A. D. 557—569) by Paramârtha.

GUṆAPRABHA 瞿拏鉢剌婆 or 德光 lit. light of goodness. A native of Parvati, who deserted the Hinâyâna for the Mahâyâna School, assailed the former in many tracts, and composed the Tattva satya and other s'âstras. Burnouf identifies him with Guṇamati.

GUṆARATNA SAÑKUSUMITA PARIPRITCHTCH'Â

功德寶華敷菩薩會 Title of a translation by Bodhirutchi, A.D. 618—907.

DUṆAVARMAN 求那跋摩 or 功德鎧 lit. armour of merit and goodness. A prince of Kubhâ (Cashmere), translator (about 431 A. D.) of 10 works.

GUṆAVṚIDDHI 求那毗地 or 德進 lit. advance of goodness. A S'ramaña of Central India, translator (A. D. 492—495) of 3 works.

GURUPÂDAGIRI v. Kukkuṭapâdagiri.

GURDJDJARA 瞿折羅 An ancient tribe (which subsequently moved S. and gave the name to Gujerat) and kingdom, in southern Radjpootana, around Barmir.

H.

HAHAVA v. Ababa.

HÂIMAVATÂḤ 醯摩跋多部 or 雪山住部 lit. School of dwellers on the snowy mountains. A subdivision of the Mahâsaṃghikâḥ School.

HAKLENAYAS'AS 鶴勒那夜奢 A Brâhmana, born in the palace of the king of Tukhâra. He divided himself into 1,000 individuals but made all the others invisible by his own splendour. When 22 years old, he became a hermit, and when 30 years old, having become an Arhat, he transported himself miraculously to Central India where he laboured (until A. D. 209) as the 23rd patriarch under the name Padmaratna.

HAMI 哈密 or 伊吾廬 An ancient kingdom and city, N. E. of lake Lop.

HANDJNA 韓若 A city somewhere in India, the birthplace of Rêvata.

HAÑSA SAṂGHÂRÂMA 亙娑伽藍 or 鴈伽藍 lit. wild goose monastery. A monastery on Indras'ilâguhâ, the inmates of which were once saved from starvation by the charitable self-sacrifice of a wild goose.

HARALI 褐剌縭 A fabric of the finest down.

HARCHA VARDDHANA 曷利沙伐彈那 or 喜增 lit. increase of joy. Name of kink of Kanyâkubdja, protector of Buddhists (A. D. 625).

HÂRITÎ or Aritî (Tib. Hphrog ma) 阿利帝 or 阿利底 or 鬼子母 lit. mother of demons. A woman of Râdjagriha who, having sworn to devour every baby in the place, was reborn as a Rakchasî and, having given birth to 500 children, devoured one every day. until she was converted by S'âkyamuni and became a nun. Her image is now in every nunnery.

HARIVARMAN 訶梨跋摩 A native of India, author of the 成實論 Satyasiddhi s'âstra, translated (A. D. 407—418) by Kumâradjîva.

HASARA 鶴薩羅 The 2nd capital of Tsâukûṭa, perhaps the modern Guzar on the Helmend.

HASAT 肘 lit. fore-arm. The 16,000th part of a yôdjana.

HASTIGARTA 象墮阬 lit. the ditch (formed by) the elephant's fall. A monument of S'âkyamuni's power in flinging aside a dead elephant put in his path by Dêvadatta.

HASTIKAKCHYÂ SÛTRA. Title of two translation viz. 佛說象腋經 by Dharmamitra, A. D. 420—479, and 佛說無所希望經 by Dharmarahcha, A. D. 265—316.

HASTIKÂYA 象軍 lit. the elephant corps (of an Indian army).

HAYAMUKHA v. Ayamukha.

HELMEND 羅摩印度 A river, rising in Afghanistan and falling into lake Hamoon.

HÊTUVÂDAPÛRVA STÂVIRÂḤ 醯兠婆拖部 or 因論先上座部 lit. the first School of the Stavirâs treating of the cause, or Hêtuvâdâḥ 因論部 lit. the School which treats of the causes. A subdivision of the Sarvâstivâdâḥ.

HÊTUVIDYÂ S'ÂSTRA 因明論 lit. the treatise explaining the causes. One of the Pantcha vidyâ s'âstras, a tract on the nature of truth and error.

HE VADJRA TANTRA 佛說大悲空智金剛大教王儀軌經 Title of a translation by Dharmarakcha, A.D. 1004—1058.

HIḌḌA 醯羅 A city (perhaps the modern Killa Assen, Lat. 34° 13 N. Long. 68° 40 E.) on a mountain on which S'âkyamuni, in a former life, sacrificed himself to save Yakchas.

HIMATALA 呬摩怛羅 or 雪山下 lit. below the snowy mountains. An ancient kingdom under a S'âkya ruler (A.D. 43), N. of the Hindookoosh, near the principal source of the Oxus.

HIMAVAT (Siam. Himaphant) 雪山 lit. snowy mountains. The Himalaya, Hindookoosh, and other mountains N. of India.

HÎNAYÂNA 小乘 lit. the small conveyance, i.e. the simplest vehicle of salvation. The primitive form of the

Buddhist dogma, the first of the 3 phases of development through which the Buddist system passed (v. Triyâna), corresponding with the first of the 3 degrees of Arhatship (v. S'râvaka). The characteristics of the Hînayâna School, of which the Chinese know 18 subdivisions, are the preponderance of active moral asceticism and the absence of metaphysical speculation and mysticism.

HÎNAYÂNÂBHIDHARMA 小乘阿毗達磨 or 小乘論 The philosophical canon of the Hînayâna School, now consisting of about 37 works, the earliest of which, the 分別功德論 Guṇanirdês'a s'âstra, was translated into Chinese, A.D. 25—220.

HIÑGU 興瞿 Assa foetida, a noted product of Tsâukûṭa.

HIRAṆYA PARVATA 伊爛拏鉢伐多 or 伊爛拏 An ancient kingdom, noted for a volcano being near its capital (the present Monghîr, Lat. 25° 16 N. Long. 86° 26 E.)

HIRAṆYAVATÎ or Hiraṇya or Adjitavatî 尸頼拏伐底 or 尸離刺拏伐底 or 阿利羅跋提 or 阿持多伐底 explained by 無勝 lit. invincible, or by 金沙跋提 lit. gold sand Vatî or by 跋提河 lit. the river Vati. A river rising in Nepaul and flowing past Kus'inagara, the modern Gaṇḍakî or Gunduck. Chinese texts confound it with the Nâiraṇdjana.

HOMA 鶴秣 A city (perhaps the modern Humoon) on the eastern frontier of Persia.

HOSNA or Ghazna 鶴悉那 the capital of Tsâukûṭa (q. v.), the modern Ghuznee.

HṚI 紇哩 explained by 心 lit. the heart. A mystic sound, used, in sorcery and litanies accompanied with mudrâ manipulations, to comfort the souls of the dead.

HROSMINKAN or Semenghân 紇露悉泯健 An ancient kingdom, the region of Koondooz, Lat. 35° 40 N. Long. 68° 22. E.

HUCHKARA 護瑟迦羅 A city of Cashmere, the modern Uskar, on the Behat.

HUDJIKAN 胡實健 An ancient kingdom, S. W. of Balkh, the region of Djuzdjân, Lat. 35° 20 N. Long. 65° E.

HUMI 護密 A tribe of Tamasthiti.

HUPIÂN 護苾那 The ancient capital of Urddhasthâna, N. of Cabul.

I.

ÎCHADHARA (Pâli. Îsadhara. Singh. Ishadhara. Siam. Tsinthon. Tib. Sciol darin) 伊沙陁羅 or 伊沙馱羅 explained by 持軸 lit. hinging on a pivot, or by 持轉 lit. revolving. A chain of mountains whose peaks resemble linchpins. The second of the 7 concentric circles of mountains surrounding the Mêru.

IKS'VÂKU VIRUDHAKA or Vidêhaka (Singh. Amba or Okkaka. Tib Bhu ram ching pa hphgsskyespo) 懿師魔 (Is'ma) or 甘蔗王 (Kama king). A descendant of Gautama (q. v.), the last king of Pôtala of the Kama (god of love) dynasty. When he heard that his four sons, whom he had banished for the sake of a concubine, refused to obey his summons to return, he exclaimed 釋迦 (S'âkya), meaning to say, 'is it possible'? Thenceforth his descendants were called the race of S'âkya.

INDRA (Siam. Phras in. Tib. Dvango or Bdosogs or Kaus'ika. Mong. Khurmusda kutchika or Khurmusda tegri) 因陀羅 explained by 帝 lit. supreme ruler, or by 王 lit. ruler. A popular god of Brahminism, adopted by Buddhism as representative of the secular power, protector of the church, but as inferior to any Buddhist saint. Further particulars see under S'akra, Sakchi, S'atamanya, Traiyastrims'as, Vadjra.

INDRADHVADJA 帝相 lit. image of Indra. A fictitious contemporary of S'âkyamuni, being Buddha of the S. W. of our universe, an incarnation of the 7th son of Mahâbhidjña djñânâ bhibhû.

INDRANÎLAMUKTÂ 因陀羅尼羅目多 explained by 帝 (Indra) 青 (azure) 珠 (pearl). i.e. a blue pearl called Indra (because it is the lord of pearls). A fabulous jewel forming the basis of the throne of Indra (v. Nyagrôdha).

INDRAS'ÂILAGUHÂ 因陀羅勢羅窶訶 explained by 帝釋窟 lit. the cavern of S'akra, or by 小孤石山 lit. the mountain of small isolated rocks. A cavernous mountain with rock temple, near Nâlanda.

INDRYA or Pantcha Indryâni (Pali. Indrayas) 五根 lit. 5 roots, explained by 發生 lit. productive of life. One of the 37 Bodhi pakchika dharma, 5 positive agents producing sound moral life, viz. (1.) faith v. S'raddêndriya,

(2.) energy v. Viryêndriya, (3.) memory v. Smritîndriya, (4.) ecstatic meditation v. Samadhîndriya, (5.) wisdom v. Pradjñêndriya. These 5 Indriyas differ from the 5 Balas (v. Balâ) only by being, in the latter case, viewed as negative moral agents preventing the growth of evil.

INDU 印度 (Indu) or 印特伽 (Indica sc. regio) or 身毒 (Sindhu, Scinde) or 賢豆 (Hindu) or 天竺 explained by 月 lit. the moon (sc. because the saints of India illumine the rest of the world), or 因陀羅婆他那 (Indravadana) explained by 主處 lit. the region (guarded by) Indra. General term for India which is described as resembling, in shape, the moon at her half, measuring 90,000 *li* in circumference, and placed among other kingdoms like the moon among the stars. See also Djambudvîpa.

INDU DHARMA ÂRAṆYA v. Dharmarakcha.

INDUS v. Sindh.

INVAKAN or Khavakan or Avakan (Afghân) or Vakhan 淫薄健 or 刼薄健 or 阿薄健 or 薄健 An ancient kingdom, the S.E. of Afghanistan, the original home of the Afghans.

IS'ANAPURA (lit. city of S'iva) 伊賞那補羅 An ancient kingdom in Burmah.

ISCHKESCHM 訖栗瑟摩 An ancient kingdom near the principal source of the Oxus.

ISFIDJAB 白水城 lit. the white river city. A city in Turkestan, on a small tributary of the Jaxartes.

ISKARDU v. Khas'a.

ÎS'VARA 伊葉波羅 or 伊溼伐羅 or 自在 lit. independent existence (sovereign). (1.) A title given to S'iva, Avalôkitês vara and other popular deities. (2.) A S'ramaṇa of the West, who made (A.D. 426) a translation (lost since 730 A. D.) of the Samyuktâbhidharma hridayas'âstra. (3.) A bhikchu of India, commentator of 菩提資糧論 a s'âstra by Nâgârdjuna, translated (A. D. 590—616) by Dharmagupta.

IS'VARADÊVA 自在天 lit. sovereign dêva. (1.) A name of S'iva. (2.) A deity revered by the Pâmsupatas.

ITIYUKTAS or Itivrittakam 伊帝目多 or 伊帝目多伽 explained by 本事 lit. original events. One of the 12 classes of Buddhist literature, biographical narratives.

K.

KACHANIA 屈霜你迦 An ancient kingdom, W. of Samarkand, near Kermina.

KACHAYA 濁 lit. corruption. There are 5 spheres of corruption, viz. (1.) the kalpa (刧) or existence of any universe, (2.) doctrinal views (見), (3.) miseries of transmigration (煩 惱), (4.) universal life (衆 生), and (5.) destiny (命).

KACHÂYA 迦羅沙曳 or 袈裟 explained by 染色衣 lit. dyed garments. The clerical (coloured) vestments.

KACHGAR 佉沙 or (after the name of the capital) 疏勒 An ancient kingdom (Casia regio), the modern Cashgar.

KADJIÑGARA or Kadjiñga or Kadjûghira (Pâli. Kadjanghêlê) 羯蝇揭羅 or 羯殊昷祇羅 An ancient kingdom, in Agra province, near Farakabad, the modern Kadjeri.

KAKUDA KÂTYÂYANA 迦旃延 One of 6 Brahmins who opposed S'âkyamuni, called Kabandhin Kâtyâyana in the Upanishads of the Atharvavêda.

KALA 時 lit. a season. A division of time, 4 hours.

KALANTAKA v. Karaṇḍaka.

KALÂNUSÂRIN 細末堅黑旃檀 lit. Tchaṇdana (yielding) a hard black dust. A species of sandalwood (Styrax benzoin).

KÂLAPINÂKA 迦羅臂拏迦 A city of Magadha, near Kulika, S. of Bahar.

KÂLARUTCHI 彊梁婁至 or 眞喜 lit. true joy. A S'ramaṇa of the West, who (A. D. 281) translated one sûtra.

KÂLASÛTRA (Siam. Kalasuta) 黑繩 lit. black ropes. The second of 8 hells where the culprits are loaded with heatedochains.

KALAVIÑGKA or Kuravikaya 迦陵頻伽 or 羯羅頻迦 or 迦陵毗迦 or 歌羅頻迦 or 好音鳥 lit. sweet voiced bird, or 仙鳥 lit. immortal bird. The Cuculus melan leicus.

KÂLAYAS'AS 畺良耶舍 or 時稱 lit. ever famous. A S'ramaṇa of the West, translator (A.D. 442) of 2 works.

KALIÑGA 羯陵伽 An ancient kingdom, S. E. of Kôs'ala, a nursery of heretics; the modern Calingapatam.

KALIRÂDJA 羯利王 or 歌利王 or 加利王 or 迦藍

浮 or 鬬諍王 lit. the quarrelsome king. A king of Magadha (reborn as Kâuṇḍinya), converted by the stoicism displayed by Kchântirichi when the latter's hands and feet were cut off, owing to the king's concubines having visited the richi's hermitage.

KÂLODAKA 迦羅留陀伽 or 時水 lit. time (kâla) water (udaka). A S'ramaṇa of the West, translator (A.D. 383) of one work.

KÂLÔDÂYIN 迦留陀夷 or 迦留陀夷 or 黑光 lit. (a man with a face of) black lustre. A disciple of S'âkyamuni, to be reborn as Samantaprabhâsa.

KALPA (Pâli. Kappa. Tib. Bskalpa. Mong. Galab) 刧波 or 刧波簸陀 or 刧 explained by 大時分 lit. a great period (not to be reckoned by months and years). A period during whick a physical universe is formed and destroyed. There are great kalpas (大刧) and small kalpas (小刧). Every great kalpa or mahâkalpa (Pâli. Mahakappa. Siam. Mahakab. Tib. Bskal pa cen po), or period elapsing from the moment when a universe is formed to the moment when another is put in its place, is divided into 4 Asaṁkhyêa kalpas (v. Vivartta, Vivarttasiddha, Samvartta, Samvarttasiddha), corresponding with the 4 seasons of the year and equal to 80 small kalpas or 1,344,000 years. Every small kalpa or Antara or interim kalpa (Singh. Antahkalpaya. Tib. Bar gyi bskal pa. Mong. Saghoratu or Sabssarum or Dumdadu Galab) is divided into a period of increase (增刧) and decrease (減刧). The former (Tib. Bskalpa bzang po), successively ruled by 4 Tchakravartis, called kings of iron, copper, silver and gold), is divided into 4 ages (iron, copper, silver, gold), during which human life gradually increases to 84,000 years and the height of the human body to 84,000 feet. The kalpa of decrease (Tib. Bskal pa ngan pa) is divided into 3 periods (三災) of distress (viz. pestilence, war, famine), during which human life is reduced to 10 years and the height of the human body to 1 foot. There is another distinction of 5 kalpas, viz. (1.) the interim (Antara) kalpa, divided, as above, into a period of increase and decrease; (2.) the kalpa of formation v. Vivartta; (3.) the kalpa of continued existence v. Vivarttasiddha; (4.) the kalpa of destruction, v. Saṁvartta; (5.) the kalpa of continued destruction v. Saṁvarttasiddha; (6.) the great kalpa v. Mahâkalpa. A third division gives, (1.) Antara kalpas (別刧), (2.) Vivartta kalpas (成刧), (3.) Saṁvartta kalpas (壞刧), and (4.) Mahâkalpas (大刧). A fourth division gives, (1.) Antara kalpas (小刧) of 16,800,000 years, (2.) Middling kalpas (中刧) of 336,000,000 years, (3.) Mahâkalpas of 1,344,000,000 years.

KÂMA v. Mâra.

KÂMADHÂTU or Kâmalôka or Kâmâvatchara (Tib. Dod pai khsma) 欲界 lit. the region of desire. (1.) The first of the Trâilôkya, the earth and the 6 Dêvalôkas, constituting the physical world of form and sensuous gratification. (2.) All beings subject to metempsychosis on account of the immoral character of desire.

KAMALADALA VIMALA NAKCHATRA RÂDJA SAMKUSUMITÂBHIDJÑA 淨華宿王智佛 lit. the king of the constellotion (called) pure flower and Buddha of wisdom. A fictitious Buddha, to appear in Vâirôtchana ras'mi praṭimanḍita.

KÂMALAÑKÂ 迦摩浪迦 An ancient kingdom, in Chittagong, opposite the mouth of the Ganges,

KAMALAS'ÎLA 迦摩羅什羅 A native of India (contemporary of Padmasambhava) who opposed the Mahâyâna School in Tibet.

KAMAPÛRA 迦摩縷波 An ancient kingdom, the modern Gohati, in western Assam.

KAMBALA 頷鉢羅 A fabric of fine wool.

KAṀKARA 甄迦羅 A numeral, equal to 10,000,000,000.

KANADÊVA 迦那提婆 A native of southern India, a Vais'ya by birth, disciple of Nâgârdjuna; laboured (B. C. 212—161), in Kapila and Pâṭaliputtra, as the 15th Indian patriarch, a great opponent of heretics.

KANAKA 羯尼迦 or 羯尼 The Butea frondosa. See also Palâs'a.

KAṆAKAVARṆA PÛRVAYOGA SÛTRA 佛說金色王經 Title of a translation (A. D. 542) by Gautama Pradjñârutchi.

KANAKAMUNI (Pâli Konâgamana. Siam. Phra Kônakham. Tib. Gser thub. Mong Altan tchidaktchi) 迦諾迦牟尼 or 拘那含牟尼 explained by 金寂 lit. a recluse (radiant as) gold A Brahman of the Kâs'yapa family, native of Subhanavati, the 2nd of the 5 Buddhas of the Bhadra kalpa, the 5th of the 7 ancient Buddhas, who converted 30,000 persons when human life lasted 30,000 years.

KANDAT 犍駄多 The capital of Tamasthiti, the modern Kundoot, 40 miles above Ishtrakh.

KANICHKA 迦膩色迦 or 迦膩伽王 A king of the Tochari, conqueror of a great part of India, patron of Buddhism, who built the finest stûpas in the Punjab and in Cabulistan. He reigned, B.C. 15 to 45 A.D., when the 3rd (or 4th) synod met in Cashmere and revised the canon finally.

KANTAKANAM AS'VARÂDJA (Singh. Kantaka) 犍陟 or 馬王 lit. king of horses. The horse by which S'âkyamuni escaped from home.

KÂÑTCHANAMÂLÂ 眞金鬘 lit. (wearing) headgear of pure gold. The wife of Kuṇâla, noted for her fidelity to her disgraced husband.

KÂÑTCHÎPURA 建志補羅 or 建志城 The capital of Drâviḍa, the modern Condjeveram, near Madras.

KANYÂKUBDJA 羯若鞠闍 or 罽饒夷城 explained by 曲女城 lit. city of humpbacked maidens. A kingdom and city of Central India, the modern Canouge, where the 1000 daughters of Brahmadatta, who refused Mahâvrikcha, became deformed.

KAPÂLIRAS or Kapâladhârinas 迦波釐 explained by 髏鬘 lit. (wearing a) headgear of skull bones. A heretical (Shivaitic) sect.

KAPILA 迦比羅 or 赤色仙 lit. the red-coloured richi. The founder of the Sâm̃khya (q. v.) philosophy, who, several centuries before S'âkyamuni, composed the heretical 金十七論 Sâm̃khyâkârikâ bhâchya s'âstra, translated (A. D. 557—569) by Paramârtha.

KAPILAVASTU (Pâli. Kapilavattu. Singh. Kimbulvat. Siam. Kabillaphat. Tib. Serskya ghroug. Mong. Kabilik) 刧比羅伐窣堵 or 迦毗羅蘇都 or 迦毗羅皤窣都 or 迦毗羅衛 or 迦毗羅 or 伽毗黎 or 迦夷 or 迦維 explained by 妙德城 lit. city of wonderful virtue or by 黄處 lit. yellow dwelling. An ancient city, birth place of S'âkyamuni, destroyed during the lifetime of the latter, situated (according to Hiuen-tsang) a short distance N.W. of present Gorucpoor, Lat. 26°46 N. Long. 83°19 E.

KAPIMALA 迦毗摩羅 A natixe of Patna, 13th

Indian patriarch, teacher of Nâgârdjuna, died (by samâdhi) about A. D. 137.

KAPIÑDJALA RÂDJA 迦頻闍羅王 or 雉王 lit. pheasant king. Name of S'âkyamuni, since, in a former life, he appeared as a pheasant (phoenix) to extinguish a conflagration.

KAPIS'A 迦畢試 Ancient kingdom and city, in the Ghûrbend valley, N. E. of Opiân, S. of the Hindookoosh, where a Han prince was once detained as hostage.

KAPITHA 劫比他 (1.) Ancient kingdom, also called Saṁkâs'ya, in Central India. (2.) A Bhraman, persecutor of Buddhists, reborn as a fish,c onverted by S'âkyamuni.

KAPÔTANA 劫布呾那 Ancient kingdom, the modern Kebûd or Keshbûd, N. of Samarkand.

KAPÔTIKÂ SAṀGHÂRAMA 迦布德伽藍 or 鴿伽藍 lit. pigeon monastery. A vihâra of the Sarvâstivâdâh, where S'âkyamuni, in the form of a pigeon, rushed into a fire to convert a sportsman.

KAPPHIṆA or Kamphilla 劫賓那 or 劫比拏 explained by 房宿 lit. the constellation Scorpio. A king of southern Kôs'ala, born in answer to prayer addressed to the regent of Scorpio; a disciple of S'âkyamuni; entered the priesthood as Mahâkapphiṇa to be reborn as Samantaprabhasa.

KARAṆḌA or Karaṇḍaka or Kalanda (Siam. Karavek) 迦蘭陀 or 阿蘭陁 or 迦蘭馱迦 or 羯蘭鐸迦 A bird of sweet voice (Cuculus melanoleucus), which waked Bimbisara to warn him against a snake.

KARAṆḌAHRADA 迦蘭陀池 A pond near Karaṇḍa vêṇuvana, a favourite resort of S'âkyamuni.

KARAṆḌA VÊṆUVANA 迦蘭陀竹園 The bamboo park (called after the bird Karaṇḍa), dedicated by Bimbisara first to a sect of ascetics, then to S'âkyamuni, for whom he built there the vihâra called Karaṇḍanivasa (Singh. Vêluvana).

KARAṆḌAVYÛHA SÛTRA 佛說大乘莊嚴寶王經 Title of a translation, A. D. 980—1,001.

KARATCHÎ v. Khadjîs'vara.

KARAVÎKA or Khadiraka (Siam. Karavik) 佉得羅柯 or 羯地洛迦 explained by 檐木山 lit. Djambu wood mountain. The 3rd of 7 concentric circles of rocks which surround the Meru; 10,000 feet high; separated by oceans from the 2nd and 4th circles.

KARCHÂPAṆA 羯利沙鉢那 or 迦利沙鉢拏 explained by 兩 lit. an ounze. A weight, equal to 80 Raktikâs or 175 grains.

KARMA (Tib. Du̥ byed) 羯摩 or 葛哩麻 explained by 業報 lit. retribution, or by 作法 lit. the law of action, or by 行 lit. action. The 11th Nidâna, the 4th of the 5th Skandhas viz. (the resultant of) moral action, which ethical term Chinese Buddhism substitutes for the metaphysical term Saṁskâra. Karma is that moral kernel (of any being), which alone survives death and continues in transmigration,

KARMADÂNA (Siam. Tscho khun balat) 羯摩陀那 or 維那 explained by 知事 lit. expert. The sub-director of a monastery.

KARMASIDDHA PRAKARAṆA S'ÂSTRA. Title of 2 translations of a tract by Vasubandhu, viz. 業成就論 by Vimokchapradjña A. D. 541, and 大乘成業論 by Hiuen-tsang, A. D. 681.

KAMAVARAṆA PRATISARAṆA 大乘三聚懺悔經 Title of a translation by Djṇânagupta and Dharmagupta, A.D. 590.

KARMÂVARṆA VIS'UDDHI SÛTRA 佛說淨業障經 Title of a translation, A. D. 350—431.

KARMAVIBHÂGA DHARMAGRANTHA 佛說分別善惡所起經 Title of translation (total abstinence tract), A.D. 25—220.

KARMAYA v. Tchatur Yôni.

KÂRMIKÂḤ 施設論部 lit. the School of Karma. A philosophical School which taught the superiority of morality over intelligence.

KARṆASUVARṆA (Pâli. Lata) 羯羅拏蘇伐剌那 or 金耳 lit. golden ears. Ancient kingdom in Gundwana, near Gangpoor.

KARPÛRA 羯布羅 or 香龍腦 lit. nâga brain perfume. Camphor.

KÂRTIKA 迦剌底迦 The 2nd month in autumn.

KARUṆÂPUṆḌARÎKA SÛTRA 悲華經 Title of a translation by Dharmarakcha, A. D. 397—439.

KÂS'Â 迦奢 A kind of grass (Saccharum spontaneum). A broom made of this grass, used by S'âkyamuni, is still an object of worship.

KASA'NNA 羯霜那 A kingdom, 300 *li* S. W. of Kharismiga, on the Oxus, the modern Koorshee.

KÂS'APURA 迦奢布羅 A kingdom, probably the country between Lucknow and Oude.

KÂS'Î v. Vârânas'î.

KAS'MÎRA 迦葉彌羅 or 迦溼彌羅 or 迦濕蜜羅 Cashmere, anciently called Kophene (v. Kubhâna), was converted through Madhyantika and became, during Kanichka's reign, the headquarters of northern Buddhism. Here the last synod assembled and hence Buddhism, saturated with Shivaitic ideas and rites, spread to Tibet and thence to China.

KÂS'YAPA v. Mahâkâs'yapa.

KÂS'YAPA BUDDHA (Pâli. Kassapa. Singh. Kasyapa. Siam. Phra Kasop. Tib. Odsrung. Mong. Kasjapa or Gerel zadiktchi) 迦葉波 or 迦葉 explained by 飲光 lit. (one who) swallowed light (viz. sun and moon which caused his body to shine like gold). The 3rd of the 5 Buddhas of the Bhadra Kalpa, the 6th of the 7 ancient Buddhas, a Brahman, born at Benares. His father was Brahmadatta, his mother Dharmavarti (財主), his favourite tree was the Nyagrôdha, his disciples were Tissa (提舍) and Bharadvadja (婆羅婆). He converted 20,000 persons whilst human life lasted 20,000 years. S'âkyamuni was formerly (as Prabhâpâla) his disciple and received from him the prediction of future Buddhaship.

KÂS'YAPAMÂTAṄGA 迦葉摩騰 or 竺葉摩騰 or 攝摩騰 or 摩騰 (Mâtanga) (1.) A disciple of S'âkyamuni (2.) The same, reborn as a Brâhmaṇa of Central India, famous as an expositor of the Suvarṇa prabhâsa, followed Mingti's Indian embassy from Tukhâra to China, and translated (A. D. 67), togethei with Dharmarakcha, the first Sûtra into Chinese, viz. 佛說四十二章經 the Sûtra of 42 Sections.

KÂS'YAPAPARIVARTA. Title of 4 translations (of the same Sûtra), viz. (1.) 普明菩薩會; (2.) 佛遺日摩尼寶經 A. D. 25-220; (3.) 佛說摩訶衍寶嚴經 A.D. 265-420; (4.) 佛說大迦葉問大寶積正法

經 A. D. 980—1,000.

KÂS'YAPA TATHÂGATA same as Kâs'yapa Buddha.

KÂS'YAPÎYÂḤ or Kâs'yapanikâya (Tib. Kâchyapriyâs) 迦葉臂耶部 or 迦葉遺部 or 迦葉比部 or 迦葉惟部 or 柯尸悲與部 or 飲光部 lit. the School feeding on light. (1.) Another name of the Mahâsaṃghikâḥ, also called 聖上座部 or 尊上座部 Âryasthaviranikâya. (2.) A subdivision of the Sarvâstivâdâḥ. See also Suvarchakâ.

KAṬABHÛTANA or Kaṭapûtana 迦吒富單那 or 羯吒布怛那 explained by 極臭鬼 lit. demons of extremely bad odour. A class of Prêtas.

KATCHA or Katch 契吒 An ancient kingdom tributary to Malava, now the peninsula Cutch.

KATCHÂNA v. Yas'ôdharâ.

KATCHTCH'ÊSVARA v. Khadjîs'vara.

KATINA 迦絺那 or 功德衣 The garment of merits.

KÂTYÂYANA 迦多衍那 or 迦旃延 or 迦延 explained by 文飾 lit. ornament of literature. (1.) A disciple of S'âkyamuni, also called Mahâkâtyâyana, author of the Abhidharma djñâna prasthâna s'âstra, to reappear as 閻浮那提金光 Buddha Djambûnadaprabha. (2.) Name of many different persons.

KÂTYÂYANA KÔCHA S'ÂSTRA 迦延俱舍論 A work on the Abhidharma by Kâtyâyana.

KATYÂYANÎPUTRA 迦旃延子 or 迦多衍尼子 The son of Mahâkâtyâyana, author of 4 philosophical works.

KATUN 可賀敦 A Mongol term for 'queen' or 'princess.'

KÂUṆḌINYA (Singh. Kondanya) 憍陳如 or 憍陳那 or 拘隣隣 explained by 火器 lit. a utensil for (holding) fire or by 本際第一解法 lit. chief of his time in expounding the law. (1.) A prince of Magadha, uncle and chief disciple of S'âkyamuni (v. Adjñâtakâuṇḍinya). (2.) A grammarian, mentioned in the Prâtis'akhya sûtras. (3.) Vyâkaraṇakâuṇḍinya (q. v.) See also under Kâlirâdja and Kâlidatta.

KAUS'ÂMBÎ or Vatsapattana (Pâli. Kôsambi. Singh. Kosamba) 拘睒彌 or 俱賞彌 or 俱睒彌 An ancient city, either the modern Kusia near Kurrha, or the modern Kosam near Allahabad.

KÂUS'ÊYA 憍奢耶 or 野蠶絲 Silk from wild silk-worms.

KAUS'IKA PRADJÑA PÂRAMITÂ 佛說帝釋般若波羅蜜多心經 Title of a translation (A. D. 980—1,000) by Dânapâla.

KÂYA (Singh. Kayan) 葛耶 or 身 lit the body. One of the 6 Ayatanas, the sense of the body, *i. e.* touch. See Chaḍâyatana and Vidjñâna.

KÂYA SMRITY UPASTHÂNA (Pâli. Kâya rupa passana) 念身不淨 lit. remembrance of the impurities of the body. One of the 4 categories of Smrityupasthâna (q. v.), the knowledge that all corporeity is impure.

KCHÂMÂKÂRA BODHISATTVA SÛTRA 菩薩生地經 Title of a translation, A. D. 222—280.

KCHAMÂVATÎ VYÂKARAṆA SÛTRA 佛說差摩婆帝受記經 Title of a translation by Bodhirutchi, A. D. 519—524.

KCHAṆA 刹那 A moment, the 90th part of a 念 thought, the 4,500th part of a minute, during which 90 or 100 births and as many deaths occur.

KCHÂNTIDÊVA 羼提提婆 A richi who taught Sâkyamuni gymnastics.

KCHÂNTI PÂRAMITÂ 羼提波羅蜜多 or 忍辱 lit. enduring insult. The 3rd of the 6 Pâramitâ (q. v.), the virtue of patient equanimity.

KCHÂNTIRICHI 辱忍仙 lit. the richi who patiently suffered insult. S'âkyamuni, in a former life, being a richi, suffered mutilation to convert Kâlirâdja.

KCHÂNTISIM̃HA 羼底僧訶 explained by 師子忍 lit. lion's patience. A native of Hiraṇyaparvata, follower of the Sarvâstivâdâḥ.

KCHATTRIYA 刹怛利耶 or 刹帝利 or 刹利 explained by 土田主 lit. landowners. The caste of warriors and kings, pure Hindus by descent, forming, next to the Brahmans, the only caste from which Buddhas come forth.

KCHÂUMA 芻摩 A species of hemp.

KCHUṆADÊVA 稿那天神 A Hindu deity worshipped by Tirthakas.

KCHUNAHILA 稿那呬羅 A mountain in Tsâukûṭa.

KÊSHINÎ 多髮 lit. much hair. Name of a Rakchasî.

KHADGA 渴伽 or 佉加 or 朅伽 explained by 獨居山林 lit, solitary dweller in forests. The rhinoceros.

KHADIRA 竭陀羅 or 朅地羅 or 羯達羅 explained by 檜山林 lit. timber of the Djambu mountains. The Mimosa catechu. See also Karavîka.

KHADJÎS'VARA or Katchtchês'vara or Karatchî 朅齰涇伐羅 The capital of Vitchâlapura, the modern Kurachie.

KHAKKHARAM or Hikkala 隙棄羅 explained by 錫杖 lit. a staff of tin. The metal wand of the Bhikchu (originally used to knock at the doors).

KHAN 可汗 A Mongol term for 'prince.'

KHARACHAR or Kutche 庫車 or 屈茨 or 屈支 or 龜茲 Ancient kingdom and city, in eastern Turkestan.

KHARISMIGA 貨利習彌迦 Ancient kingdom (Kharizm) on upper Oxus, forming part of Tukhâra.

KHARÔCHṬHA 佉盧虱吒 explained by 驢脣 lit. (having the) lips of an ass. Name of an ancient richi.

KHAS'A 竭叉 An ancient tribe (Kasioi) on the Paropamisus. Others point to Cashmere (Rémusat), Iskardu (Klaproth), Kartchou (Beal).

KHAVAKAN v. Invakan.

KHAVANDHA 揭盤陀 An ancient kingdom and city, the modern Kartchou, S.E. of Sirikol lake.

KHOTAN v. Kustana.

KHULM 忽懔 An ancient kingdom and city, between Balkh and Koondooz, near Khooloom.

KHUSTA 闊悉多 or 闊悉多 A district of Tukhâra, S. of Talikhan.

KIKANA 稽薑那 A district of Afghanistan, the valley of Pishin, now inhabited by the Khaka tribe.

KIM̃S'UKA 甄叔迦寶 explained by 鸚鵡寶 lit. the treasure (red as the beak) of the macaw. The Butea frondosa. See also Kanaka.

KINNARA (Siam. Kinon. Tib. Miham tchi) 緊那羅 or 非人 lit. not men or 疑神 doubtful (horned) spirits. Demons (dangerous to men), the musicians (represented with horse heads) of Kuvêra.

KLICHṬA MANAS v. Vidjñâna.

KÔCHA KARAKÂ v. Adhidharma kôcha karakâ.

KÔKÂLÎ or Kukâlî or Gôkâlî 俱迦利 explained by 惡時者 lit. one of a bad time. The parent of Dêvadatta, the latter being called Kôkâliya (son of Kôkâlî). See also Gôpalî.

KÔKILA 拘耆羅 or 拘翅羅 A bird, probably same as Kalaviñgka.

KÔLITA 拘隸多 or 俱利迦 or 俱律陀 or 拘栗 The father of Mahâmaudgalyâyana.

KÔÑKAṆAPURA 恭建那補羅 An ancient kingdom, the modern Goa and North-Canara.

KÔÑYÔDHA 恭御陀 An ancient kingdom, the modern Ganjam, on the East coast of India.

KÔSALA or Kôs'ala (Singh. Kosol) 憍薩羅 or 喬薩摩 (1.) Southern Kôsala or Dakchiṇakôsala, an ancient kingdom, the present Gundwana and Berar. (2.) Northern Kôsala or Uttarakôsala, an ancient kingdom, the modern Oude.

KÔS'AS 俱舍 Dictionaries or repertories.

KÔṬI (Pâli. Kathi) 俱胝 or 拘胝 or 戈追 explained by 億 lit. ten myriads. A numeral, equal to 10,000,000. See also Lakkha.

KOTLAN 珂咄羅 An ancient kingdon, W. of Tsungling mountains, S. of Karakul lake.

KÔVIDARA 拘鞞陀羅 The Bauhinia variegata.

KRAKUTCHTCHANDA (Pâli. Kakusanda. Siam. Phra Kukusom. Tib. Hkor vah djigs. Mong. Ortchilong ebdektchi or Kerkessundi) 迦羅鳩村馱 or 迦羅迦村馱 or 羯羅迦忙陀 or 羯洛迦孫馱 or 枸樓孫佛 or 枸留孫佛 explained by 所應斷已斷 lit. (one who) readily makes the right decision. The first of the 5 Buddhas of the Bhadrakalpa, the 4th of the 7 ancient Buddhas, native of 安和城 Kchemavati, descendant of the Kâs'yapa family, son of 禮德 (Singh. Aggidatta) and 善枝 (Singh. Wisakha), teacher of 薩尼 (Singh. Sanjawi) and 毗樓 (Singh. Wadhura). His favourite tree was the Sirîsa; he converted 40,000 persons, whilst human life lasted 40,000 years.

KRIS'ṆAPAKCHA 黑分 lit. the black portion. A division of time, 14—15 days. See S'uklapakcha.

KRIS'NAPURA v. Mathûra.

KRITYA (fem. Krityâ) 吉蔗 explained by 起尸鬼 lit. demons digging up corpses, or 訖利多 explained by 買得 lit bought (slaves). (1.) A class of demons, including Yakchakrityas and Manuchakrityas. (2.) A term of contempt, applied to mischievous persons.

KRÔS'A 枸盧舍 or 拘樓賒 or 俱盧舍 or 拘屢 or 拘盧 explained by 大牛音 lit. the lowing of a big ox. A measure of distance, the 8th part of a Yôdjana, or 5 *li*.

KUBHÂ 罽賓 The river Kophes (Kabul).

KUBHÂNA 護苾那 or 罽賓 Kophene . (v. Kas'mîra), the modern Kabul.

KUKÂLÎ v. Kôkâlî.

KUKEJAR 子合國 A country W. of Khoten, 1,000 *li* from Kaschgar, perhaps Yerkiang.

KUKKUṬA PADAGIRI 屈屈吒波陀山 or Gurupadagiri 窶盧播陀山 explained by 鷄足山 lit. chicken foot mountain, or by 狼足山 lit. wolf's foot mountain, or by 尊足山 lit. Buddha's foot mountain. A mountain 7 miles S.E. of Gâya, in which Mahâkâs'yapa is believed to be living even now.

KUKKUTÂRÂMA or Kukkutapada saṃghârâma 屈屈吒阿濫摩 or 屈屈吒波陀僧伽藍 or 鷄足園 lit. chicken foot park. A monastery on Kukkuṭapadagiri, built by As'ôka.

KULAPATI 俱羅鉢底 or 家主 lit. landlord. A title of honour.

KULIKA 拘理迦 A city 9 *li* S.W. of Nâlanda in Magadha.

KULUTA 屈露多 An ancient State, in northern India, famous for its rock temples; the modern Cooloo, N. of Kangra.

KUMÂRA 拘摩羅 or 童子 lit. a youth. (1.) Name of a certain king. (2.) General appellation of royal princes.

KUMÂRA BHÛTA 鳩磨羅浮多 explained by 童子 lit. a youth. A child of about 10 years.

KUMÂRABUDHI 鳩摩羅佛提 or 童覺 lit. youthful intelligence. A S'ramaṇa of the West, translator (A. D. 369—371) of the 四阿含暮抄解 explanation of an abstract of the 4 Agamas by Vasubhadra.

KUMÂRADJÎVA 鳩摩羅耆婆 or 鳩摩羅什婆 or 鳩摩羅十 or (abbrev.) 鳩摩羅 or 羅十 explained by 童壽 lit. youthful and aged. A native of Kharachar, son of Kumârâyana and Djîvâ, disciple of Vandhudatta, Vimalâkcha and Sûryasoma, great expositor of the Mahâyâna, carried as prisoner to China (A. D. 383), where he was styled 'one of the 4 suns of Buddhism,' introduced a new alphabet and translated some 50 works.

KUMÂRALABDHA 拘摩羅邏多 explained by 童授 lit. gift of a youth. A follower of the Sâutrântikaḥ, author of many philosophical works,

KUMÂRARÂDJA 太子 or 王子 or 王太子 lit. crown-prince, or 法王之子 lit. son of a Dharmavarti. (1.) An epithet of Buddhas of royal descent. (2.) An epithet of Mandjus'ri.

KUMARATA 鳩摩羅多 or 矩摩邏多 or 鳩摩 explained by 童首 lit. chief of princes. A dêva in Paranirmita vas'avartin, reborn in Tuchita, disciple of Kaus'ika, reborn in a Brahmalôka, reborn among the Tukhâra as a Brahman, laboured in Central India as the 19th patriarch, died A. D. 22.

KUMBHÂṆḌAS or Kumbhâṇḍakas (Siam. Thepa Kumphan) 鳩槃茶 or 究槃茶 or 恭畔茶 or 弓槃茶 explained by 陰囊 lit. scrotum (of monstrous size). A class of monstrous demons (perhaps identic with the 船遮 of Fah-hien).

KUMBHÎRA 金毗羅 or 宮毗羅 explained by 鰐魚 lit. crocodiles; or by 蛟龍 lit. boa-dragons. A crocodile, described as 'a monster with the body of a fish, but shaped like a snake and carrying pearls in its tail'; perhaps identic with the 室獸摩羅 or 失收摩羅 described as 'a four-footed crocodile, over 20 feet long.'

KUMIDHA 拘謎陀 An ancient kingdom (Vallis Comedorum), on the Beloortagh, N. of Badakchan.

KUṆÂLA or Dharmavivardhana 拘拏羅 The son of As'ôka; father of Sampadî (who succeeded As'ôka, 226 B.C.); of Gândhâra; his eyes, beautiful as those of the bird Kunâla, were gouged out by order of a concubine of his father. See also Ghôcha.

KUṆḌIKÂ 捃稚迦 or 軍持 explained by 澡罐 or 澡瓶

lit. a watering pot. The water bowl of the bhikchu.

KUṆḌINYA s.a. Kâuṇḍinya.

KUÑKUMA 鬱金香 Perfume, prepared from the Turmeric (rhizome) plant, either Curcuma longa or Curcuma aromatica.

KUÑKUMASTÛPA 鬱金香窣都波 A stûpa (covered with a paste of Kuñkuma), in honour of Avalôkitês'vara, at Gâya.

KUNTI 臯帝 Name of a certain Rakchasî.

KURAṆA 屈浪那 An ancient kingdom, originally a district of Tukhâra, the modern Garana (with mines of lapis lazuli), S. of Robat.

KURUDVÎPA s.a. Uttarakuru.

KURYANA or Kuvayana 鞠利衍那 or 鞠和衍那 An ancient kingdom, N. of the upper Oxus, S. E. of Ferghana, the present Kurrategeen.

KUS'A 矩奢 or 茆草 or 上茅 explained by 吉祥草 lit. grass of lucky augury. Sacred odoriferous grass, Poa cynosuroides.

KUS'ÂGÂRAPURA 矩奢揭羅補羅 or 上茅宮城 lit. the city of Kus'a grass palaces, or 山城 lit. the mountain city. The ancient capital of Magadha, 14 miles S. of Behar, deserted by Bimbisâra in favour of Râdjagriha (6 miles farther West).

KUS'ALAMÛLA SAMPARIGRAHA SÛTRA 佛說華手經 Title of a translation by Kumâradjîva, A.D. 384—417.

KUS'INAGARA or Kus'igrâmaka (Pâli. Kusinâra. Singh. Cusinana or Cusinara. Tib. Rtsa mtchogh grong) 拘尸那揭羅 or 拘夷那竭 or 拘尸城 or 拘尸那 explained by 九士生地 lit. the birthplace of 9 scholars. An ancient kingdom and city, near Kusiah, 180 miles N. of Patna; the place where S'âkyamuni died.

KUSTANA 瞿薩怛那 or 豁旦 or 澳那 or 屈丹 or 于闐 or 于遁 or 和闐 the metropolis of Tartar (Tochari) Buddhism (since A. D. 300), until the invasion of Mohammedanism; the modern Khoten.

KUSUMA 拘蘇摩 or 白菊花 The white China aster.

KUSUMAPURA 拘蘇摩補羅 or 花宮城 lit. the city of palaces of flowers. The ancient name of Pâtaliputtra.

KUSUMA SAÑTCHAYA SÛTRA 稱揚諸功德經 Title of a translation (A.D. 386—534).

KUVAYANA v. Kuryana.

KUVÊRA v. Vais'ramana.

LAḌA v. Lâra.

L.

LADAKH (Tib. Ladag) 於麾 The upper Indus valley, under Cashmerian rule, inhabited by Tibetans.

LÂGHULA s.a. Râhula.

LAHUL v. Lôhara.

LAKCHAṆAS (Pâli. Assulakunu. Singh. Maha purusha lakshana) 三十二相 lit. 32 signs. The marks visible on the body of every Buddha.

LAKKHA (Singh. Lakhan. Tib. Laksh) 洛叉 or 洛沙 explained by 十萬 lit. 100,000. The 100th part of a Kôṭi.

LALA v. Lâra.

LALITAVISTARA (Tib. Rgya cer rol pa). Title of several translations of a biography of S'âkyamuni, viz. (1.) 方等本起經 or 普曜經 (lit. Samanta prabhâsa sûtra), by Dharmarakcha, A. D. 308; (2.) 方廣大莊嚴經 or 神童遊戲經 or 神通遊戲經 by Divâkara, A.D. 683.

LAMBÂ 藍婆 A certain Rakchasî.

LAMBINÎ see Lumbinî.

LAMBURA or Lambhara 藍勃羅 A mountain (with a famous Nâgahrada), the present Laspissor, in Kohistan, N. of Kabul.

LAMPÂ or Lampâka 濫波 An ancient kingdom on the Laghmân mountains, N. of the Kabul, E. of the Alingar and W. of the Kunar rivers.

LAÑGALA 狼揭羅 An ancient tribe of Shivaites in western Pundjab (now located near Katch Gandava, in Beluchistan).

LAÑKÂ (Tib. Sing ga glin) 楞伽 or 駿伽 or 楞求羅伽 explained by 不可住 lit. uninhabitable. (1.) A mountain in S.E. corner of Ceylon with a city of demons (Lañkâpurî). (2.) The island of Ceylon.

LAÑKÂVATÂRA SÛTRA. Title of 3 translations of a polemical philosophical treatise, based on the teaching said to have been given by S'âkyamuni on mount Lañkâ, viz. (1.) 楞伽阿跋多羅寶經 by Guṇabhadra, A.D. 443, (2.) 入楞伽經 by Bodhirutchi, A. D. 513, (3.) 大乘楞

伽經 by S'ikchânanda, A.D. 700—704.

LÂRA or Laḍa 羅 (1.) Mâlava 南羅 lit. southern Lâra. (2.) Vallabhi 北羅 lit. northern Lâra.

LAṬA s.a. Karṇasuvarṇa.

LÂVA 臘縛 or 羅婆 The 900th part of a Takchatra, equal to 1 minute and 36 seconds.

LIKCHÂ 蟣 lit. a nit. The 131,712,000th part of a Yôdjana.

LIMBINÎ v. Lumbinî.

LINGA S'ARÎRA s. a. Dharmakâya.

LITCHHAVI (Singh. Lichawi. Tib. Lidschawji) 梨車 or 黎車 or 栗呫婆 explained by 力士 lit. mighty heroes. The republican rulers of Vâis'âlî, the earliest followers of S'âkyamuni.

LÔHARA or Lahul 洛護羅 Kingdom and tribe (Malli, who subsequently moved S. and founded Mâlava), anciently N. of Kuluta.

LÔHITAKA v. Rôhitaka.

LÔKADJYÊCHṬHA (Siam. Lôkavithu. Tib. Ndjig rtengyi) 世尊 lit. honoured by the universe. An epithet of every Buddha.

LÔKÂNTARIKA v. Naraka.

LÔKANUVARTANA SÛTRA 佛說內藏百寳經 Title of a translation by Lôkarakcha, A.D. 25—220.

LÔKAPÂLA 護世者 lit. guardian of the universe. Title given to valorous deities and saints, as the Tchatur Mahârâdjas, Avalôkitês'vara, and others.

LÔKÂYATIKA or Lôkâyata 路伽耶陀 explained by 惡論 lit. wicked talk or by 順世外道 lit. heretics who follow (the ways of) the world. A brahminical sect of 'teachers who injure their pupils and return acts of kindness by wicked replies,' corresponding with an atomistic sect (attached to the atheistic doctrines of the Tchârvâkas) of 'pupils who injure their teachers and return acts of kindness by wicked queries,' called 逆路伽耶陀 lit. Antilôkâyatikas.

LÔKÊS'VARARÂDJA 盧迦委斯諦 or 世尊 lit. lord of the universe. (1.) Name of a certain Buddha. (2.) Epithet of Avalôkitês'vara and other deities and saints.

LÔKÔTTARAVÂDINÂḤ 盧倶多婆拖部 or 說出世部 or 出世說部 lit. the School of those who pretend to have done with the world. A subdivision of the Mahâsamghikâh, attached to the Hinâyâna School.

LUMBINÎ or Limbinî or Lavirî or Lambinî (Mong. Lampa) 嵐毗尼 or 龍彌你 or 論民 or 林微尼 or 臘伐尼 or 解脫處 lit. the place of delivery (v. Pratimôkcha). The park in which Mâyâ gave birth to S'âkyamuni, 15 miles E. of Kapilavastu.

M.

MACHA 摩沙 explained by 豆 lit. pea. A weight, equal to 5 Raktikâs $10\frac{15}{16}$ grains (Troy).

MADHAKA or Madhuka 末杜迦 or 末度迦 or 摩頭 explained by 美果 lit. a pleasant fruit. The Bassia latifolia.

MADHAVA v. Mâthava.

MADHURA 美 lit. pleasant. A king of Gandharvas.

MADHURASVARA 美音 lit. pleasant sound. (1.) A king of Gandharvas. (2.) A son of Sudhîra and Sumêtra, converted by Ananda.

MADHYAMIKA 中論性教 A School, founded by Nâgârdjuna, teaching a system of sophistic nihilism, which dissolves every proposition into a thesis and its antithesis and denies both.

MADHYADÊS'A (Pâli. Madjdjadêsa. Siam. Matxima prathet) 中國 lit. the middle kingdom. Common term for Central India.

MADHYAMÂGAMA v. Âgama.

MADHYÂNTA VIBHÂGA S'ÂSTRA. Title of 2 works by Vasubandhu, viz. (1.) 中邊分別論 translated by Paramârtha, A. D. 557–569, and (2.) 辨中邊論 translated by Hiuen-tsang, A.D. 661.

MADHYÂNTA VIBHÂGA S'ÂSTRA GRANTHA 辨中邊論頌 A work ascribed to Maitrêya, translated by Hiuen-tsang, A.D. 661.

MADHYÂṆTIKA (Tib. Nimaigung) 末由底迦 or 末由地 An Arhat of Dahala, disciple of Ananda, who converted Cashmere.

MADHYIMÂYÂNA 中乘 lit. the middling conveyance (sc. to Nirvâṇa). An abstract category, unknown to Southern Buddhists, in which are classed all systems poised between Mahayâna and Hinâyâna, It corresponds with the state of a Pratyêka Buddha who 'lives half for himself and half for others, as if sitting in the middle of a vehicle, leaving scarcely room for others.'

MAGADHA 摩揭陀 or 摩竭

提 or 摩伽陀 explained by 善勝 lit. virtuous conqueror or by 星處 lit. starry dwelling. (1.) A richi, reborn in heaven, who gave the name to South Bahar. (2.) A kingdom of Central India (Southern Bahar), the cradle of Buddhism (up to 400 A. D.), covered with vihâras and therefore called Bahar.

MAGHA 磨祛 The second winter month.

MAHABALA 竺大力 A S'ramaṇa of the West, a translator (A.D. 197) of a Tcharyâ nidâna sûtra 修行本起經, a life of S'âkyamuni.

MAHÂBHADRÂ v: Gañgâ.

MAHÂBHERI HÂRAKA PARIVARTA 大法鼓經 Title of a translation by Guṇabhadra, A.D. 420—479.

MAHÂBHIDJÑA DJÑÂNÂBHIBHU 大通智勝 lit. conqueror of all-pervading wisdom. A fabulous Buddha, whose realm is Sambhâva, in the Mahârûpa kalpa. Having spent 10 middling kalpas in ecstatic meditation, he became a Buddha and retired again in meditation for 84,000 kalpas, during which time his 16 sons continue (as Buddhas) his teaching, being incarnate as Akchôbhya, Mêrukûta, Siṁhaghôcha, Siṁhadhvadja, Akâsapratichṭhita, Nityaparivrita, Indradhvadja, Brahmadhvadja, Amitâbha, Sarvalôkadhâtu padra vôdvêga pratyuttîrna, Tamâlapatra tchandanagandha, Mêrukalpa, Mêghasvara, Mêghasvararâdja, Sarvalôka bhayâstambhitatva vidhvaṁsanahara, and S'âkyamuni.

MAHÂBODHI SAṀGHÂRÂMA 摩訶菩提寺 lit. the monastery of great intelligence. A vihâra near the Bodhidrûma at Gâyâ.

MAHÂBRAHMÂ 大梵天王 A title of Brahma, as lord of the inhabitants of the Brahmalôkas.

MAHABRAHMÂṆAS (Singh. Mahabrahmas. Tib. Tchangs pa tchen po) 大梵 lit. great Brahma. The 3rd Brahmalôka, the 3rd region of the lst Dhyâna.

MAHÂBRAHMÂ SAHÂṀPATI v. Brahma Sahâṁpati.

MAHÂDAṆḌA DHÂRAṆÎ 大寒林聖難拏陀羅尼經 Title of a translation, by Dharmadêva, A.D. 973—981.

MAHÂDÊVA 摩訶提婆 or 大天 lit. great dêva. (1.) A former incarnation of S'âkyamuni, as a Tchakravarttî. (2.) An Arhat, author of many S'âstras, who fell into heresy. (3.) A title of Mahês'vara.

MAHADÊVÎ 摩訶提鼻耶 or 功德天 lit. the dêva of merits. Title of Mahês'vara's wife. See also Bhima, Marichi, Sarasvati.

MAHÂDHARMA 妙法 lit. wonderful law. A king of Kinnaras.

MAHÂKÂLA (Tib. Nag po tchen po. Mong. Jeke charra) 大神王 lit. great spirit king. (1.) A disciple of Mahâdêva, now guardian deity of monasteries. His image (with black face) is placed in the dining hall. (2.) A title of Mahês'vara.

MAHÂKALPA v. Kalpa.

MAHÂKARUṆA PUṆḌABIKA SÛTRA. Title of two translations, viz. 大乘大悲分陀利經 A. D. 350—432, and 大悲經 by Narendrayas'as and Dharmapradjña, A.D. 552.

MAHÂKÂS'YAPA or Kâs'yapa (Singh. Kasyapa. Tib. Ods-rung tchen po. Mong. Gascib) 摩訶迦葉波 or 摩訶迦葉 or 迦葉頭陀 (Kas'yapadhâtu) explained by 食光 lit. (he who) swallowed light, ('because his mother, having in a former life obtained a relic of Vipas'yin in form of a gold-coloured pearl, became radiant with gold-coloured light'). A Brahman of Magadha, disciple of S'âkyamuni, after whose death he convoked and acted as chairman (Ârya, Sthavira, 上座) of the first synod. He was the first compiler of the canon, and the first patriarch (until 905 or 499 B.C.), and is to be reborn as Buddha Ras'miprabhâsa. See also Kâs'yapîyâḥ.

MAHÂKÂS'YAPA SAṀGHITI 摩訶迦葉會 Title of a translation (A. D. 541) by Upas'ûnya.

MAHÂKATYÂYANA v. Kâtyâyana.

MAHÂKÂUCHṬHILA 摩訶俱絺羅 or 摩訶拘絺羅 or 俱祇羅 explained by 大膝 lit. (one who had) large knees. A disciple of S'âkyamuni, maternal uncle of S'âriputtra, author of the Saṁghâṭîparyâya s'âstra.

MAHÂKÂYA 大身 lit. large body. A king of Garudas.

MAHÂMÂITRÎ SAMÂDHI 大慈定 lit. samdâhi of great benevolence. A degree of ecstatic meditation.

MAHÂMANDÂRAVA 摩訶曼陀羅 s.a. Mandârava.

MAHÂMAÑDJÛCHAKA 摩訶殊沙 v. Mañdjûchaka.

MAHÂMAṆI VIPULA VIMÂNA VIS'VA SUPRATIS'ṬHITA GUHYA PARAMA RAHASYA KALPARÂDJA DHARAṆÎ. Title of 3 translations, viz. (1.) 牟梨曼陀羅咒經 A. D. 502—557, (2.) 廣大寶樓閣善住秘密陀羅尼經 by Bodhirutchi, A.D. 706, and (3.) 大寶廣博樓閣善住秘密陀羅尼經 by Amoghavadjra, A. D. 746—771.

MAHÂMATI 馬曷麻諦 or 大慧 lit. great wisdom. A fictitious Bodhisattva mentioned in the Laṅkâvatâra sûtra.

MAHÂMAUDGALYÂYANA or Maudgalyâyana or Maudgalaputtra (Singh. Mugalan. Tib. Mouh dgalyi bu) 摩訶目犍羅夜那 or 摩訶目建連 or 大目犍連 or 大目乾連 or 目連 or 目伽略 or 沒特伽羅子 (Maudgalaputtra) or 沒力伽羅子 or 毛馱伽羅子 or 勿伽羅子 explained by 胡豆 Mudga (lentil), because 'one of his maternal ancestors lived exclusively on lentils'. (1.) The left-hand disciple (侍佛左邊) of S'âkyamuni, also called Kôlita, distinguished by magic power (神通第一) by which he viewed S'âkyamuni in Tuchita and made a statue of him, and went to hell to release his mother. He died before his master, but is to be reborn as Buddha Tamâla patra tchanda nagandha. (2.) Name of two great leaders of the Buddhist Church who lived several centuries later.

MAHÂMÂYÂ or Mâyâ or Mâtrikâ 摩訶摩邪 or 摩耶第脾 (Mâyâ dêvi) or 摩耶夫人 (lady Mâyâ) or 佛母 lit. mother or Buddha, explained by 幻 lit. illusion, or by 大術 lit. great mystery, or by 大清 lit. great purity. The immaculate mother of S'âkyamuni, whom the latter visited and converted in Tuchita. She reappeared on her son's death and bewailed his departure.

MAHÂMÂYÂ SÛTRA 摩訶摩耶經 Title of a translation, A. D. 560—577.

MAHÂMAYÛRÎ VIDYÂRÂDJÑÎ SÛTRA. Title of 6 translations, viz. (1.) 佛說大孔雀王神咒經 by S'rîmitra, A. D. 317—420, (2.) 佛說大孔雀王雜神咒經, by S'rîmitra, A.D. 317—420, (3.) 大金色孔雀王咒經

by Kumâradjîva, A.D. 384—417, (4.) 佛說孔雀王咒經 by Saṁghapâla, A. D. 502—557, (5.) 佛母大孔雀明王經 by Amoghavadjra, A. D. 618-907, and (6.) 佛說大孔雀咒王經 A.D. 705.

AHÂMUTCHILINDA or Mu-Mtchilinda 摩訶目眞鄰陀 or 目詣隣陀 or 牟眞鄰陀 or 目支隣陀 or 支隣 explained by 解脫處 lit. place of redemption. (1.) A Nâga king, tutelary deity of a lake (near Gayâ) at which S'âkyamuni engaged 7 days in meditation under his protection. (2.) A mountain (Mahâmutchilinda parvata) and forest surrounding that lake.

MAHANADA v. Mahî.

MAHÂNÂMAN (Singh. Mahanamâ) 摩訶男 A son of Drônôdana râdja, one of the first five disciples of S'âkyamuni.

MAHÂNDHRA or Mahêndrî 大安達羅 or Râdjamahêndri. A city, near the mouth of the Godavery, the present Radjamundry.

MAHÂNÎLA 摩訶尼羅 explained by 大靑珠 lit. a large blue pearl. A precious stone, perhaps identic with Indranîla mukta.

MAHÂPARINIRVÂṆA SÛTRA. Title of 5 translations, viz. (1.) 大般涅槃經 by Dharmarakcha, A. D. 416—423; (2.) 大般泥洹經 by Fah-hien and Buddhabhadra, A.D. 217—418; (3.) 佛臨涅槃記法住經 by Hiuen-tsang, A.D. 652; (4.) 佛說方等泥洹經 A.D. 317-420; (5.) 佛般泥洹經 A.D. 290—306.

MAHÂPRADJÂPATÎ or Gâutamî 摩訶波闍波提 or 摩訶波闍波提 explained by 大愛道 lit. path of great love, or by 大生主 lit. great lord of life (Pradjâpati), or by 衆主 lit. superior of the community (of nuns). The aunt and nurse of S'âkyamuni, the first woman admitted into the priesthood, first superioress of the first convent; to reappear as a Buddha called Sarvasattva priya dars'ana.

MAHÂPRADJÑÂPÂRAMITÂ SÛTRA 大般若波羅蜜多經 A collection of 16 Sûtras, expounding the philosophy of the Mahâyâna School.

MAHÂPRATIBHÂNA 大樂說 lit. one who discourses pleasurably. A fictitious Bodhisattva.

MAHÂPRATIHÂRYOPADES'A 大神變會 Title of a

translation by Bodhirutchi, A.D. 618—907.

MAHÂPRATISARA VIDYÂ-RÂDJÑÎ 普徧光明燄鬘清淨熾盛如意寶印心無能勝大明王大隨求陀羅尼經 Title of a translation by Amoghavadjra, A. D. 746—771.

MAHÂPÛRṆA 大滿 lit. great and full. A king of Garuḍas.

MAHÂPURUCHA LAKCHAṆÂNI v. Lakchaṇas.

MAHÂPURUCHA S'ÂSTRA 大丈夫論 Title of a work by Devala, translated A. D. 397-439.

MAHÂRÂCHṬRA 摩訶刺佗 An ancient kingdom in the N.W. of the Deccan; the Mahratta country.

MAHÂRÂDJA v. Tchatur mahârâdja kayika.

MAHÂRATNAKÛṬA SÛTRA 大寶積經 A collection of 49 Sûtras, arranged by Bodhirutchi.

MAHÂRÂURAVA (Siam. Maharôruva) 大號叫 or 大叫 or 大呼 lit. great crying. The 5th of the 8 hot hells, where 24 hours equal 800 mundane years, surrounded by volcanoes which bar all escape.

MAHARDDHIPRÂPTA 如意 lit. at pleasure. A king of Garuḍas.

MAHÂRÛPA 大相 lit. great signs. The kalpa of Mahâbhidjña djñanâbhibhu.

MAHÂSAM̃BHAVA 大成 lit. great completion. A fabulous realm in which innumerable Buddhas, called Bhîchmagardjita ghôchasvararâdja, appeared.

MAHÂSAM̃GHA VINAYA 摩訶僧祇律 The Vinaya of the Mahâsam̃ghikâḥ, translated by Buddhabhadra, A.D. 416.

MAHÂSAM̃GHIKÂḤ or Mahâsam̃ghanikâya 摩訶僧祇部 or 大衆部 lit. School of the great assembly (priesthood). A School, formed after the 2nd synod (B.C. 443), in opposition to the Mahâsthâvirâḥ School. Followers of Mahâkâs'yapa. Their textbook is the Pratimôkcha. After the 3rd synod (B. C. 246) this School split into 5 branches, v. Pûrvas'âilḥâ, Avaras'âilâḥ, Hâimavatâḥ, Lôkôttara vâdinâḥ, and Pradjñaptivâdinâḥ. See also Dharmakala.

MAHÂSANNIPÂTA 大集部 A division of the Sûtra piṭaka, containing Avadânas (q. v.)

MAHÂSÂRA 摩訶娑羅 Ancient city, the present Masar, near Patna.

MAHÂSAHASRA PRAMARDANA 佛說守護大千國

士經 Title of a translation by Dânapâla A.D. 980—1000.

MAHÂSATTVA 嫣哈薩督呀 or 摩訶薩埵 The perfected Bodhisattva, as greater(Maha) than any being (sattva) except Buddhas, or as using the Mahâyâna to save other beings.

MAHÂSATTVA KUMARA RADJA 摩訶薩埵王子 lit. the great being and royal prince. Title of S'âkyamuni.

MAHÂS'RAMAṆA 大沙門 lit. the great S'ramaṇa. Epithet of S'âkyamuni.

MAHÂS'RÎ SÛTRA 佛說大吉祥天女十二名號經 Title of a translation by Amoghavadjra, A. D. 746—771.

MAHASTHÂMA or Mahasthanaprapta 大勢至菩薩 A Bodhisattva (perhaps Mâudgalyâyana) belonging to the retinue of Amitâbha.

MAHÂSTHÂVIRÂḤ v. Sthâviraḥ.

MAHÂTÂPANA v. Pratâpana.

MAHÂTÂRAKA 摩訶怛羅 explained by 道官 lit. officer of the road. An official guide or escort.

MAHÂTCHAKRAVÂLA 大鐵圍 lit. the great iron enclosure. The larger one of the two Tchakravâlas.

MAHÂTCHAMPÂ 摩訶瞻波 An ancient kingdom in Burmah.

MAHÂTCHÎNA 摩訶至那 lit. great China. Name of China (since the Tsin dynasty, A.D. 265). See Tchîna.

MAHÂTÊDJAS 大威德 lit. great dignity and virtue. A king of Garuḍas.

MAHÂVÂDÎ 大論師 lit. doctor of philosophy. Title of eminent scholars, especially of expositors of the Saṁkyâ and Vais'êchika systems.

MAHÂVADJRAMÊRU S'IKHARA KÛṬÂGÂRA DHÂRAṆI 大金剛妙高山樓閣陀羅尼經 Title of a translation by Dânapâla, A D. 980—1,000.

MAHÂVAIPULYA v. Vaipulya.

MAHÂVAIPULYA MAHASANNIPÂTA BODHISATTVA BUDDHÂNUSMṚITI SAMÂDHI 佛說大方等大集菩薩念佛三昧經 Title of a translation by Dharmagupta, A.D. 589—618.

MAHÂVAIPULYA MAHÂSANNIPÂTA BHADRAPÂLA SÛTRA 大方等大集賢護經 Title of a translation by Djñânagupta and others, A.D. 594.

MAHÂVANA SAMGHÂRÂMA 摩訶伐那伽藍摩 or 大林寺 lit. the monastery of the great forest. A famous monastery, S. of Mongali.

MAHAVIHÂRA VÂSINÂḤ 摩訶毗訶羅住部 lit. School of dwellers in large vihâras. A subdivision of the Mahâsthâvirâḥ, opposing the Mahâyâna doctrines.

MAHÂVIBHÂCHÂ S'ASTRA 大毗婆沙論 A philosophical (Hinâyâna) treatise by Buddhâsa.

MAHÂVIHÂRA 摩訶毗訶羅 A monastery in Ceylon, where Fah-hien (A. D. 400) found 3000 inmates.

MAHÂVRIKCHA RICHI 大樹仙 lit. the hermit of the great tree. An ascetic called Vâyu, whose body finally resembled a decayed tree. See Kanyâkubdja.

MAHÂVYÛHA 大莊嚴 lit. great ornament. The kalpa of Mahâkâs'yapa Buddha.

MAHÂYÂNA (Mong. Jeke Kü) 摩訶衍那 or 摩訶衍 or 摩訶乘 explained by 大乘 lit. great conveyance. (1.) A later form of the Buddhist dogma, one of the 3 phases of its development (v. Triyâna), corresponding to the 3rd degree of saintship, the state of a Bodhisattva, who, being able to transport himself and others to Nirvâṇa, may be compared with a large vehicle (大乘). A School formed by Nâgârdjuna, which flourished especially in Tchakuka, but influenced more or less the whol Buddhist church. The characteristics of this system are an excess of transcendental speculation tending to abstract nihilism, and the substitution of fanciful degrees of meditation (Samâdhi and Dhyâna) in place of the practical asceticism of the Hinâyâna School. It is not known to Southern Buddhists as a separate system, though it appears to have influenced Singhalese Buddhists, whom Hiuentsang classed among the followers of the Mahâyâna School. (2.) A S'ramaṇa of the West, translator of the Vinaya of the Sthâvirâḥ, A.D. 483—493.

MAHÂYÂNÂ BHIDHARMA SAMGÎTI S'ÂSTRA 大乘阿毗達磨集論 A philosophical treatise by Asamgha, translated by Hiuen-tsang, A.D. 652.

MAHÂYÂNÂ BHIDHARMA SAMYUKTASAMGITI S'ÂSTRA 大乘阿毗達磨雜集論 A commentary on the preceding work, compiled by Sthitamati, translated by

Hiuen-tsang, A. D. 646.

MAHÂYÂNADÊVA 摩訶那那提婆 lit. the dêva of the Mahâyâna School. Epithet of Hiuen-tsang (釋玄奘 or 陳禕), who travelled (A. D. 629—645) through Central Asia and India, author of the 大唐西域記 Record of Western Kingdoms, published under the T'ang dynasty, A. D. 648; translator and editor of some 75 works on the Mahâyâna system. See also Môkcha dêva.

MAHÂYÂNA SAMPARIGRAHA S'ÂSTRA 攝大乘論 A collection of philosophical treatises on the Mahâyâna system, by Asamgha, translated by Paramartha, A. D. 563.

MAHÂYÂNA YOGA v. Yoga s'âstra.

MAHÂYÂNOTTARA TANTRA S'ÂSTRA 究竟一乘寶性論 Title of a translation by Ratnamati, A. D. 508.

MAHÊNDRA (Pâli. Mahinda. Singh. Mahindo) 摩哂陀 or 哂陀 or 魔醯因陀羅 or 摩訶因陀羅 explained by 大帝 lit. great ruler. A younger brother (or son) of As'ôka who, as viceroy of Udyana, led a dissolute life, but, when fallen into disgrace, he repented, became an Arhat, and went to Ceylon where he founded the Buddhist church still flourishing there.

MAHÊS'VARA 摩醯溼伐羅 or 魔醯首羅 or 魔醯 explained by 大自在 nt. great sovereign, or by 天王 lit. a king of dêvas. Shiva, "a deity with 8 arms and 3 eyes, riding on a white bull and worshipped by heretics;" the "Lord of one great chiliocosmos," who resides above Kâmadhâtu. Hiuen-tsang specially noticed Shiva temples (built of blue sand stone) in the Pundjab.

MAHÊS'VARA DÊVA 大自在天 lit. the great independent dêva. An epithet of Shiva.

MAHÊS'VARAPURA or Matchivâra 魔醯溼伐羅補羅 Ancient city and kingdom in Central India, the present Machery.

MAHÎ or Mahânada 莫訶 (1.) A small tributary of the Nâiramdjanâ, in Magadha. (2.) The modern Mhye, flowing into the gulf of Cambay.

MAHINALÂ 拔提 A vihâra on Ceylon, near Anuradhapura, famous when Dharmagupta lived there.

MAHIRAKULA 魔醯邏矩

羅 explained by 大族王 lit. king of a great tribe. A king who persecuted Buddhists in the Punjab (A. D. 400), fled, when defeated by Bâlâditya, to Cashmere, assassinated its king and persecuted Buddhists there until "hell swallowed him up."

MAHÎS'ÂSAKÂḤ or Mahîs'âsikas 磨醯奢娑迦部 or 彌喜捨娑阿部 or 彌沙塞部 explained by 化地部 lit. the School of the earth transformed (i.e. by the influence of Buddhism), or by 正地部 lit. the School of the rectified earth. A subdivision of the Sarvâstivâdâḥ.

MAHÎS'ÂSAKA VINAYA 彌沙塞部五分律 Title of a translation by Buddhadjîva, A.D. 424, the standard code of the foregoing School.

MAHORAGA (Tib. Ltohphye tchen po) 摩睺羅伽 or 摩睺羅伽 or 牟呼洛 or 莫呼洛 or 摩休勒 or 摩護羅議腹 lit. large belly or by 蟒神 lit. boa spirit. A class of demons, shaped like a boa.

MAITRÂYAṆÎPUTTRA v. Pûrṇa maitrâyaṇî putra.

MAITRÊYA (Pâli. Mettêyo. Singh. Maitri. Siam. Phrai. Tib. Byampspa mgon po or Chamra. mong. Maidari) 梅怛麗邪 or 昧怛履曳 or 彌勒 explained by 慈氏 li he whose name is charity. A fictitious Bodhisattva often called Aditja, a principal figure in the retinue of S'âkyamuni, though not a historic disciple. It is said S'âkyamuni visited him in Tuchita and appointed him to issue thence as his successor after the lapse of 5,000 years. Maitrêya is the expected Messiah of the Buddhists and even now controls the propagation of the faith. A philosophical School (五性宗 lit. School of the five-fold nature) regards him as their founder. Statues were erected in his honour as early as B. C. 350. See also Avalokitês'vara, Pûrṇamaitrâyaṇi and Mañdjus'ri.

MAITRÊYABHADRA 慈賢 A native of Magadha, translator of 5 works (A.D. 1125).

MAITRÊYA PARIPṚITCHTCHA. Title of 3 translations, viz. (1.) 佛說大乘方等要慧經 A.D. 25—220, (2.) 彌勒菩薩入法會 and (3.) 彌勒菩薩所問會, the latter two by Bodhirutchi, A. D. 386—534.

MAITRÊYA VYÂKARAṆA.

Title of 3 translations, viz. (1.) 佛說彌勒下生經 by Kumâradjîva, A.D. 314—417, (2.) 佛說彌勒來時經 A. D. 317—420, and (3.) 佛說彌勒下生成佛經 A.D. 701.

MAITRÎBALA RÂDJA 慈力王 lit. the King of strength of affection. A former incarnation of S'âkyamuni, when he shed his blood to feel starving Yakchas.

MAKARA 摩竭羅 or 摩竭 A monster shaped like a fish.

MAKHAI (Mong. Gobi) 莫賀延 The desert of Gobi. See also Navapa.

MÂLÂDHARÎ 持瓔珞 lit. holding a necklace of pearls. A certain Rakchasî.

MÂLÂGANDHA VILÊPANA DHÂRANA MAṆḌANA VIBHUSA NAṬṬHÂNÂ 不着香華鬘不香塗身 lit. thou shalt not adorn thyself with wreaths of fragrant flowers nor anoint thy body with perfume. The 8th Sikchâpada.

MÂLÂKUṬA 秣羅矩吒 or Malâya 摩賴耶 explained by 光明國 lit. the kingdom of light and brightness. Ancient State on the coast of Malabar, once (A.D. 600) the headquarters of the Nirgranthas.

MÂLÂKUṬADANTÎ 曲齒 lit. curved teeth. A certain Rakchasî.

MALASA 秣羅娑 A valley in the upper Punjab.

MÂLAVA or Lâra 摩臘婆 Ancient State in Central India, the present Malva, famous for its heretical sects.

MALÂYA v. Mâlâkuṭa.

MALÂYAGIRI 南海摩羅耶山 (1.) A mountain range S. of Mâlâkuṭa. (2.) A mountain on Ceylon with a city (Lañkâ) of Yakchas on its summit.

MALLA 末羅 explained by 力士 lit. mighty heroes. Epithet of the inhabitants of Kus'inagara and Pâvâ.

MALLIKA 末利 or 摩利 explained by 柰 lit. plum. (1.) The wife of Prasênadjit. (2.) The narrow leaved Nyctanthes (with globular berries 柰); the flower, now called Casturi (musk) because of its odour.

MANAS 意 lit. the mind. The 6th of the Chaḍâyatana, the mental faculty which constitutes man as an intelligent and moral being. See also Vidjñâna.

MÂNASA or Manasvin 摩那斯 explained by 意流出 lit. efflux of the mind (sc. of

Brahma), or by 大身 lit. large body. (1.) The lake Manasa sarovara (or Anavatapta). (2.) The tutelary deity (nâga) of that lake.

MÂNAVA 摩那婆 or 摩納縛迦 (Manavaka) or 那羅摩那 (Naramana) or 那羅摩納 (Naramava) explained by 人 lit. a man or by 年少淨行 lit. a young Brahman. General designation for a Brahman youth (lit. a descendant of Manu).

MAṆḌAKA 門擇迦 Elementary sounds (so called in Pâṇini's grammar).

MAṆḌALA 曼荼羅 (1.) The circle of continents around the Mêru. (2.) Magic circles used in sorcery. (3.) Circular plate (with 5 elevations representing the Mêru and the 4 continents) placed on every altar.

MANDÂRA or Mandarâva 曼陀羅 explained by 意適 lit. according with the wish, or by 天妙花 lit. wonderful celestial flower. One of the 5 shrubs of Indra's heaven, resembling the Erythrina fulgens or Erythrina Indica.

MAÑDJÛCHAKA 曼殊沙 or 曼殊顏 explained by 柔軟 lit. pliable. Rubia cordifolia, yielding the madder (munjeeth) of Bengal.

MAÑDJUS'RÎ or Mañdjunâtha or Mañdjudêva or Mañdjughocha or Mañdjusvara (Tib. Hdjam dvyang or Hdjam dpal) 曼殊室利 or 曼殊尸利 or 文殊師利 or 文殊 or 曼首 explained by 妙吉祥 lit. wonderful lucky omen or by 妙德 lit. wonderful virtue. (1.) A legendary Bodhisattva, also styled Mahâmati (大智 lit. great wisdom), Kumara râdja (q. v.) and 千臂千鉢教王 lit. religious king with 1,000 arms and 1,000 alms-bowls. It is said, that he attended many Buddhas in a (fabulous) universe called Ratnêya (寶氏 lit. precious family), E. of our world; that he was in the retinue of S'âkyamuni, and composed many Sûtras; that the daughter of Sâgara obtained Buddhaship through his teaching; that he is now a Buddha, called 龍種尊者 lit. the Ârya of Nâgas, and resides on a (fabulous) mountain, somewhere in the N. E. of our universe, called 清涼山 lit. the pure and cool mountain, attended by 1,000 Bodhisattvas. Mañdjus'rî has become an object of worship in all the churches of Northern Buddhism, but most especially in Shansi (China). Fah-hien (A. D. 400) found Mañdjus'rî generally worshipped by followers of the Mahâyâna School, whilst Hiuen-tsang (A. D. 603), who saw at Mathurâ a stûpa containing the remains of Mañdjus'rî's body, connects his worship especially with the Yogâtchârya School. It is supposed that Mañdjus'ri lived 250 years after Sâkyamuni's death, i.e. B. C. 293. The Mahâyâna School treated the dogma of Mañdjus'rî as the apotheosis of transcendental wisdom, identifying him with Vis'vakarman, and giving him (as the personified wisdom) the same place in their trias of Bodhisattvas (with Avalokitês'vara and Vadjrapâṇî) which Brahma occupies in the Indian Trimurti. The Yogâtchârya School placed Mañdjus'rî among their seven Dhyâni Bodhisattvas, as the spiritual son of Akchôbhya Buddha, and identified him with Vadjrapâṇi. A later branch of the Mahâyâna School (一性宗 lit. School of one nature), which asserts that all beings have the same nature as Buddha, claimed Mañdjus'rî as their founder. (2.) The son of an Indian King (circa 968 A. D.), who came to China but was driven away again by the intrigues of other priests.

MAÑDJUS'RÎ BUDDHA-KCHÊTRA GUṆA VYÛHA. Title of two translations, viz. 文殊師利授記會 by S'ikchânanda, A. D. 618—607, and 文殊說般若會 by Mandra, A. D. 502—557.

MAÑDJUS'RÎ NÂMA SAÑGÎTI 文殊所說最勝名義經 Title of a translation by Suvarṇadhâraṇi, A.D. 1113.

MAÑDJUS'RÎ PARIPRITCHTCHHA. Title of two translations, by Divâkara (A D. 983 and later).

MAÑDJUS'RÎ SADVRITTA GUHYA TANTRA RÂDJASYA VIMS'ATIKA KRODHA VIDJAYÂÑDJANA 佛說妙吉祥最勝根本大教經 Title of a translation. A. D. 982—1001.

MAÑDJUS'RÎ VIKRIḌITA SÛTRA. Title of 2 translations, viz. 佛說大淨法門品經 by Dharmarakcha, A. D. 213, and 大莊嚴法門經 by Narendrayas'as, A.D. 583.

MANDRA 曼陀羅 or 弱聲 (lit. weak sound) or 弘弱 (lit. grand but weak). A S'ramaṇa of 扶南 (Bunan, Siam ?), translator of 4 works.

MANGALA v. Moñgalî.

MAṆI 摩尼 or 末尼 explained by 無垢 lit. stainless, or by 增長 lit. increasing and enlarging, or by 珠之總名 lit. general term for pearls, or by 如意珠 lit. felicitous pearls. A fabulous pearl (v. Sapta ratna) which is ever bright and luminous, therefore a symbol of Buddha and of his doctrines, whilst among Shivaites it is the symbol of the Linga. See also Oṁ maṇi padmê hûm.

MANOBHIRÂMA 意樂 lit. joy of mind. The realm where Mâudgalyayana is to be reborn as Buddha.

MANODHATU 意界 lit. the world of the mind. The mental faculties.

MANODJÑA S'ABDÂBHI GARDJITA 妙音徧滿 lit. replete with wonderful sounds. The Kalpa in which Ânanda is to reappear as Buddha.

MANODJÑASVARA 樂音 lit. sound of music. A king of Gandharvas,

MANORHITA or Manorhata 末笯曷利他 explained by 如意 lit. in conformity (hita) with the mind (manas), or Manura 摩拏羅 or 摩奴羅 The 21st (or 22nd) patriarch, author of the Vibhâcha vinaya, who laboured (until A.D. 165) in Western India and Ferghana; originally an Indian prince, then disciple (or according to Hiuen-tsang the teacher) and successor of Vasubandhu.

MANOVIDJÑANA DHÂTU 意識界 lit. the world of mind and knowledge. The sphere of thought.

MANTRA (Tib. Gsungs sngags) 曼特羅 or 曼怛羅 or 滿怛羅 or 擟打勒 or 曼荼羅 explained by 咒 lit. magic spells, or by 神咒 lit. riddhi mantra. Short magic sentences (generally ending with meaningless Sanskrit syllables), first adopted by followers of the Mahâyâna School, then popularized in China by Vadjrabodhi. See also Dhâraṇî.

MANUCHA KRITYA 人吉庶 (1.) Demons shaped like men. (2.) Domestic slaves, introduced in Cashmere Madhyantika.

MANUCHYA (Pâli Manussa) 末奴沙 or 摩㝹沙 or 摩㝹舍南 (Manuchyânâm. Pâli. Manussânam) explained by 人 lit. a man, or by 有意 lit. rational or by 有智慧

lit. intelligent. Human beings, or divine beings in human form.

MANURA v. Manorhita.

MÂRA or Mârarâdja Kamadhâtu or Papîyân (Siam. Phajaman. Burm. Mat or Manh. Tib. Bdudsdig tchan or Hdodpa. Mong. Schimnus) 魔羅 or 末羅 explained by 殺者 lit. the murderer, or by 障礙善 lit. obstructing and hindering virtue, or by 破壞善 lit. destroying virtue; or 魔王 Mâra râdja; or 波旬 explained by 惡愛 lit. sinful love; or 波卑夜 Papîyân, explained by 欲界王 lit. Kâmadhâtu râdja. The god of lust, sin and death, represented with 100 arms and riding on an elephant. He resides, with the Mârakâyikas, in Paranirmita vas'avartin on the top of Kâmadhâtu. He assumes various monstrous forms, or sends his daughters, or inspires wicked men (like Dêvadatta, or the Nirgranthas) to seduce or frighten saints on earth.

MÂRA KÂYIKAS 魔民 lit. the subjects of Mâra, or 魔子魔女 lit. sons and daughters of Mâra. Mâra's subordinates.

MARDJAKA 阿梨樹 A tree (perhaps a banyan) which splits into 7 pieces when felled.

MARGA or As'thânga mârga (Pâli. Attangga magga. Singh. Arya ashtangikamargga. Siam. Mak. Burm. Magga) 八聖道分 or 八正道分 lit. 8 portions of the holy or correct path, or 八正門 lit. 8 correct gates (sc. to Nirvâṇa). Eight rules of conduct, the pre-requisites of every Arhat, the observation of which leads to Nirvâṇa Details see under Samyagdrichṭi, Samyaksam̃kalpa, Samyagvâk, Samyagâdjîva, Samyagvyâyâma, Samyaksamâdhi, Samyaksmriti and Samyakkarmânta.

MÂRGABHÛMI SÛTRA 道地經 Translation (A. D. 148—170) of a work by Sam̃gharakcha.

MÂRGAS'IRAS 末伽始羅 The third month of autumn (9th to 10th Chinese moons).

MÂRÎTCHI 摩里支 or 末利支 or Mârîtchi dêva bodhisâttva 摩利支菩薩天 (1.) In Brahmanic mythology, the personified light, offspring of Brahma, parent of Sûrya, ancestor of Mahâkâs'yapa (q. v.) (2.) Among Chinese Budhists, the goddess of light who holds aloft sun and moon, the protectress against war; also styled Queen of Heaven 天后 and Mother of the Dipper 斗姥 and identified with Tchundi (q.v.) and with Mahês'varî (the wife of Mahês'vara). The magic formula, 唵摩利支娑婆訶 ôm Mârîtchi svâha, is attributed to her, and Georgi, who calls her Mha-lhi-ni, explains the name as 'a Chinese transcription of the name of the holy virgin Mary'. (3.) Among Chinese Tauists, Marîtchî is styled Queen of Heaven and, with her husband (斗父天尊 lit. the worthy dêva of the Dipper) and 9 sons, located in Sagittarius.

MÂRÎTCHI DÊVA DHÂRAṆÎ 佛說摩利支天陀羅尼經 Title of a translation (A. D. 502—557).

MARUTA 摩嚕多 The sons of Rudra; demons reigning in storm

MÂSA 月 lit. a moon. A lunar month. See also Krichnapakcha and S'uklapakcha.

MASUBA SAM̃GHÂRÂMA 摩愉羅伽藍 or 豆伽藍 lit. monastery of lentils. An ancient vihâra, some 200 li S. E. of Moñgali.

MÂTAÑGA ÂRAṆYAKAḤ 摩登伽阿蘭若 The second class of Âraṇyakaḥ (q. v.), hermits living on cemeteries, forbidden to approach a village within hearing distance of the lowing of a cow, and called after the caste of Mâtañga (outcasts).

MÂTAÑGÎ SÛTRA. Title of 4 translations, viz. (1.) 摩鄧女經 A.D. 25—220; (2) 摩鄧女解形中六事經 A.D. 265—420; (3.) 摩登伽經 A.D. 222—280; (4.) 舍頭諫經 by Dharmarakcha, A. D. 265—316.

MATCHIVÂRA v. Mahês'vara.

MÂTHAVA or Madhava or Madhu 摩沓婆 A tribe of aborigenes (the Mathai of Megasthenes) living N. of Kôs'ala, in Rohilcund, and S. of Nepaul. They gave the name to Mathurâ and Matipura.

MATHURÂ or Madhurâ 摩度羅 or 摩偷羅 or 摩突羅 or 摩頭羅 or 秣兎羅 explained by 孔雀城 lit. peacock city (Krishnapura). Ancient kingdom and city (the modern Muttra), birthplace of Krishna (whose emblem is the peacock), famous for its stûpas.

MATI 有意 lit. rational. Eldest son of Tchandra sûrya pradîpa.

MATIPURA 秣底補羅 Ancient kingdom (the modern Rohilcund) and city, ruled (A. D. 600) by kings of the S'udra caste; the home of many famous priests.

MATISIM̃HÂ 末底僧訶 explained by 獅子慧 lit. a

lion's intelligence. Epithet given to men of superior talent.

MÂTRIGRÂMA (Pâli. Mâtugâmâ) 摩咀理伽羅摩 explained by 母邑 lit. mother city. The female sex.

MÂTRIKÂ (Tib. Yum or Ma mo) 摩咀里迦 or 摩德理迦 or 摩德勒伽 or 摩夷 explained by 行毋 lit. the mother of karma. Abhidharma lit. the mother of karma. The Abhidharma piṭaka, so called because it explains how karma (q. v.) 'is the productive mother of fresh karma.'

MÂTRITCHETA 摩咥哩制吒 A native of India, author of the Buddhastotrârdhas'ataka 一百五十讚頌 translated A.D. 708.

MAṬUTA TCHANDÎ 黑齒 lit. black teeth. A certain Rakchasî.

MÂUDGALAPUTTRA or Mâudgalyâyana v. Mahâmâudgalyâyana.

MÂYÂ v. Mahâmâyâ.

MÂYÂ DJÂLAMAHÂTANTRA MAHÂYÂNA GAMBHÎRA NÂYA GUHYA PARAS'I SÛTRA 佛說瑜加大敎王經 Title of a translation, A. D. 982—1001.

MÂYOPAMA SAMÂDHI 佛說如幻三昧經 Title of a translation by Dharmarakcha, A.D. 265—316.

MAYÛRA (Singh. Moriyanaga) 摩裕羅 Ancient capital of the Maurya (Morya) princes, the modern Amrouah near Hurdwar.

MAYÛRA RÂDJA 摩裕羅王 or 孔雀王 lit. peacock king. A former incarnation of S'âkyamuni, when, as a peacock famished with thirst, he sucked out of a rock water which had miraculous healing power.

MÊGHA DUNDUBHI SVARA RÂDJA 雲雷音王 lit. king of clouds and thunderbolts. A Buddha who lived, during the kalpa Priyadars'ana, in a (fabulous) realm called Sarvabuddha sam̃dars'ana.

MÊGAHSVARA 雲自在 lit. cloud sovereign. A (fabulous) Buddha who lived, N. of our universe, an incarnation of the 13th son of Mahâbhidjnâ djânâbhibhu.

MÊGHASVARARÂDJA 雲自在王 lit. sovereign king of clouds. A (fabulous) Buddha who lived, N. of our universe, an incarnation of the 14th son of Mahâbhidjña djñanâbhibhu.

MÊRU v. Sumêru.

MÊRUKALPA or Mêrudhvadja 須彌相 lit. the sign of

Mêru. A (fabulous) Buddha who lived, N.W. of our universe, an incarnation of the 12th son of Mahâbhidjña djñânâbhibhu.

MÊRUKÛTA 須彌頂 lit. the summit of Mêru. A Buddha of Âbhirati, an incarnation of the 2nd son of Mahâbhidjña djñanâbhibhu.

MIKKAKA 彌遮迦 The 6th Indian partriarch, who transported himself from Northern India to Ferghana, where he died by samâdhi, B. C. 637 (or 231). See also Vasumitra.

MIMAHA 弭秣賀 Ancient kingdom, 70 *li*. E. of Samarkand, the modern Maghîn in Turkestan.

MÎMÂM̃SARDDHIPADA (Pâli, Wimansidhi pada) 思惟足 lit. the step of meditation and reflection, explained by 衡量所修之法滿願也 lit. oversatiated by the practice of balancing and measuring (truth and error). The 4th Riddhipâda, viz., absolute renunciation of intellectual activity, a step to magic power.

MINGRULAK 千泉 lit. 1,000 sources, or Bingheul 屛律 A lake country, 30 *li* E. of Talas.

MITRAS'ÂNTA 彌陀山 or 寂友 lit. calm friend. A S'ramaṇa of Tukhâra, translator (A. D. 705) of the 無垢淨光大陀羅尼經 Vimala suddha prabhâsa mahâdhâraṇî sûtra.

MITRASÊNA 蜜多羅斯那 or 蜜多斯那 A disciple of Guṇaprabha, a teacher of Hiuen-tsang.

MLÊTCHHAS 蔑戾車 People who do not believe in Buddha; infidels.

MOKCHADÊVA 木叉提婆 The title (dêva of liberation) given by followers of the Hînayâna School to Mahâyânadêva.

MOKCHAGUPTA 木叉毱多 A priest of Kharachar, a follower of the Madhyimâyâna School, whose ignorance Mahâyânadêva exposed.

MOKCHALA 無羅叉 or 無叉羅 A S'ramaṇa of Kustana, translator of one Sûtra, author (A. D. 291) of a new alphabet for the transliteration of Sanskrit.

MOKCHA MAHÂPARICHAD v. Pañtchaparichad.

MOÑGALI or Mañgala 瞢揭釐 Ancient capital of Udyâna, now Manglavor on the Swât, in the N. of the Pundjab.

MOTCHA 茂遮 A species of Ficus religiosa.

MRIGADÂVA (Singh. Isipatana. Burm. Migadawon) 鹿野 or 鹿苑 or 鹿林 lit. deer park. A park N. E. of Varânas'i, favonred by S'âkyamuni now; Sârañganâtha near Benares.

MRIGALA 蜜利伽羅 explained by 鹿 lit. deer, or by 鹿王 lit. king of deer (Mrigarâdja). Epithet of S'âkyamuni and of Dêvadatta (each having been a deer in a former life.

MUDGA 胋豆 lit. Tartar lentil. Phaseolus mungo.

MUDRÂ (Tib. Pad sskor) 木得羅 or 目帝羅 or Mahâmudrâ 馬曷木得羅 explained 法印 lit. the seal of the law. A system of magic gesticulation, consisting in distorting the fingers so as to imitate ancient Sanskrit characters of supposed magic efficacy; a product of the Yogâtchârya School.

MUHÛRTA 牟呼栗多 A period of 18 minutes.

MUKTA (Pâli. Muttâ. Tib. Mutig). 目多 Jewels. especially pearls.

MÛLÂBHIDHARMA S'ÂSTRA 根本阿毘達摩論 A philosophical treatise of the Mahâsaṃghikâḥ.

MÛLAGRANTHA 慕羅健陀 explained by 根本 lit. original text books of Buddha's words.

MÛLASAMBURU or Mûlasthânipura 茂羅三部盧 Ancient kingdom of Western India, tributary of Tchêka; the modern Moultan.

MÛLASARVÂSTIVÂDAIKAS'ATA KARMAN 根本說一切有部百一羯磨 Title of a translation, A. D. 618—907.

MÛLASARVÂSTIVÂDA NIKÂYA VINAYA GÂTHÂ 根本說一切有部毗奈耶頌 A work on the Vinaya of the Hînayâna by Vais'âkhya, translated A.D. 710.

MUNGALI v. Moñgali.

MUNIMITRA 寂友 A native of India, author of the 佛吉祥德讚 Buddha s'rîguṇa stotra, translated by Dânapâla, A. D. 980—1000.

MUṆI 牟尼 or 摩尼 or Mahâmuṇi 馬曷摩尼 or Vimuṇi 月摩尼 An epithet (sage) of every Buddha.

MUNKAN or Mungan 瞢健 A province of Tukhâra, on the upper Oxus, W. of Badakchan.

MURDDHÂBHICHIKTA or Murddhadja 文陀竭 or 曼

馱多 or 灌頂 lit. washing the top of the head. A ceremony, common in Tibet in the form of infant-baptism, administered in China at the investiture of high patrons of the church, e. g. to the Emperor Yüan-tsung (A.D. 746) by Amoghavadjra, and to statues of Buddha (as a daily rite). A prince thus baptized is styled 文陀竭王 or 灌頂王 Murddhadja râdja.

MUSALAGARBHA or Musâragalva (Pâli. Masaragalla) 牟婆洛 or 摩沙羅 or 謨薩羅 or 摩沙羅 or 目娑 explained by 紺色王 lit. a jewel of violet colour, or by 瑪瑙色王 lit. a jewel coloured like a cornelian. One of the Saptaratna, either an ammonite or agate or coral. See also As'magarbha.

MUSÂVÂDÂ VÊRAMAṆÎ 不妄語 lit. abstaining from lies. The 4th of the S'ikchâpada.

MUTCHILINDA PARVATA v. Mahâmutchilinda.

N.

NADÎKÂS'YAPA (Burm. Nadi Kathaba. Tib. Tchu wo odsrung) 捺地迦葉波 or 那提迦葉 An Arhat, disciple of S'âkyamuni, brother of Mahâkas'yapa; to be reborn as Buddha samanta prabhâsa.

NADÎ 那提 or Puṇyopâya 布如烏伐耶 explained by 福生 lit. progeny of happiness. A. S'ramaṇa of Central India, who brought (A. D. 655) over 1500 texts of the Mahâyâna and Hinâyâna Schools to China, fetched medicines (A. D. 656) from Kwanlun, and translated (A. D. 663) three works.

NÂGA (Burm. Nat. Siam. Nagha. Tit. Klu. Mong. Lus) 那伽 or 龍神 lit. dragon spirit, or 龍鬼 lit. dragon-demon, explained as signifying, (1.) 龍 lit. dragons, (2.) 象 lit. elephants (nagaga) (3.) 不來 lit. persons exempt from transmigration. The term Nâga was perhaps originally applied to dreaded mountain tribes, and subsequently used to designate monsters generally. The worship of Nâgas (i. e. dragons and serpents) is indigenous in China and flourishes even now, dragons being regarded as mountain spirits, as tutelary deities of the five regions (i. e. 4 points of the compass and centre) and as the guardians of the 5 lakes and 4 oceans (i.e. of all lakes and seas). The worship of Nâgas has been observed as a characteristic of Turanian nations. The Aryan Buddhists, finding it too popular, connived at or adopted this worship. All the most ancient

Sûtras and biographies of Buddha mention Nâgas, who washed Buddha after his birth, conversed with him, protected him, were converted by him, and guarded the relics of his body. Chinese Buddhists view mountain Nâgas as enemies of mankind, but marine Nâgas as piously inclined. Whilst the Burmese confound Dêvas and Nâgas, the Chinese distinguish them sharply. According to an ancient phrase (龍天八部 lit. Nâgas, Dêvas and others of the eight classes) there are 8 classes of beings, always enumerated in the following order, Dêvas, Nâgas, Rakchas, Gandharvas, Asuras, Garuḍas, Kinnaras, Mahorâgas. See also Sâgara, and Virupakcha.

NÂGAHRADA 龍池 lit. dragon-tank. General term for all sheets of water, viewed as dewellings of Nâgas.

NÂGARÂDJA 龍王 lit. dragon king. Epithet of all guardian spirits of waters, many of whom are believed to have been converted and embraced monastic life.

NÂGARAHÂRA or Nâgara 那揭羅喝羅 or 曩哦羅賀羅 or 那竭 Ancient kingdom and city (Dionysopolis), 30 miles W. of Jellallabad, on the southern bank of the Cabul river.

NÂGARADHANA 那迦羅馱那 An ancient vihâra in Djalandhara.

NÂGÂRDJUNA or Gâgakrochuna (Pâli. Nâgasêna) 那伽閼刺樹那 or 龍樹 lit. the Arguna tree (Pentaptera arjuna) or 龍孟 lit. Nâga the great, or 龍勝 lit. Nâga the conqueror: A native of Western India, a hermit living under an Arguna tree, until, converted by Kapimala, he became the 14th patriarch, famous in Southern India by dialectic subtelty in disputations with heretics, chief representative of the Mahâyâna School, first teacher of the Amitâbha doctrine, founder of the Madhyamika School, author of some 24 works, the greatest philosopher of the Buddhists, viewed as "one of the 4 suns which illumine the world." He taught that the soul is neither existent nor non-existent, neither eternal nor non-eternal, neither annihilated by death nor non-annihilated. His principal disciples were Dêva Bodhisattva and Buddhapalita. In a monastery near Kôsala, he cut off his own head as an offering at the request of Sadvâsa's son (B. C. 212 or A. D. 194). He is now styled a Bodhisattva.

NÂGASENA 那先比丘 A

Bhikchu, author of a Sûtra of the same name (translated A.D. 317—420).

NAGNA or MAHÂNAGNA 諾伽那 or 摩訶諾伽那 explained by 露身 lit. naked or by 大力神 lit. spirits of great power. Warlike spirits (or bardes) of supernatural strength, who appear naked.

NAHUTA 那由他 A numeral term (100 millions).

NÂIRAM̃DJANÂ (Singh. Niranjara. Burm. Neritzara) 尼連禪那 or 希連禪 or 希連河 explained by 不樂著河 lit. the river without cheer or brightness, or by 無著河 lit. the river without brightness. (1) A river (Niladjan) which flows past Gayâ. (2.) A river (Hiranjavatî), which flows past Kus'inagara.

NÂIVASAÑDJÑA SAMÂDHI 非想定 lit. fixed (meditation) without thinking. A degree of Samâdhi, rising above thought.

NÂIVA SAÑDJÑÂNÂ SAÑDJÑÂYATANAM v. Ṭchaturarûpa brahmalôka.

NAKCHATRA RÂDJA SAMKU SUMITÂBHIDJÑA 宿王華 lit. flower of the star king. A fabulous Bodhisattva, follower of S'âkyamuni.

NAKCHATRA RÂDJA VIKRIDITA 宿王戲 lit. the sports of the star king. A degree of Samâdhi.

NAKCHATRATÂRÂ RADJÂDITYA 日星宿 lit. sun and stars. A degree of Samâdhi.

NÂLANDA 那爛陀 explained by 施無厭 lit. benevolent without wearying. The Nâga (deity) of a lake in the Amra forest near Râdjagriha.

NÂLANDAGRAMA 那爛陀 A village near Nâlanda sam̃ghârâma.

NÂLANDA SAM̃GHÂBÂMA 施無厭寺 lit. the monastery of the unwearied benefactor. A monastery, built by S'akrâditya, 7 miles N. of Râdjagriha, now called Baragong (i.e. vihâragrama).

NAMAḤ (Pâli. Namo. Burm. Namau. Tib. Nama) 捺謨 or 捺麻 or 那麻 or 那謨 or 曩謨 or 納謨 or 南無 explained by 皈依 lit. I humbly trust (adore). The Ave of the Buddhist, daily used in the liturgy, in the invocation of the Triratna, and in incantations, wherefore both Buddhist and Tauist priests and sorcerers are called 南無師 lit. masters of nanaḥ.

NÂMARÛPA 名色 lit. name

and form. One of the 12 Nidâna, signifying the unreality of both abstract notions and material phenomena.

NANDA (Tib. Dgabo) 難陀 explained by 善觀喜 lit. joy of virtuous views. (1.) A Nâga king (Singh. Nando pannanda). (2.) A person called Sundarananda. (3.) The girl Nandâ (Singh. Sujata) who supplied S'âkyamuni with milk. See also Bala.

NANDÂVARTAYA or Nandyâvarta (Pâli. Nandiyavatta) 難提迦物多 explained by 右旋 lit. rotating to the right. A conch with spirals running to the right, a mystic symbol of good omen.

NANDI 竺難提 or 喜 lit. joy. A grihapati of the West, translator (A. D. 419) of 3 works.

NANDIMITRA 難提蜜多羅 Author of the 撰集三藏及雜藏傳 translated A. D. 317—420.

NARADATTA v. Katyâyana.

NÂRAKA (Pâli. Miraya. Siam. Narok. Burm. Niria. Tib. Myalba. Mong. Tamu) 捺落迦 explained by 人 (nara) 惡 (ka), lit. men's wickedness, or by 不可樂 lit. unenjoyable, or by 苦器 lit. instruments of torture; or 泥黎 (Niraya) explained by 地獄 lit. prison under the earth, or by 冥府 lit. the prefecture of darkness. General term for the various divisions of hell. (1.) The hot hells (熱獄), 8 of which (see Samdjiva, Kâlasûtra, Samghata, Râurava, Mahârâurava, Tapana, Pratâpana, ank Avîtchi) are situated underneath Djambudvîpa in tiers, beginning at a depth of 11,900 yôdjanas, and reach to a depth of 40,000 yôdjanas; but as each of these hells has 4 gates and outside each gate 4 antechamber-hells, there are altogether 136 hot hells. (2.) The cold hells (寒獄), 8 in number (see Arbuda, Nirarbuda, Atata, Hahava, Ahaha, Utpala, Padma and Puṇḍarîka), situated underneath the 2 Tchakravâlas and ranging shaft-like one beneath the other, but so that this shaft is gradually widening down to the 4th hell and then narrowing again, the first and last hells having the shortest and the 4th hell the longest diameter. (3.) The dark hells, 8 in number, situated between the 2 Tchakravâlas; also called vivifying hells (活獄), because any being, dying in the first of these hells, is at once reborn in the 2nd, and so forth, life lasting 500 years in each of these hells. (4.) The cold Lôkântarika hells

(邊獄 lit. hells on the edge sc. of the universe), 10 in number, but each having 100 millions of smaller hells attached, all being situated outside of the Tchakravâlas. (4.) The 84,000 small Lôkântarika hells (邊小地獄 lit. small hells on the edge, divided into 3 classes, as situated on mountains, or on water, or in deserts. Each universe has the same number of hells, distributed so that the northern continent contains no hell at all, the two continents E. and W. of the Mêru have only the small Lôkântarika hells, and all the other hells are situated under the southern continent (Djambudvîpa). There are different torments in different hells; the length of life also differs in each class of hells; but the distinctions made are too fanciful to be worth enumerating. The above hells constitute one of the 6 gâti of transmigration and people are reborn in one or other class of hells according to their previous merits or demerits. It is not necessary that each individual should pass through all the above hells. The decision lies with Yama, who, assisted by 18 judges and hosts of demons, prescribes in each case what hells and tortures are appropriate. His sister performs the same duties with regard to female criminals. Chinese fancy has added a special hell for females (血盤池 lit. placenta tank), consisting of an immense pool of blood. From this hell, it is said, no release is possible, but all the other hells are mere purgatories, release being procured when sin has been sufficiently expiated or through intercession of the priesthood.

NARAPATI v. Djambudvîpa.

NARASAṂGHÂRÂMA 人伽藍 lit. the monastery of men. An ancient vihâra near the capital of Kapis'a.

NARASIṂHA 那羅僧訶 An ancient city (Nrisiñhavana?) near the E. frontier of Tchêka.

NÂRÂYAṆA or Nârâyaṇadêva 那羅野拏 or 那羅延 or 那羅延天 explained by 人生本 lit. the originator of human life (Brahma, or by 天力士 lit. hero (nara) of divine power, or by 堅固 lit. firm and solid. (1.) An epithet of Brahma as creator. (2.) A (wrong) designation of Narendrayas'as.

NARENDRAYAS'AS 那黎提拏耶舍 A native of Udyâna, translator (A. D. 557—589) of many Sûtras.

NARIKÊLA 那利薊羅 The cocoanut tree.

NARIKÊLADVÎPA 那羅稽羅州 An island, several

thousand *li* S. of Ceylon, inhabited by dwarfs who have human bodies with beaks like birds and live upon cocoanuts.

NARMMADÂ 耐秣陀 The river Nerbudda, forming the southern frontier of Barukatchêva.

NAS'AS'ATA or Basiasita 婆舍斯多 A Brahman of Kubhâ who became the 25th patriarch (in Central India) and died (A. D. 325) by samâdhi.

NATCHTCHAGÎTA VÂDITA VISUKADASSANÂ VÊRAMAṆÎ 不歌舞倡伎不往觀聽 lit. thou shalt not take part in singing or dancing in musical or theatrical performances, nor go to look on or listen. The 7th of the 10 S'ikchâpada.

NAVADÊVAKULA 納縛提婆矩羅 An ancient city (now Nohbatgang) on the Ganges, a few miles S. E. of Kanyâkûbdja.

NAVAMÂLIKÂ 那婆摩利 explained by 雜花 lit. variegated flowers. A perfume used for scenting oil. See Mallika,

NAVAPA 納縛波 or 鄯善 now called 闢展 (Pidjan). An ancient kingdom on the eastern border of Gobi. See Makhai.

NAVASAÑGHÂRÂMA 納縛僧伽藍 An ancient vihâra near Baktra, possessed of a tooth, basin and staff of S'âkyamuni.

NÂYAKA 天人導師 lit. the guide of dêvas and men (Nâyaka dêva mânuchyânâm). An epithet of S'âkyamuni. See Mânuchya.

NEMIMDHARA (Siam. Neminthon) 尼民陀羅 or 尼民達羅 or 彌樓 explained by 地特 lit. what earth grasps, or by 魚嘴山 lit. fish mouth mountain. (1.) A fish with a curiously shaped head. (2.) The lowest of the seven concentric mountain ranges (600 yôdjanas high) which encircle Mêru.

NÊPÂLA 尼波羅 An ancient kingdom (now Nepaul). E. of Khatmandu, 10,000 *li* from China, noted for the amalgamation of Brahminism and ancient Buddhism, which took place there, also as a station in the route of Indian and Chinese embassies, and as possessing fire (naphtha) wells.

NICHKLÊS'A 無復煩惱 lit. no return to trouble and vexation. Freedom from passion, a characteristic of the state of an Arhat.

NICHṬAPANA 涅疊般那 or 闍維 or 焚燒 lit. burning. Cremation, as performed in China at the funerals of priests.

NIDANA (Tib. Rten brel) 尼陀那 explained by 十二因緣 lit. the 12 causes of existence. (1.) The fundamental dogma of Buddhist thought, the concatenation of cause and effect in the whole range of existence through 12 links (see Djarâmarana, Djâti, Bhava, Upâdâna, Trichnâ, Vêdana, Spars'a, Chaḍâyatana, Nâmarûpa, Vidjnana, Saṁskâra and Avidya) the understanding of which solves the riddle of life, revealing the inaninity of existence and preparing the mind for Nirvâṇa. (2.) All sûtras or pamphlets written for some special reason (nidâna), either to answer a query, or to enforce a precept, or to enhance a doctrine.

NIDÂNA BUDDHA s.a. Pratyêka Buddha.

NILAKAṆṬHA 千眼千臂觀世音菩薩陀羅尼神咒經 Title of a translation, concerning the ritual and ceremonies used in the worship of Avalokitês'vara.

NILANÊTRA v. Dêva.

NÎLAPIṬA or Nîlapiṭaka 尼羅蔽荼 or 靑藏 'lit. the azure collection. A collection of annals and royal edicts.

NINYA 泥壤 A city in Central Asia.

NIRARBUDA 尼羅浮陀 explained by 疱裂 lit. bursting blisters. (1.) The 2nd large cold hell (v. Naraka), where cold winds blister the skin of criminals. (2.) The 2nd of the 10 cold Lokântarikâ hells (v. Naraka). (3.) A numeral, equal to 1 followed by 33 cyphers.

NIRGRANTHA 泥犍陀 or 薩遮尼揵 or 薩遮尼乾連陀 or 尼乾 explained by 離繫 or 不繫 lit. unfettered (sc. by want of food or clothes) or by 露形外道 lit. nude heretics. (1,) A Tîrthaka (q. v.), a son of Djñâti and therefore also called Nirgranthadjñâti (尼揵陀若提), who taught fatalism, recommended fasting and condemned the use of clothes. (2.) The followers of Nirgrantha.

NIRMAṆAKÂYA (Tib. sprul ba) 化身 or 應身 or 應化身 lit. a body capable of transformation. (1.) One of the Trikâya (q.v.), the power of assuming any form of appearance in order to propagate Buddhism. (2.) The incarnate avatâra of a deity (Tib. Chutuktu. Mong. Chubilgan). See also Anupapâdaka,

NIRMÂṆARATI (Pâli. Nimmanaratti. Siam. Nimmanaradi. Tib. Hphrul dga) 尼摩羅天須蜜羅天 or 化樂天 or 樂變化天 lit. dêvas who delight in transformations. The 5th Dêvaloka, situated 640,000 yôdjanas above the Mêru. Life lasts there 8,000 years.

NIRUKTI v. Pratisaṁvid.

NIRVÂṆA (Pâli. Nibbâna. Siam. Niphan. Burm. Neibban. Tib. Mya ngan las hdas pa i.e separation from pain. Mong. Ghassalang etse angkid shirakasan i.e. escape from misery) 湼盤 or 泥洹 explained by 離生滅 lit. separation from life and death (i.e. exemption from transmigration), or by 出離煩惱 lit. escape from trouble and vexation (i.e. freedom from passion, Klês'a nirvâṇa), or by 圓滿淸淨 lit. absolutely complete moral purity, or by 滅盡一切習氣 lit. complete extinction of the animal spirits, or by 無爲 lit. non-action. (1.) The popular exoteric systems agree in defining Nirvâṇa negatively as a state of absolute exemption from the circle of transmigration, as a state of entire freedom from all forms of existence, to begin with freedom from all passion and exertion, a state of indifference to all sensibility. Positively they define Nirvâṇa as the highest state of spiritual bliss, as absolute immortality through absorption of the soul into itself, but preserving individuality so that e.g. Buddhas, after entering Nirvâṇa, may reappear on earth. This view is based on the Chinese translations of ancient sûtras and confirmed by traditional sayings of S'âkyamuni who, for instance, said in his last moments "the spiritual body (法身) is immortal." The Chinese Buddhist belief in Sukhavatî (the paradise of the West) and Amitâbha Buddha is but confirmatory of the positive character ascribed to Nirvâṇa (湼盤), Parinirvâṇa (般湼盤) and Mahâparinirvâṇa (大般湼盤). (2.) The esoteric or philosophical view of Nirvâṇa is based only on the Abhibharma which indeed defines Nirvâṇa as a state of absolute annihilation. But this view is not the result of ancient dogmatology. The philosophical Schools which advocate this nihilistic view of Nirvâṇa deal in the same way with all historical facts and with every positive dogma: all is to them mâya *i.e.* illusion and unreality.

NITYA PARIVRITA 常滅 lit. continuous extinction. A fabulous Buddha living S. of our universe, an incarnation of the 6th son of Mahâbhidjña djñanâbhibhu.

NIVARTTANA STÛPA 回駕窣堵波 lit. the stûpa erected on the spot where S'âkyamuni's) coachman parted from him.

NIVÂSANA 泥伐散那 or 那縛些那 explained by 裙 lit. a skirt. The coloured garment (without buttons or girdle) of a S'ramaṇa.

NIVRITTI 無爲自然 A philosophical term, non-acting self-existence, opposed to Pravritti 無不爲 constant action.

NIYATÂNI YATAGATI MUDRÂVATÂRA Title of two translations, viz. (1.) 不必定入定入印經 A. D. 542 by Pradjñârutchi, and (2.) 入定不定印經 A.D. 700.

NIYUTA 那庾多 A numeral, equal to 1,000 kôṭi.

NUTCHIKAN or Nuchidjan (Nudjketh) 笯赤建 An ancient kingdom, between Taras and Kodjend, in Turkestan.

NYAGRODHA 尼拘律 or 尼拘律陀 or 尼俱律 or 尼俱陀 or 尼俱類陀 or 尼俱盧陀 or 尼拘屢阿 explained by 無節樹 lit. a tree without knots (and described as being the highest tree of India.) The Ficus Indica.

NYÂYA ANUSÂRA S'ÂSTRA 順正理論 lit. the orthodox s'âstra. A designation of the Abhidharma kôcha s'âstra.

NYÂYA DVÂRA TÂRAKA S'ÂSTRA 因明正理門論本 A work by Mahâdignâga, translated (A. D. 648) by Hiuen-tsang.

NYÂYA PRAVÊS'A TÂRAKA S'ÂSTRA 因明入正理論 A work by Saṁkarasvâmin, translated (A. D. 647) by Hiuen-tsang.

O.

OCH or Ûsch 烏鎩 or 鏺沙 or 依耐 or 英吉沙彌 (Yingeshar). An ancient kingdom N. of the S'itâ.

ÔM or aûm 唵 or 烏菴 A mystic interjection, of magic and sin-atoning efficacy, used in prayers and in sorcery, originally derived by Tibetan

Buddhists from later Hindooism (*a* standing for Vishnu, û for Shiva and *m* for Brahma) and introduced in China by the Yogâtchârya School.

ÔM̃ MAṆI PADMÊ HÛM̃ 唵摩呢八爾吽 or 菴乜呢必滅堪 explained by 藏字能辟邪鎮煞 lit. Tibetan characters able to ward off noxious influences. A set of six Sanskrit sounds (lit. thou jewel in the lotus, hûm!) of mystic and magic import, used in prayers and in sorcery, inscribed on amulets, cash, tombstones and at the end of books, and (especially in Tibet) most commonly addressed to Avalokitês'vara. These 6 syllables are sometimes applied to the 6 gâti and to the 6 pâramitâ. They are more popular in Tibet than in China where another set of 6 syllables (南無阿彌陀佛 namaḥ Amitâbha) is largely used in the same sense.

P.

PADMA 波頭摩 or 波曇摩 or 波暮 or 鉢特忙 or 鉢特摩 explaiaed by 赤蓮花 lit. red lotus flowers. (1.) The waterlily, lotus, nymphaea, and specially the rose coloured species (Nelumbium speciosum). (2.) A symbol of Buddhaship, s. a. Raktapatmaya. (3.) The 7th, of the 8 cold hells (where the cold produces blisters like lotus buds).

PADMAPAÑI see under Avalokitês'vara.

PADMAPRABHA 華光佛 The name under which S'âriputtra reappears as Buddha.

PADMARGÂA 鉢曇摩羅迦 or 赤刼球 lit. a true red pearl. A ruby.

PADMARATNA v. Haklenayas'as.

PADMA SAM̃BHAVA (Tib. Padma byung gnas, or Urgyan padma) 蓮華生上師 lit. the lotus-born superior teacher. A Buddhist of Kabul (Urgyan) who, invited by king 乞栗雙提贊 Khri-srong-lde-btsan, introduced in Tibet (A. D. 740—786) a system of magic and mysticism (saturated with Shivaism) which fonnd its way also to China.

PADMAS'ÎLA 蓮華戒 A Bodhisattva, author of the 廣釋菩提心論 Bodhi hridaya vaipulya prakarana s'âstra.

PADMAS'RÎ 華德菩薩 A Bodhisattva in the retinue of S'âkyamuni; re-incarnation of S'ubhavyûha; to re-appear as Buddha S'alendra râdja.

PADMA TCHINTÂMAṆI DHÂRAṆÎ SÛTRA. Ttile of 5 translations, viz., (1.) 觀世音菩薩秘密藏神咒經 by S'ikchânanda, A. D. 618—907; (2.) 觀世音菩薩如意摩尼陀羅尼經 by Ratna tchinta A.D. 618—907; (3) 觀自在菩薩如意陀羅尼經 A.D. 710; (4.) 如意輪陀羅尼經 by Bodhirutchi, A. D. 709; (5.) 佛說如意摩尼陀羅尼經

PADMAVATÎ 蓮華色 A wife of As'ôka, transformed into a Tchakravarti.

PADMA VRICHABHA VIKRÂMIN 華足安行 The name under which Dhritiparipurṇa reappears as Buddha.

PADMA VYÛHA BODHISATTVA 華嚴菩薩 A fabulous Bodhisattva worshipped in China on New Year's eve.

PADMÔTTARA 殊妙身 Name of the 729th Buddha of the present Bhadra Kalpa.

PALA or Satamâna 波羅 explained by 斤 lit. a catty. A weight, equal to 10 dharana.

PALÂS'A 波羅奢 explained by 赤花樹 lit. a tree with red flowers (also said to yield a red dye). The Butea frondosa. See also Kanaka.

PALI 波利 A village, with an ancient stûpa, 90 *li* N. N. W. of Baktra.

PÂLI 舊言 lit. the ancient dialect (*i. e.* of the ancient country). The vernacular of Magadha, or Magadhî Prâkrit.

PAMIRA 波謎羅 The plateau of Pamir, the centre of the Tsung-ling range, including Anavatapta lake.

PÂM̃S'UPATAS or Pâs'upatas 波輸鉢多 or 波輸鉢多 explained by 塗灰外道 lit. heretics who besmear themselves with ashes. A Shivaitic sect of worshippers of Mahês'vara, clad in plain rags. Some shaved their heads.

PANASA or Djaka 波那娑 or 半櫋娑 or 般裹娑 The Artocarpus integrifolia (jacktree). See also under Udumbara.

PÂṆÂTI PÂTÂ VÊRAMAṆÎ 不殺生 lit. kill no living being. The first of the S'ikchâpada (10 rules for novices).

PAṆḌAKA 般荼迦 or 半擇迦 or 般吒 explained by 黃門 lit. eunuchs. General term for (1.) Paṇḍakas (properly so called) 般吒 who, though impotent; have perfect organs; (2.) Irs'âpaṇḍakas 伊利沙般荼迦 who are impotent except when jealous; (3.) Chaṇḍakas 扇荼迦 whose organs are incomplete; (4.) Pakchapaṇḍakas 博义般荼迦 who are for half a month males and for half a month females; (5.) Ruṇapaṇḍakas 留拏般荼迦 who are emasculated males.

PAṆḌITA (Tib. Pan-shen) 班彌達 A title (scholar, teacher), given to learned (especially Tibetan) priests.

PÂNINI 波你尼 A Brahman (B.C. 350) of S'âlâtula, editor of the Vyâkaraṇam, author of a Sanskrit grammar.

PAÑTCHÂBHIDJÑÂ (Singh. Pancha abignya. Tib. Phungpo) 五神通 lit. five supernatural talents. See under Abhidjñâ.

PAÑTCHA DHARMA KÂYA 五分法身 lit. the spiritual body in five portions. Five attributes of the Dharma kâya, viz., (1.) 戒 lit. precept, explained by 超色陰 exemption from all materiality (rûpa), (2.) 定 lit. tranquillity, explained by 超受陰 exemption from all sensations (vêdanâ), (3.) 慧 lit. wisdom, explained by 超想陰 exemption from all consciousness (samdjña), (4.) 解脱 lit. emancipation (mokcha) explained by 超行陰 exemption from all moral activity (karman), (5.) 知見 lit. intelligent views, explained by 超識陰 exemption from all knowledge (vidjñâna).

PAÑTCHA INDRYÂNI v. Indrya.

PAÑTCHA KACHÂYA v. Kachâya.

PAÑTCHA KLÊS'A 五鈍使 lit. 5 dull messengers, or 五重滯 lit. 5 serious hindrances. Five moral imperfections, viz. (1.) 貪 cupidity, (2.) 嗔 anger, (3.) 癡 foolishness, (4.) 慢 irreverence, (5.) 疑 doubts. Victory over these 5 vices constitutes the 5 virtues or Pañtcha s'îla.

PAÑTCHA MAHÂRHATCHTCHATANI 五百大羅漢 (1.) The 500 great Arhats who formed the synod under Kanichka, supposed authors of the Abhidharma mahâvibhâcha s'âstra.

PAÑTCHANADA or Bhiḍa 毗荼 Ancient kingdom (now the Pundjab), called Bhiḍa after its capital.

PAÑTCHÂNANTARYA 五逆 lit. the 5 rebellions. Five deadly sins, viz. matricide, parricide, killing an Arhat, causing divisions among the priesthood, and shedding the blood of a Buddha.

PAÑTCHA PARICHAD or Pañtcha varchikâ parichad or Mokcha mahâparichad 般闍于瑟 or 般遮跋利沙 or 般遮婆栗史迦 or 般遮大會 explained by 五年大會 lit. the great quinquennial assembly. An ecclesiastical conference held once in 5 years, established by As'oka for the purpose of confession of sins and moral exhortations.

PAÑTCHARÂCHṬRA or Pañtchasattva v. Punatcha.

PAÑTCHAS'ÎLA see under Pañtcha Klês'a

PAÑTCHA SKANDHA v. Skandha.

PAÑTCHA SKANDHAKA S'ÂSTRA 大乘五蘊論 A work of Vasubandhu, translated by Hiuen-tsang (A. D. 647).

PAÑTCHA SKANDHAKA S'ÂSTRA KÂRIKÂ 五蘊論釋 A commentary by Vinîtaprabha.

PAÑTCHA SKANDHA VAIPULYA S'ÂSTRA 大乘廣五蘊論 A commentary by Sthitamati, translated by Divâkara (A.D. 685).

PAÑTCHA VÊRAMAṆÎ 五戒 lit. 5 precepts. The first half of the S'ikchâpada.

PAÑTCHA VIDYÂ S'ASTRA 五明 lit. the 5 luminaries. The 5 elementary schoolbooks of India. See S'abda, S'ilpasthâna, Tchikitsa, Hêtu, and Adhyâtma vidyâ.

PÂPIYÂN v. Mâra.

PÂRÂDJIKÂ or Phârâdjikâ 波羅闍巳迦 or 波羅夷 explained by 無餘 lit. extreme (measures). The first section of the Vinaya pitaka, containing rules regarding expulsion from the priesthood.

PARAMA BOḌHI 鉢羅摩菩提 explained by 正覺 lit. correct intelligence. A state of superior intelligence (v. Bodhi).

PARAMALAGIRI 跋邏末羅耆釐 explained by 黑峰 lit. the dark peak. A mountain S.W. of Kos'âla, where Sadvaha built a monastery for Nâgârdjuna.

PARAMÂṆU 極細塵 lit. an atom of dust. A measure of length, the 7th part an Aṇu.

PARAMÂRTHA 波羅末陀 or 眞諦 also styled 拘那

羅陀 Guṇarata. A S'ramaṇa of Udjdjayana, translator (A. D. 548—569) of some 50 works.

PARA MÂRTHA DHARMA VIDJAY ASÛTRA. Title of 2 translations, viz., 佛說第一義法勝經 by Gautama Pradjñârutchi (A. D. 534—550), and 佛說大威燈光僊人問疑經 by Djñânagupta (A.D. 586).

PARAMÂRTHA SAṂVARTI SATYA NIRDES'A SÛTRA. Title of 3 translations, viz. (1.) 佛說文殊師利淨律經 by Dharmarakcha (A.D. 289), (2.) 清淨毗尼方廣經 by Kumâradjîva (A.D. 30I—409), and (3.) 寂調音所問經 A.D. 420—479.

PARAMÂRTHA SATYA S'ÂSTRA 勝義諦論 A work by Vasubandhu.

PÂRAMITÂ 波羅蜜多 or 六度 lit. 6 means of passing (to Nirvâṇa), explained by 到彼岸 lit. arrival at the other shore (i.e. at Nirvâṇa), but with the note, "it is only Pradjñâ (the 6th virtue) which carries men across the Sañsâra to the shores of Nirvâṇa." Six cardinal virtues, essential to every Bodhisattva, but representing generally the path in which the saint walks, viz. (1.) Dâna, charity, (2.) S'îla, morality, (3.) Kchânti, patience, (4.) Vîrya, energy, (5.) Dhyâna, contemplation, and (6.) Pradjñâ, wisdom. Sometimes ten Paramitâs 十度 are counted by adding (7.) Upâya, use of proper means, (8.) Djñâna, science, (9.) Prañidhana, pious vows, and (10.) Bala, force of purpose.

PARANIRMITA VAS'AVARTIN (Pâli. Wasawarti. Siam. Paranimit. Tib. Gjan hphrul dvang byed or Bab dvang phpugh. Mong. Bussudum chubilghani erkeber or Maschi baya suktchi ergethu) 波羅尼密婆舍跋提天 or 他化自在天 lit. dêvas who, whilst others are transformed, remain independent, or dêvas who control the transformation of others. The last of the 6 Dêvalokas, the dwelling of Mâra, where life lasts 32,000 years.

PARASMAIPADA 般羅颯迷 A form of conjugation, each tense having a peculiar termination for the transitive voice, so-called (lit. words for another) because the action is supposed to pass (parasmai) to another.

PARATCHITTADJÑÂNA (Pâli. Parassa tchêtôpariyâ yañâna) 他心 lit. the minds of others. The 5th of the 6 Abhidjñas, intuitive knowledge of the minds of all other beings.

PÂRAVÂ 波羅越 explained by 鴿 lit. pigeon. A rock temple in the Dekkhan, dedicated to Kâs'yapa Buddha.

PÂRIDJÂTA 波利質多 A sacred shrub (growing in a circle in front of Indra's palace).

PARINIRVÂṆA 般泥洹 or 般涅槃 or 波利涅縛南 or 般利涅槃那 explained by 無餘寂滅 lit. extreme stillness and extinction (&c. of sense), or by 圓寂 lit. complete stillness, or by 滅度 lit. the passase of extinction, or by 普究竟出離煩惱結 lit. final termination and escape from the bonds of trouble and vexation. The 2nd degree of Nirvâṇa, corresponding with the mental process of resigning all thought (無想門). See under Nirvâṇa.

PARINIRVÂṆA VAIPULYA SÛTRA 方等般泥洹經 A work of 5,000 stanzas delivered by S'âkyamuni previous to his entrance into Nirvâṇa.

PARÎTTHÂBHAS (Tib. Ôd bsal or Od tchhung) 少光 lit. limited light The 4th Brahmaloka; the 1st region of the 2nd Dhyâna.

PARÎTTAS'UBHAS (Singh. Parittasubha. Tib. Dge tchhung) 少淨 lit. limited purity. The 7th Brahmaloka; the 1st region of the 3rd Dhyâna.

PARIVRÂJIKAS (Singh. Paribrâjikas) 般利伐羅勾迦 or 簸利婆羅闍迦 or 删闍耶 explained by 普行 lit. (those who) walk about everywhere. A Shivaitic sect, worshippers of Mahês'vara, who wear clothes of the colour of red soil. They shave the head excepting the crown.

PARṆAS'AVARI DHÂRAṆÎ 葉衣觀自在菩薩經 Title of a translation by Amoghavadjra (A. D. 746—771).

PARSA 波刺斯 or 波刺私 or 波斯 Persia, situated "near the western ocean," the principal mart for precious stones, pearls and silks, possessing at its capital (Surasthâna) the almsbowl of S'âkyamuni. The favourite deity of the country is Dinabha.

PÂRS'VA or Pârs'vika or Ârya pârs'vika 波栗溼縛 or 脅尊 lit. the Ârya (who used to lie) on his side, or 脅比丘 (Pârs'va bhikchu). A Brahman of Gandhâra, originally called 難生 lit. born with difficulty. As a Bhikchu, he swore to remain lying on his side till he had mastered the 6 Abhidjñas and 8 Pâramitâs. He is counted as the 9th (or 10th) patriarch (died B.C. 36).

PARVATA 鉢伐多 or 鉢羅伐多 Ancient province and city of Tchêka, 700 *li* N. E. of Mûlusthânîpura, perhaps the modern Futtipoor (between Multan and Lahore).

PARVATÎ s. a. Bhîmâ.

PARYAÑGKA BANDHANA 結跏趺坐 or 跏趺坐 A sacred phrase; binding a cloth round the knees, thighs and back, as seated on the hams.

PÂRYÂTRA 波里衣多羅 Ancient kingdom (now Birat, W. of Mathurâ), a centre of heretical sects.

PÂS'UPATAS v. Pâms'upatas.

PÂṬALA or Pâṭali (Tib. Skyanar) 波羅羅 or 波吒釐 explained by 熏花樹 lit. a tree whose flower emit steam or by 女婿樹 lit. the tree of the son-in-law. The Bignonia suave olens (trumpet flower).

PÂṬALIPUTTRA or Kusumapura (Tib. Skya nar gyi bu) 波吒梨耶 or 巴蓮弗 or 熙蓮弗 or 波吒釐子城 lit. the city of the son of the Pâṭali flower, or 華氏城 lit. the city of flowers (Pus'papura). An ancient city originally known as Kusumapura, where the 3rd synod (B. C. 246) was held; the present Patna.

PATRA 梖多樹 (Peito tree) or 梖多葉 (Peito leaves) or 葉樹 lit. leave tree, or 思惟樹 lit. meditation tree. A palm, the Borassus flabelliformis, often confounded with the Pippala. See Bodhidruma and Tâla.

PÂTRA (Pâli. Patto. Singh. Patra. Burm. Thabeit. Tib. Lhung bsed. Mong. Baddir or Zögösã) 波多羅 or 鉢盂 or 鉢多羅 or 鉢 (1.) The almsbowl (patera) of S'âkyamuni to be used by every Buddha, first preserved at Vâis'ali, then taken to Gandhâra, Persia, China, Ceylon, to the heaven Tuchita, to the palace of Sâgara (at the bottom of the sea), where it awaits the advent of Maitrêya, whereupon it will divide into 4 pieces, each of which is to be guarded by a Mahârâdja, as with its absolute disappearance the religion of Buddha will perish. (2.) The almsbowl of every Budhist mendicant.

PÂTRA DÊVA 鉢天 The dêva of the almsbowl, invoked by conjurors.

PATTIKÂYA 步 lit. infantry. A division of every Indian army.

PÂUCHA 報沙 The first of the 3 winter months, beginning on the 16th day of the 12th (Chinese) moon.

PHÂRÂDJIKA v. Pârâdjika.

PHÂTCHITTYÂ DHAMMA (Pâli) 波逸提法 (Singh. Pâchiti), explained by 墮 lit. fall (into hell). A section of the Vinaya, containing 90 prohibitions.

PHÂṬIDÊSANÎYÂ v. Pratidês'anîyâ.

PILINDA VATSA 畢隣陀婆蹉 An Arhat, one of the disciples of S'âkyamuni.

PÎLUSÂLAGIRI 比羅娑洛山 or 象堅山 A mountain (S.W. of Kapis'a city), the guardian spirit of which was converted by S'âkyamuni.

PÎLUSÂRA STÛPA 象堅窣都波 A stûpa erected by As'okha on the top of Pîlusâragiri.

PIPPALA or Pippala vrikcha 畢鉢羅 or 波波羅 or 賓撥梨力叉 One of the many names of Ficus religiosa. See under Bodhidruma and Patra.

PIS'ÂTCHA (Tib. Scha za) 畧舍閣 or 臂奢柘 or 畢舍遮 or 畧舍遮 A class of demons (vampires), more powerful than Prêtas. The retinue of Dhritarâchṭra.

PIS'UNA v. Mâra.

PIṬAKA (Singh. Pitakattayan. Burm. Pitagat) 藏 lit. a receptacle. General term for canonical writings. See Tripiṭaka.

PITÂ PUTRA SAMÂGAMA 菩薩見實會 Title of a translation (A. D. 562) by Narendrayas'as.

PITÂS'ILÂ 臂多勢羅 Ancient kingdom and city (in Sindh), 700 *li* N. of Adhyavakîla, 300 *li* S. W. of Avaṇḍa.

POCHADHA or Upochaṇa 布薩 explained 相句說罪 lit. mutual confession of sin. The ceremony of confession, performed on 1st and 15th of every month.

POTALA or Potaraka (Tib. Ri Potala or Ghru hdzin) 補陁 or 普陀 or 布呾洛迦 or 補怛洛迦 or 普陀洛迦 or 布達拉 explained by 小白花 lit. small white flowers. (1.) A port (now Tatta) at the mouth of the Indus, a centre of ancient trade, the home of S'âkyamuni's ancestors. (2.) A mountain range (Nilgherries?) E. of Malâya mountains, S.E. of Malakûṭa. The original resort of Avalokitês'vara. (3.)

The island of Pootoo (near Ningpo), a centre of the worship of Kwanyin (v. Avalokitês'vara). (4.) The three-peaked hill near Lhassa, with the palace of the old kings of Tibet, now the seat of the Dalai Lama (who is an incarnation of Avalokitês'vara). (5.) A fabulous resort of Bodhisattvas, "somewhere in the western ocean."

POṬṬHABHA (Pâli. Pottaban. Singh. Phassâ) 觸 lit. touch. The sense of touch. See Chaḍâyatana.

PRABHÂKARAMITRA or Prabhâmitra 波羅頗迦羅蜜多羅 or 作明知識 or 波頗 or 明友 or 光智 A S'ramaṇa of Central India, a Kchatriya by caste, who came to China (A. D. 627) and translated 3 works.

PRABHÂKARA VARDDHANA 波羅頗羯邏伐彈那 or 作光增 lit. one who causes increase of light. The father of Karcha varddhana, king of Kanyâkubdja.

PRABHÂPÂLA 護明菩薩 A former incarnation of S'âkyamuni, when he was a disciple of Kâs'yapa Buddha.

PRABHU (1.) A term in philosophy, primordial existence, 元始 (2.) A title of Vishnu (the sun) 波羅赴 or 鉢利部 See Vasudâva.

PRABHÛTARATNA 鉢羅部多羅怛曩 or 多寶 One of the Sapta Tathâgata, patron of the Saddharma puṇḍarika who divided himself into seven Buddhas (十方佛) to labour in as many different places, and appears sometimes in the form of a Stûpa. See Ratna vis'uddha.

PRADAKCHINA 循環 The (Brahmanic and Buddhist) ceremony of circumambulating a holy object with one's right side turned to it.

PRADÂNAS'ÛRA 勇施菩薩 A Bodhisattva in the retinue of S'âkyamuni.

PRADÎPADÂNÎYA SÛTRA 佛說施燈功德經 Title of a translation (A. D. 558) by Narendrayas'as.

PRADJÂPATÎ v. Mahâpradjâpatî.

PRADJÑA (Pâli. Panna. Singh. Pragnyâwa) 般若 explained by 智慧 lit. intelligence. (1.) The highest of the 6 Pâramitâ, intelligence, the principal means of attaining to Nirvâṇa, as a knowledge of the illusory character of all existence. (2.) A S'ramaṇa of Kubhâ (Cabul), translator (about A.D. 810) of 4 works, author of a new alphabet.

PRADJÑÂBARA (Pâli. Pannâbala, Singh. Pragnyawabala) 慧力 lit. power of intelligence. Wisdom, one of the 5 Balâ.

PRADJÑÂBHADRA 般若跋陀羅 A learned priest from Tiladhâka, native of Bâlapati, adherent (about 630 A. D.) of the Sarvâstivâdaḥ.

PRADJÑADÊVA 慧天 A learned and pious priest of Mahâbodhi saṁghârâma.

PRADJÑÂGUPTA 般若毱多 or 慧護 A learned Brahman, teacher of Sîladitya.

PRADJÑÂKARA 般若羯羅 or 慧性 A learned priest of Nâvasaṁghârâma, native (about 630 A.D.) of Tchêka.

PRADJÑÂKÛṬA 智積 A fictitious Bodhisattva, living in Ratnavis'uddha, attending on Prabhûtaratna.

PRADJÑÂPARAMITÂ 般若波羅密多 explained by 到彼岸 lit. landing on the other shore. Intelligence as a means to reach Nirvâṇa. See Pradjña and Pâramitâ.

PRADJÑÂPARAMITÂ ARDHAS'ATIKÂ. Title of 4 translations of the 10th Sûtra of the Mahâpradjñâparamitâ, viz. (1.) 實相般若波羅蜜經 by Bodhirutchi (A. D. 618—907); (2.) 金剛頂瑜伽理趣般若經 by Vadjra bodhi (A.D. 723—730); (3.) 大樂金剛不空眞實三麼耶般若波羅蜜多理趣經 by Amoghavadjra (A. D. 746—771); (4.) 佛說五十頌聖般若波羅蜜經 by Dânapâla (A.D. 980—1000).

PRADJÑAPÂRAMITÂ SÛTRA s.a. Mahâpradjña paramitâ sûtra.

PRADJÑÂPÂRAMITÂ SAṀKA. YAGÂTHÂ 佛母寶德藏般若波羅密經 Title of a translation (A. D. 982—1001).

PRADJÑÂPRADÎPA S'ÂSTRA 般若燈論 A work of Nâgârdjuna and Nirdês'aprabha (分別明), translated (A. D. 630—632) by Prabhâkaramitra.

PRADJÑAPTIPÂDAS'ÂSTRA 施設論 A work of Mahâmaudgalyâyana, translated by Dharmarakcha (A. D. 1004—1058).

PRADJÑAPTIVÂDINAḤ 波羅若底婆拖部 or 說度

部 or 說假部 lit. the School which discusses redemption or illusions. A subdivision of the Mahâsaṁghikaḥ.

PRADJÑÂTARA 般若多羅 The 27th patriarch, native of Eastern India; laboured in Southern India; died A. D. 457.

PRADJÑÊNDRYA (Pâli. Pannêndriya. Singh. Pragnyawa indra) 慧根 The organ of intelligence (v. Pradjña), one of the 5 organs (or roots) of life (v. Indrya).

PRÂGBODHI 鉢羅笈菩提 explained by 前正覺 lit. anterior to correct perceptions. A mountain in Magadha, which S'âkyamuni ascended "before entering upon Bodhi."

PRAHÂṆA 修 or 修文法 Conversion and entering ecclesiastical life.

PRAKARAṆAPÂDA VIBHÂCHÂ S'ÂSTRA 衆事分毗婆沙論 A philosophical treatise by Skandhila.

PRALAMBA 毗藍婆 A certain Rakchasî.

PRAMITI 般刺蜜帝 or 極量 A S'ramaṇa of Central India, co-translator (A. D. 618—907) of a Sûtra.

PRANIDHANA 願度 lit. salvation by vows. The virtue of (faithfulness in) prayers and vows.

PRÂṆYAMÛLA S'ÂSTRA ṬÎKÂ 中論 lit. discourse on the (due) mean (*i.e.* Madhyamika). The principal text book (by Nâgârdjuna and Nîlanêtra) of the Madhyamika School, translated (A. D. 409) by Kumâradjîva.

PRÂSÂDA (Singh. Poega. Tib. Dgedun gji du khang or Mtchhod khang or Du khang) 跋路娑陀 explained by 堂 lit. the hall. The assembly hall (in a monastery); the confessional.

PRAS'ÂNTA VINIS'KAYA PRATIHÂRYA SAMÂDHI SÛTRA 寂照神變三摩地經 Title of a translation (A. D. 663) by Hiuen-tsang.

PRASÊNADJIT (Pâli. and Singh. Pasênaḍi. Burm. Pathanadi. Tib. Gsal rgyal. Mong. Todorchoi Ilaghaksan) 鉢羅犀那恃多 or 鉢邏斯那恃多 or 波斯匿 explained by 勝軍 lit. conqueror of an army. A king of Kos'ala, residing in S'ravasti; one of the first royal converts and patrons of S'âkyamuni; originator of Buddhist idolatry (by having a statue of Buddha made before his death).

PRAS'RABDHI (Pâli. Passadhi) 除 lit. removal (sc. of misery) or 除覺 lit. the Bodhyanga (called) removal, explained by 斷除煩惱 lit. the cutting off and removing of trouble and vexation. A state of tranquillity. See Bodhyanga.

PRATÂPANA or Mahâtâpana (Siam. Mahadapha) 大燒然獄 lit. the hell of great burning, or 極熱 lit. extreme heat, or 大炎熱 lit. great flame and heat. The 7th of the 8 hot hells, where life lasts half a kalpa.

PRATIBHÂNA (Pâli. Patibhâna) 樂説 lit. pleasant discourses. (1.) A fictitious Bodhisattva, one of 14 Dêva Arya 天尊 worshipped in China. (2.) One of the 4 Pratisaṃvid (q. v.).

PRATICHṬHÂNA v. Prayâga.

PRATIDÊS'ANÎYÂ (Pâli. Phatidesanîyâ. Singh. Patidêsanidhamma) 波羅提提舍尼法 explained by 向彼悔 lit. confession of sins before others. A section of the Vinaya concerning public confession of sins.

PRATIMOKCHASAÑGHIKA VINAYAMÛLA 波羅提木叉僧祇戒本 Translation by Buddhabhadra (A.D. 416) of an abstract of the Mahâsañgha vinaya.

PRATIMOKCHA SÛTRA. Title of 2 translations (of works on the Sarvâstivâda vinaya), viz. 十誦律比丘戒本 by Kumâradjîva (A. D. 404), and 根本説一切有部戒經 A. D. 710.

PRATISAÑVID (Pâli. Patisambhida. Singh. Pratisambhidâ) 四無礙智 lit. 4 unlimited (forms of) wisdom. Four modes of knowledge, characteristic of an Arhat, viz. (1.) Artha (Pâli. Attha) 義無礙智 lit. unlimited knowledge of the sense (of the laws); (2.) Dharma (Pâli. Dhamma) 法無礙智 lit. unlimited knowledge of the canon; (3.) Nirukti (Pâli. Nirutti) 詞 or 辯無礙智 lit. unlimited knowledge of agreements or 得解 lit. facility in explanations; (4.) Pratibhâna (Pâli. Patibhâna) 樂説無礙智 lit. unlimited knowledge of pleasant discourses (sc. on the 12 Nidânas).

PRATÎTYA SAMUTPÂDA S'ÂSTRA (Singh. Paticha samuppâda. Tib. Rten tching hbrel barbhyur pa) 十二因緣論 lit. S'âstra on the Dvâdas'a (twelve) nidânas. A translation by S'uddhamati (A. D. 508—534).

PRATYÊKA BUDDHA or Pratyêka Djina (Pâli. Patiêkan. Singh. Pasê Buddha. Burm. Ptetzega. Tib. Rangs sang dschei. Mong. Pratikavudor Ovörö Törölkitu) 畢勒支底伽佛 or 辟支佛 explained by 獨覺 lit. individually intelligent, or by 圓覺 lit. completely intelligent, or by 緣覺 lit. intelligent as regards the Nidânas. A degree of saintship (unknown to primitive Buddhism), viewed as one of the 3 conveyances to Nirvâna (v. Madhyimâyâna), and practised by hermits who, as attaining to Buddhaship individually (*e.i.* without teacher and without saving others), are compared with the Khadga and called Ekas'ringa richi. As crossing Sañsâra, suppressing errors, and yet not attaining to absolute perfection, the Pratyêka Buddha is compared with a horse which crosses a river, swimming, without touching the ground. Having mastered the 12 Nidânas, he is also called Nidâna Buddha.

PRATYÊKA BUDDHA NIDÂNA S'ÂSTRA 辟支佛因緣論 Translation (A. D. 350—431) of a work on the Abhidharma of the Hinayâna.

PRAYÂGA or Pratichṭhâna 鉢羅耶伽 Ancient kingdom and city (now Allahabad), at the junction of Yamûna and Ganges.

PRÂYA S'TCHITTA (Pâli. Phâtchittiya) 波逸提法 explained by 墮 lit. fall (into hell). A section of the Vinaya, concerning 90 misdemeanours of priests.

PRÊTAS (Siam. Pret. Burm. Preitha. Tib. Yidwags or Yid btags. Mong. Birrid) 畢利多 or 薜荔多 or 閉黎多 or 彌多 explained by 餓鬼 lit. hungry demons. One of the 6 Gâti; 36 classes of demons with huge bellies, large mouths and tiny throats, suffering, unappeasable hunger, and living either in hell, in the service of Yâma, or in the air, or among men (but visible only at night). Avaricious and rapacious men are to be reborn as Prêtas.

PRITHAGDJANA (Pâli. Puthudjana) 獨人 lit. solitary (extr aecclesiam). The unconverted, as compared with the Ârya.

PRÎTI (Pâli. Piti. Singh. Pritiya) 喜 lit. joy. The 4th Bodhyanga, spiritual joy and content, leading to Samâdhi.

PRYADARS'ANA 喜見 lit. joyful view. The (fictitious) kalpa of S'ubhavyuha, Meghadundubhisvara and others.

PUCHPADANTÎ 華齒 lit. flowery teeth. A certain Rakchasî.

PUCHPAGIRI SAṂGHÂRÂMA 補澀波祇釐僧伽藍 A monastery on mount Puchpagiri in Uḍa.

PUCHPAKÛṬA SÛTRA. Title of 4 translations, viz. (1.) 華積陀羅尼神咒經 (A.D. 222—280); (2.) 師子奮迅菩薩所問經 (A. D. 317—420); (3.) 佛說華聚陀羅尼經 (A. D. 317—420); (4.) 佛說華積樓閣陀羅尼經 (A. D. 980—1,000).

PUCHYA (Tib. Skar ma rgyal) 弗沙 or 富沙 or 佛星 or 彗星 (comet). (1.) Name of an ancient richi. (2.) Name of a constellation formed by 3 stars.

PUDGALA 補 (or) 富特伽羅 or 弗 (or 福 or 富) 伽羅 explained by 有情 lit. affectionate beings, or by 數取趣 lit. entering several paths. (1.) Human beings as subject to metempsychosis. (2.) Personality (as a philosophical term).

PÛDJÂ (Singh. Poya) 供養 lit. to support and nourish. Offerings, as the Buddhist substitute for the Brahmanic sacrifices (Yadchna).

PÛDJASUMÎRA 富闍蘇彌羅 A learned Arhat of Salaribhu, disciple of Ananda.

PÛGA 檳榔 (Pinang). Areca catechu; betel nut palm.

PULAKÊS'A 補羅稽舍 A king (A. D. 630) of Mahârâchṭra.

PULASTYA 補攞悉底耶 An ancient richi.

PUNATCHA or Pantchasattra or Pantcharâchtra 半笯嗟 Ancient province and city (now Poonah) of Cashmere.

PUṆḌARIKA 分陀利 or 芬利 or 奔茶 explained by 大 or 白蓮華 lit. great (or white) lotus. The last of the 8 large and cold hells, where the cold lays bare the bones of criminals like white lotus flowers.

PUṆḌARA VARDDHANA 奔那伐戰那 Ancient kingdom and city (now Burdvan) in Bengal.

PUṆYABALÂVADÂNA 佛說福力太子因緣經 Title of a translation (A. D. 987—1000) by Dânapâla.

PUṆYAPRASAVÂS 福生 lit. happy birth, or 生天 lit. living dêvas. (1.) The 10th Brahmaloka. (2.) The 1st region of the 4th Dhyâna.

PUṆYAS'ÂLÂ 奔攘舍羅 Houses of refuge, for the sick or poor.

PUṆYATÂRA 弗若多羅 explained by 功德 lit. merit and virtue. (1.) One of the 24 Dêva Arya 天尊 worshipped in China. (2.) A S'ramaṇa of Cabul, co-translator (A. D. 404) of the Sarvâstivâda vinaya.

PUṆYAYAS'AS 富那耶舍 or 富那夜奢 The 10th (or 11th) patriarch; died B. C. 383; a descendant of Gâutama; born in Pâṭaliputtra; laboured in Vâranâs'i; converted As'vaghocha.

PUṆYOPÂYA 布如烏伐耶 or Nadi 耶提 explained by 福生 lit. happy birth. A S'ramaṇa of Central India; brought to China (A. D. 663) 3 works.

PURÂNA v. Dharana.

PÛRAṆA KÂSYAPA 富蘭那迦葉 or 棓刺拏 One of the 6 Tirthyas; maternal descendant of the Kas'yapa family; brahminical ascetic; opponent of S'âkyamuni.

PURÂNAS 富蘭那 or 布 (or 補) 刺拏 explained by 滿 lit. complete. A class of Brahmanic, mythological, philosophical and ascetic literature.

PURJA MITRA or Putnomita 不如密多 The 26th patriarch, son of a king of Southern India, laboured in Eastern India, died (A.D. 388) by Samâdhi.

PURNNA v. Bala.

PÛRṆA (Singh. Punna) v. Pûrṇamaitrâyaṇîputtra.

PÛRṆA KALASAYA (Siam. Bat keo inthanan) 本裹伽吒 explained by 滿瓶 lit. a full jar. One of the mystic figures of the S'ripâda.

PÛRṆAMAITRÂYAṆÎ (PUTTRA) or Maitrâyaṇîputtra or Pûrṇa (補刺那) 梅呾麗衍尼弗呾羅 or (富樓那) 彌多羅尼子 or 耨邠文陀尼子 or 邠耨文陀弗 or 富那曼陀弗多羅 explained by 滿慈子 lit. son of completeness (Pûrṇa) and charity (Maitrâyaṇi), or by 滿嚴飾女子 lit. the son of completeness and of the lady of dignified beauty, or by 滿見子 lit. the son of complete view. A disciple of S'âkyamuni; son of Bhava by a slave girl; illtreated by his brother, he engaged in business, forsook wealth for the priesthood, saved his brothers from shipwreck by conquering Indra through Samâdhi; built a vihâra for

S'âkyamuni; became a Bodhisattva, expected to reappear as Dharmaprabhâsa Buddha. He is often confounded with Maitrêya.

PÛRṆAMUKHA AVADÂNA S'ATAKA 撰集百緣經 Title of a translation (A. D. 223-253) of 100 legends.

PÛRṆA PARIPRITCHTCHHÂ 富樓那會 Title of a Sûtra, translated (A. D. 405) by Kumâradjîva.

PÛRṆAVARMMA 補剌拏伐摩 explained by 滿胄 lit. complete helmet. A king of Magadha, the last descendant of As'okha.

PURUCHA 補盧沙 or 富樓沙 or 士夫 (lit. master) explained by 神我 lit. the spiritual self. The spirit which, together with Svabhâvaḥ, produces, through the successive modifications of Guna, all forms of existence.

PURUCHAPURA 布路沙布羅 or 佛樓沙 Ancient capital (now Peshawur) of Gandhâra.

PÛRVANIVÂSÂNU SMRITI DJÑÂNA (Pâli. Pubbeni vâsânugatamnânem) 宿命 lit. destiny of the dwellings. Knowledge of all forms of pre-existence of oneself and others. See Abhidjña.

PÛRVAS'ÂILÂḤ 佛槃勢羅部 or 東山部 lit. the School of the eastern mount. One of the 5 subdivisions of the Mahâsaṃghikaḥ.

PÛRVAS'ÂILA SAṂGHÂRÂMA 佛槃勢羅僧伽藍 or 東山寺 lit. temple of the eastern mount. A monastery on a hill E. of Dhanakatchêka.

PÛRVAVIDÊHA or Vidêha. (Singh. Purwa widêsa. Siam. Buphavithe Thavib. Tib. Char gii lus pag dwip. Mong. Dorona oulam dzi beyetou dip) 佛婆毗提訶 or 脯利婆鼻提賀 or 布嚕婆毗提訶 or 毗提訶 or 佛婆提 or 佛于逮 or 哺兒幹微的葛 explained by 勝神州 lit. island of conquerors of the spirit, or by 離體 lit. separate from the body. One of the 4 continents (of every universe), E. of the Mêru, semicircular in shape, the inhavitants having also semi-circular faces and "seeing the sun rise before we see it."

PUS'PAPURA v. Pâṭaliputtra.

PUTANA 富單那 A class of Prêtas who control fever.

PUTCHÊKAGIRI 補磔迦山 A mountain in Eastern India on which Avalokitês'vara appeared.

R.

RÂCHTRAPÂLA 護國菩薩 A Bodhisattva among demons.

RÂCHTRAPÂLA PARIPRITCHTCHHÂ. Title of 2 translations, viz. (1.) 護國菩薩會 by Djñânagupta (A.D. 589—618); (2.) 佛說護國尊者所問大乘經 by Dharmadêva (A.D. 973—981).

RÂDJÂVAVÂDAKA SÛTRA. Title of 4 translations, viz. (1.) 佛說諫王經 (A.D. 420—479); (2.) 如來示敎勝軍王經 by Hiuen-tsang (A. D. 642); (3.) 佛爲勝光天子說王法經 (A. D. 705); (4.) 佛說勝軍王所問經 by Dânapâla (A. D. 980—1,000).

RÂDJA BALÊNDRÂ KÊTU 力尊幢 The prince who possessed the Devêndra samaya.

RÂDJAGIRIYÂS s. a. Abhayagirivâsinaḥ.

RÂDJAGRIHA or Radjagrihapura (Pâli. Râdjagaha. Singh. Rajagahanuwara. Burm. Radzagio. Mong. Vimaladjana ün kundi. Tib. Dchal poikap) 曷羅闍姞利呬 or 羅閣城 or 王舍城 lit. the city of royal palaces. The residence, at the foot of Gridhrakûṭa, of the Magadha princes from Bimbisara to As'oka; meeting place of the first synod (B. C. 540); the modern Radghir (S. W. of Bahar) venerated by Jain pilgrims. See Kus'âgarapura.

RÂDJAKUMÂRA or Râdjaputtra (Tib. Ghial sres. Moug. Khan kubakhun) s.a. Kumâra râdja.

RÂDJAMAHÊNDRÎ v. Mahândhra.

RÂDJAPURA 曷羅闍補羅 Ancient city and province (now Rajoar), near S. W. frontier of Cashmere.

RADJATA v. Rûpya.

RÂDJAVARDDHANA 王曷邏闍伐彈那 or 王增 King of Kanyâkubdja, son of Harchavardhana.

RÂDJÂVAVÂDAKA SÛTRA 佛說勝軍王所問經 Title of a translation by Dânapâla (A.D. 980—1000).

RAHÂN or Rahat v. Arhat.

RÂHU (Tib. Sgra gtchan) 羅睺 or 羅虎那 explained by 障蔽 lit. stoppage. A king of Asuras, who seeks (in the shape of a dog) to devour sun and moon, and thus causes eclipses.

RÂHULA or Râhulabhadra or Lâghula (Burm. Raoula. Tib. Sgra gtchan hdsin. Mong. Raholi) 羅睺羅 or 羅吼羅 or 曷羅怙羅 or 何羅怙羅 or 羅云 explained by 覆障 lit. (he who) upset the hindrances (viz. of Kâhus against his birth). The eldest son (by Yas'odhara) and disciple of S'âkyamuni; descendant of Gâutama Râhugaṇu; founder of the Vâibhâchikaḥ; now revered as patron saint of novices; to be reborn as the eldest son of every Buddha, especially of Ananda. See Djalâmbara.

RÂHULATA 羅睺羅多 The 16th patriarch, native of Kapila, laboured (till B. C. 113) in S'râvasti. See Saṁghânandi.

RÂIVATA or Rêvata (Singh. Revato) 利波多 or 離波多 or 黎婆多 or 頡隷伐多 explained by 室星 lit. the constellation (2 stars in Pegasus) called "the house." (1.) A Brahman hermit; one of the principal disciples of S'âkyamuni; to be reborn as Samanta prabhâsa. (2.) A native of Handjna, president of the 2nd synod (B.C. 443). (3.) A member of the 3rd synod B.C. 246).

RÂKCHASA or Rakchas (Tib. Srin boi din. Mong. Manggu) 羅叉娑 or 羅刹 or 藥叉 explained by 食人鬼 lit. demons which devour men, or by 可畏 lit. terrible. (1.) The aborigines of Ceylon, dreaded as cannibals by ancient mariners, extirpated by Siṁhala. (2.) The demons attending Vâis'ramaṇa, invoked by sorcerers.

RAKCHAS'Î 羅叉斯 or 羅叉私 or 羅刹女 The wives and daughters Rakchasa demons, invoked by sorcerers.

RAKTAPATMAYA or 鉢特忙 The red lotus; one of the figures of the S'ripâda.

RAKTAVITI 絡多未知 explained by 赤泥 lit. red soil. A saṁghârâma, erected near the capital of Karṇasuvarṇa, on the spot where a Buddhist priest from Southern India defeated a heretic in public disputation.

RAKTIKÂ or Retti 賴提 explained by 草子 lit. a seed of (the Gunjâ) creeper. An Indian weight, equal to $2\frac{3}{16}$ grains.

RÂMA or Râmagrâma 藍摩 or 藍莫 Ancient city (N.W. of Goruckpoor) and kingdom, between Kapilavastu and Kus'inagara.

RAS'MINIRHÂRA SAṀGIRATHÎ or Prabhâ sâdhanâ 出現光明會 Title of a translation by Bodhirutchi (A. D. 618—907).

RAS'MIPRABHÂSA 光明 lit. light and brightness. The name under which Mahâkâs'yapa is to be reborn as Buddha. See Mahâvyûha and Avabhâsa.

RAS'MI S'ATASAHASRA PARIPÛRṆA DHVADJA 具足千萬光相 lit. one whose feet display innumerable luminous figures (like the S'rîpâda). The name under which Yas'odharâ is to appear as Buddha.

RATHAKAYA 車軍 lit. the chariot corps. A division of an Indian army.

RATIPRAPÛRṆA 喜滿 lit. complete joy. The kalpa during which Mâudgalyâyana is to appear aa Buddha.

RATNA v. Sapta ratna.

RATNADVÎPA 寶渚 lit. island of treasures (pearls). Ancient name of Simhala (Ceylon).

RATNAGHIRI 寶山 lit. precious mount. A mountain near Râdjagriha.

RATNÂKARA 寶積 lit. treasure store. (1.) A native of Vâis'âli, contemporary of S'âkyamuni. (2.) The 112th Buddha of the Bhadra kalpa.

RATNAKÊTU 寶相 lit. precious figure. (1.) One of the Sapta Tathâgata. (2.) The name under which S'âkyamuni's 2,000 disciples, and especially Ânanda, will reappear as Buddha at different points of the compass.

RATNAKÛṬA 寶積部 A section of the Sûtra piṭaka, including the Mahâratnakuṭa, the Ratnakûṭa sûtra and some 36 other works.

RATNAKÛṬA SÛTRA Title of 2 translations, viz. (1.) 寶積三昧文殊師利菩薩問法身經 A. D. 25—220, and (2.) 入法界體性經 by Djñânagupta, A.D. 595.

RATNAMATI 勒那摩 or 婆提 or 寶意 lit. precious intentions. (1.) The 4th son of Tchandra sûrya pradîpa. (2.) A S'ramana of Central India, translator (A. D. 508) of 3 works.

RATNAMÊGHA DHARANI 佛說雨寶陀羅尼經 Title of a translation by Amogha vadjra (A.D. 746—771).

RATNAMÊGHA SÛTRA. Title of 3 translations, viz., (1.) 佛說寶雲經 by Mandra and Samghapâla (A. D. 503); (2.) 佛說寶雨經 by Dharmarutchi (A. D. 693); (3.) 佛說除蓋障菩薩所問經 by Dânapâla, Dharmarakcha etc. (A. D. 1000—1010).

RATNAPARÂS'I 寶梁聚會 Title of a translation (A. D. 397—439), forming part of the Mahâratnakûṭa sûtra.

RATNASAMBHAVA 寶生 lit. precious birth. (1.) One of the Pañtcha Dhyâni Buddhas, attended by Ratnapâṇi. (2.) The realm of S'asikêtu Buddha.

RATNAS'IKHIN v. S'ikhin.

RATNATCHINTA 阿儞眞那 or 寶思惟 lit. precious thought. A S'ramana of Cashmere, translator (A. D. 693—706) of 7 works.

RATNATÊDJOBHYUDGARÛDJA 寶威德上王 lit. superior king of precious dignity and virtue. A fabulous Buddha, living E. of our universe, attended by Samantabhadra.

RATNATRAYA v. Triratna.

RATNÂVABHÂSA (1.) 寶明 lit. precious brightness. The kalpa of Dharmaprabhâsa. (2.) 有寶 lit. possessor of treasures. The kalpa of S'asikêtu.

RATNAVIS'UDDHA 寶淨 lit. precious purity. The fabulous realm of Prabhûtaratna.

RÂURAVA (Siam. Rôruva) 號叫 or 叫呼 or 叫喚 lit. crying. The 4th of the 8 large hot hells where life lasts 4,000 (or 400) years, but where 24 hours are equal to 4000 years on earth.

RÂVAṆA 羅婆那 or 婆羅那 A King of Siṁhala.

RAVI v. Trâvatî.

RÊVATA v. Râivata.

RICHI (Burm. Racior rathee. Tib. Drang srong) 仙人 lit. immortals, 遷道 lit. the gâti of immortals. A man, transformed into an immortal, by asceticism and meditation. Nâgârdjuna, who counts 10 classes of richis, ascribes to them only temporary exemption (for 1,000,000 years) from transmigration, but Chinese Buddhists (and Tauists) view them as absolutely immortal, and distinguish 5 classes, viz. (1.) Dêva richis 天仙 residing on the 7 concentric rocks around Mêru, (2.) Purucha (or Atman) richis 神仙 roaming about in the air, (3.) Nara richis 人仙 dwelling as immortals among men, (4.) Bhûmi richis 地仙 residing on earth in caves. and (5.) Prêta richis 鬼仙 roving demons. These richis form a 7th gâti (q. v.) or a 7th class of sentient beings.

RIDDHI (Pâli. Iddhi. Mong. Riddi chubilghan) 如意身 lit. a body (transmutable) at will. The dominion of spirit over matter. implying (1) possession of a body which is exempt from the laws of gravitation and space, and (2) power to assume any shape or from and to traverse space at will.

RIDDHIMANTRA 神咒 or 如意咒 Incantations or prayers used to gain or exercise the power of Riddhi.

RIDDHIPÂDA (Pâli. Iddhipado. Tib. Rdzu hphrul gyi rkang pa) 四如意足 lit. 4 steps to Riddhi. Four modes of obtaining Riddhi, by the annihilation of desire, energy, memory and meditation See Tchhanda, Vîrya, Tchitta and Mimamsa riddhi pâda.

RIDDHI SÂKCHÂTKRI YÂ (Pâli. Iddhippabhêdo) 神足力 lit. the power of the supernatural (riddhi) steps. The power to assume any shape or form (see Riddhi), the third of the 6 Abhidjñas.

RIDDHI VIKRÎḌITA SAMÂDHI 神通遊戲三昧 A degree of samâdhi, called "the idle sports of spiritual penetration."

RIG VÊDA 讚誦 lit. hymns of praise. The most ancient portion of the Vèda, consisting of a collection of hymns (Sanhitá) and a number of prose works (Brahmanas and Sûtras).

ROHINILÂ 洛殷膩羅 An ancient monastery, visited by S'âkyamuni; the modern Roynallah, near Balgada, in E. Bahar.

ROHITAKA or Lohitaka 盧醯呾迦 (1) Red or opal colour. (2) The ruby or balasruby.

ROHITAKA STÛPA 盧醯呾迦窣都波 explained by 赤塔 lit. the red stûpa. A stûpa built by As'oka, 50 *li* W. of Moñgali, where Maitribala râdja fed starving Yakchas with his blood.

ROHITA MUKTI 盧呬胝訶目多 Red pearls or rubies. See Sapta ratna.

ROHU 曷羅胡 Ancient province and city of Tukhâra, S. of the Oxus.

RUDRA (Tib. Yu lang) 盧陀羅耶 A name of Shiva, as ruler of the wind, and lord of the Khumbandhas.

RUDRAKA RÂMAPUTTRA 鬱頭藍子 lit. Rudraka the son of Râma. A richi of Magadha, a teacher of S'âkyamuni.

RÛPA (Tib. Gzugs) 色 lit. form. (1.) The perception of form; one of the Chaḍâyatana. (1.) Form, as one of the aggregates of the 色身 physical body. See Skandha.

RÛPADHÂTU or Rûpâvatchara (Tib. Gzugs-kyikhams) 色界 lit. the region of form. The 2nd of the Trâilokya; the world of form, comprishing 18 Brahmalokas, divided into 4 Dhyânas, where life lasts from 16,000 kalpas down to half a kalpa, and the height of the body measures from 16,000 yodjanas down to half a yodjana, the inhabitants being sexless and unclothed.

RÛPYA 銀 lit. silver. The 2nd of the Sapta Ratna.

RUTCHIRA KÊTU 妙幢 lit. wonderful banner. A fabulous Bodhisattva.

S.

S'ABDA or Sadda (Pâli. Saddan) 聲 lit. sound. The perception of sound; one of the Chaḍâyatana.

S'ABDA VIDYÂ S'ÂSTRA 聲明論 lit. lucid treatise on sounds. One of the Pañtcha Vidyâ S'âstras, a work on etymology by Añs'uvarmma.

SADÂPARIBHÛTA' 常不輕 lit. never slighting (others). (1.) A Bodhisattva, famous for his unselfish meekness. (2.) A former incarnation of S'âkyamuni, when he displayed unselfish meekness though slighted by Bhadrapâla (with 500 Bodhisattvas), by Simhatchandra (with 500 Upasakas) and by Sugata tchêtana (with 500 Bhikchuṇis).

SADDA v. S'abda.

SADDHARMA (Pâli. Saddhamma) 妙法 lit. the wonderful law. A fabulous Mahâbrahmâ (also called Sudharma), devotee of Mahabhidjñâdjñânâbhibhu.

SADDHARMA LAÑKAVATÂRA s. a. Laṅgkâvatâra sûtra.

SADDHARMA PRATIRÛPAKA 像法 lit. law of images. The 2nd of the 3 stages of development through which Buddhism passes under each Buddha, the first being 正法 lit. the period of true religion, the 2nd 像法 lit. the period of fanciful religion, the 3rd 後法 lit. the period of declining religion. In the case of S'âkyamuni, the 1st period continued for 200 years after his death, the 2nd lasted 1000 years, and the 3rd will last 3000 years, whereupon Maitrêya renews this triple process, and each of his successors likewise.

SADDHARMA PUṆḌARÎKA SAMADHI 法華三昧 (1.) A degree of samâdhi, mastered by Vimalanêtra. (2.) Title of a translation (of a portion of the Saddharma puṇḍarîka sûtra), A. D. 427.

SADDHARMA PUṆḌARÎKA SÛTRA. Title of 4 translations, forming the standard books of the Lotus School

蓮宗 viz (1.) 正法華經 by Dharmarakcha (A. D. 286), (2.) 薩曇芬陀利經 (incomplete, A.D. 265-316), (3.) 妙法蓮華經 by Kumaradjîva (A. D. 406), (4.) 添品妙法蓮華經 by Djñânagupta and Dharmagupta (A. D. 589—618).

SADDHARMA PUṆḌARÎKA SÛTRA S'ÂSTRA. Title of 2 translations of Vasubandhu's commentary on the preceding work, viz. 妙法蓮華經優波提舍 by Bodhirutchi and others (A. D. 386—534) and 妙法蓮華經論優波提舍 by Ratnamati and another (A.D. 508).

SADDHARMA SMRITYUPASTHÂNA SÛTRA. Title of 2 translations. viz 正法念處經 by Gautama, Pradjñârutchi (A.D. 539), and 妙法聖念處經 by Dharmadêva (A.D. 973—981).

SADVAHA 沙多婆何 or 引善 or 引正 lit. guide of goodness or truth. A king of Kosala, patron of Nâgârdjuna.

SADVÂHANA v. Djñâtaka.

SÂGALA v. S'âkala.

SÂGARA 娑竭羅 or 娑伽羅 One of the 24 Dêva Ârya (天尊), a Nâga king (龍王), whose daughter (8 years old) became a Buddha under the tuition of Mañdjus'ri. He is said to dwell in a palace of pearls at the bottom of the sea, and is worshipped as a god of rain.

SÂGARAMATI 海慧 A priest of Nâlanda, defender of the Mahâyâna in disputations with heretics.

SAGARAMATI PARIPRITCHTCHHÂ 海意菩薩所問淨印法門經 Title of a translation, by Dharmarakcha and another (A. D. 1009—1058), of a chapter from the Mahâvaipulya mahâsannipâta sûtra (大方等大集經).

SÂGARA NÂGARÂDJA PARIPRITCHTCHHÂ. Title of 3 translations, viz. (1.) 佛說海龍王經 by Dharmarakcha (A. D. 265—316), (2.) 佛爲海龍王說法印經 (A.D. 618—937), (3.) 佛爲娑伽羅海龍王所說大乘法經 by Dânapâla (A.D. 980—1000).

SÂGARA VARADHARA BUDDHI VIKRÎḌITÂBHIDJÑA 山海慧自在通王 The name under which Ânanda reappears as Buddha, in Anavanâmita vâidjayanta, during the kalpa

Manodjña s'abdabhigardjita.

SAHA or Sahaloka or Sahalokadhâtu (Mong. Ssava jirtintchu) 娑婆 or 索阿 or 娑婆 explained by 堪忍世界 lit. the world of suffering, or by 千世界之都 lit. the capital of a chiliocosmos. The inhabited portion of every universe, including all persons subject to transmigration and needing a Buddha's instruction, and divided into 3 worlds (v. Trâilokya) ruled by Sahâm̃pati.

SAHÂM̃PATI (Singh. Sampati) v. Mahâbrahma Sahâm̃pati.

S'ÂIKCHA or S'âikchya (Pâli. Sekhiyâ) 式乂迦羅尼 explained by 應當學 lit. one who ought to study, or subjects to be studied; or 突吉羅 explained by 惡作 lit. wicked deeds. (1.) Catechumens, especially laynovices. See Arhan. (2.) A section of the Vinaya, called laws for the community of disciples 衆學法 being a series of 100 regulations for novices.

SAKCHI or S'akti or S'as'i 舍支 or 設施 (lit. sacrifice.) (1.) The hare (which threw itself into the fire to save starving people), transferred by Indra to the centre of the moon. (2.) A name of Vêmatchitra. (3.) The consort of any deity (according to the Tantra School). (4.) Female energy (Yoni).

S'ÂKALA (Pâli. Sâgala. Singh. Sangala) 奢羯羅 The capital of Tchêka and (under Mahirakula) of the whole Pundjab. The Lagala of Ptolemy. The modern Sanga near Umritsir.

S'ÂKRA (Pâli. Sakka. Singh. Sekra) 釋迦 or 帝釋 or 釋 or 釋迦婆 explained by 能天主 lit. the mighty Lord (Indra) of Dêvas, or 釋迦提婆 (S'akra Devêndra) or 釋提桓因 explained by 天帝釋 lit. S'akra the Lord (Indra) of Dêvas, or 忉利帝釋 or 忉利天王 lit. king of Trâyastrims'as. Common epithets of Indra q. v.) as rules of the Dêvas.

S'AKRÂDITYA 鑠伽羅阿逸多 or 帝日 lit. sun of the ruler (S'akra). A king of Magadha (after S'âkyamuni's death).

SAKRIDÂGÂMIN (Pâli. Sakadâgâmi. Singh. Sakradâgâmi. Burm. Thakagan. Tib. Leneik cir honghaba) 娑羯利陀伽彌 or 斯陀含 explained by 一來 lit. coming once more. The 2nd degree of saintship (v. Ârya), involving rebirth among dêvas and among men, whereupon Arhatship is reached.

S'AKYA (Singh. Sâkya. Burm. Thakia) 釋迦 explained by 仁 lit. charily or 能仁 lit. charitable. The ancestors and descendants of Iks'vaku Virudhaka (q. v.), viz. 5 kings of the Vivartta kalpa (成刧五王) headed by Mahasammata (大三末多); 5 Tchakravarttis (五轉輪王) headed by Murdhadja (頂生王); 19 kings, the first being Tchêtrya (拾帝) and the last Mahâdêva (大天); 5000 kings; 7000 kings; 8000 kings; 9000 kings; 10,000 kings; 15,000 kings; 11,000 kings, the first being Gautama (q.v.) and the last Iks'vaku (q. v.) who reigned at Potala, and whose 4 sons reigned at Kapilavastu, after the destruction of which 4 surviving princes founded the kingdoms of Udyana, Bamyan, Himatala and S'ambi. See also S'âkyamuni.

S'AKYA BODHISATTVA 釋迦菩薩 A title of Prabápala.

S'ÂKYA BUDDHA s. a. S'âkyamuni.

S'ÂKYA MITRA 釋迦密多羅 or 能友 lit. powerful friend An author of commentaries on philosophical works of the Madhyimâyâna School.

S'ÂKYAMUNI (Burm. Thakiamuni. Tib. Shakja thubpa. Mong Shigamunior Burchan bakshi) 釋迦牟尼 or 釋伽文 explained by 能仁 (S'âkya) 寂默 (Muni) lit. mighty in charity, seclusion and silence. The last of the Sapta Buddha, one of Sapta Tathâgata, the 4th of the 1000 Buddhas of the Bhadra kalpa. The name by which Chinese books refer to Gautama Buddha. The Lalitavistara and the popular aphorisms of Wang Puh (釋迦如來成道記) tell the story of his life, which is an indispensable key to the understanding of Buddhist doctrines. Some 5000 Djâtakas (q.v.) are on record, in the course of which he worked his way up through as many different stages of transmigration, from the lowest spheres of life to the highest, practising all kinds of asceticism and exhibiting in every form (v. Maitribalarâdja, Kapindjala râdja, Mayûra râdja etc.) the utmost unselfishness and charity. Having attained to the state of Bodhisattva as Prabhâpala, he was reborn in Tuchita and there considered where he ought to be reborn on earth to become Buddha. The S'âkya (q.v.) family of Kapilavastu was selected and in it Mâyâ, the young wife of S'uddhodhana, as the purest on earth. In the form of a white elephant (v. Bodhisattva) he descended and entered through Mâyâ's right side into her womb (8th day of the 4th moon, B.C. 1028 or 622), where he was visited thrice a day by all the Buddhas of the universe (v. Prabhûta ratna). On the 8th day of the 2nd (or 4th) moon, B.C. 1024 or 621, Mâyâ, standing in Lumbini under an As'oka (or Sâla) tree, painless gave birth to a son who stepped out of her right side, being received by Indra (the representative of popular religion) and forthwith baptized (v. Murddhâbhichikta) by Nâga kings. Thereupon the newborn babe walked 7 steps towards each of the 4 points of the compass and, pointing with one hand to heaven and with the other to earth, said, with a lion's voice (v. Simhanâda), "I have received the body of my final birth; of all beings in heaven above and beneath the heavens, there is none but myself to be honoured." At the moment of his birth an Udambara flower sprouted up, and a series of 42 miraculous events (earthquakes, flashes of five coloured light, lotus flowers etc.) announced to the universe the birth of Buddha. His skin exhibited 32 fanciful tracings (v. Lakchana); on the soles of his feet there were 65 mystic figures (v. S'rîpâda), and his body possessed 80 forms of beauty, which were interpreted by Asita as the characteristic marks of Buddhaship. He was named Sarvârthasiddha. Mâyâ having died 7 days after his birth, Mahâ pradjapati (q.v.) nursed him. When 3 years old, he was presented in a Shiva temple, when all the statues of Shivaitic deities did obeisance to the infant Buddha, who was then named Dêvatidêva. When he was 7 years old, Arata Kâlâma and Rudrakarâma taught him the Pañtcha Vidyâ S'âstras, and Kchanti dêva (羼提提婆) taught him gymnastics. When 10 years old, he was peerless in strength, hurled an elephant to some distance (v. Hastigarta), and opened an artesian well (v. S'arakûpa) by the discharge of an arrow. He was married to Yâs'odhara and took several concubines. When 19 years old, he was converted through S'uddhavâsa dêva who presented himself successively in the form of an old man, a sick man, a corpse, a religious mendicant, and excited in him disgust regarding domestic life. His father sought to divert his mind, by sensual excitements and by proposing to him the career of a Tchakravartti as a military conqueror of the world, but, strengthened by

S'uddhavâsa dâva, he overcome the temptations of lust and ambition and fled from home in the night of the 8th day of the 2nd moon, B. C. 1003 or 597. Yakchas, Dêvas, Brahma, Indra and the Tchatur Mahârâdjas assisted him to escape. He cut off his locks and swore to save humanity from the misery of life, death and transmigration. After a brief attempt to resume study under Arata, he spent 6 years as a hermit on the Himâlaya, testing the efficacy of Brahmanic and Shivaitic meditation. Dissatisfied with the result, he visited Arata and Rudraka and then repaired to Gayâ, where he practised ascetic self-torture. [About that time his son Râhula was born.] Having spent 6 years at Gayâ, on a daily allowance of one grain of hemp (opium ?) and one grain of wheat, and seeing the uselessness of such fasting, he determines to strike out a new path henceforth. Dêvas minister to the needs of his body, which threatens to break up, by bathing him with perfumes, and induce Nanda and Bala (q.v.) to nurse him with rice boiled in milk. Resting on a couch prepared by Indra under the Bodhidruma, he new gives himself up to Samâdhi (q. v.), whilst Mâra and his armies endeavour, in vain, to tempt him in various disguises and finally through Mâra's 4 beautiful daughters. Unmoved he continues in Samâdhi, until he reaches at last the state of Bodhi (q.v.), and becomes a Buddha, in the night of the 8th day of the 12th moon, B. C. 998 or 592. The spirits of the earth forthwith announce the glad tidings to the spirits of the atmosphere and those again report it to the spirits in the various heavens. Heaven and earth rejoice. Seven days afterwards two merchants, Trapus'a (提謂) and Bhallika (波利), passing by, present him with offerings of barley and honey. Soon he gathers round himself 5 disciples, Kâuṇḍiṇya, Bhadrika, Vâchpa, As'vadjit and Mahânâma. With them he starts from the Bodhidruma (B.C. 997 or 592) and preaches his new gospel at Mrigadâva, where his 5 disciples attain to the state of Arhat and 1000 persons are converted. In the course of the following year, he preached chiefly to Nâga kings (i. e. against popular worship of snakes). The year 995 or 589 B.C. is marked by the conversion of S'âriputtra and Mâudgalyâyana with 250 others. In the course of the following year Anâthapiṇḍika presented Buddha with the Djêtavana. In the year 991 or 585 B.C., a victory having been gained over Shivaism by the conversion of Añgulimâlîya and his followers, Buddha ascended to Trayastrims'as in order to convert his mother, and stayed there 90 days. Meanwhile Prasênadjit, frightened by his prolonged absence, ordered Mâudgalyâyana and the dêva Vis'vakarman, transformed as artists, to ascend to Traiyastrims'as and to take a likeness of S'âkyamuni. They did so and carved, in sandal wood, a statue which thenceforth became an object of worship. Here we have the origin of Buddhist idolatry. On S'âkyamuni's return, the statue lifted itself into mid-air and saluted him, whereupon he uttered a prophesy which was fulfilled when Kâs'yapa Mâtaṇga took that statue to China. In 990 (or 584) B.C. S'âkyamuni visited Magadha and converted Vatsa. In the following year he predicted the future of Maitreya, and in the next year he revisited Kapilavastu, when he preached to his putative father. From the year 983 (or 577) B.C. to the time of his death, he gave particular attention to doctrinal exposition, delivering the Samyuktasañtchaya in 983 (or 577) B. C., the Pradjñâparamitâ in 982 (or 576), the Suvarṇaprabhâsa and Saddharmapuṇḍarika in 950 (or 544), and the Parinirvâṇa sûtra in 949 (or 543). Ânanda was converted in 977 (or 571) B. C. and Pradjâpatî admitted to rights of priesthood together with other women. When S'âkyamuni, in the year B. C. 949 or 543, felt his end drawing near, he went to Kus'inagara. Heaven and earth began to tremble and loud voices were heard, all living beings groaning together and bewailing his departure. On passing through Kus'inagara, he took his last meal from the hands of one of the poorest (Tchunda), after refusing the offerings of the richest. Declaring that he was dying, he went to a spot where eight Sâla trees stood in groups of two. Resting on his right side, he gave his last instructions to his disciples, reminding them of the immortality of the Dharma kâya, and then engaged in contemplation. Passing mentally through the 4 degrees of Dhyâna, and thence into Samâdhi, he lost himself into Nirvâṇa and thus his earthly career was ended. His disciples put his remains into a coffin which forthwith became so heavy that no power on earth could move it. But his mother Mâya suddenly appeared in the air, bewailing her son, when the coffin rose up, the lid sprang open and S'âkyamuni stepped forth for a moment with folded hands to salute his mother. On attempting cremation, his disciples found that his body, being that of a Tchakravartti, could not be consumed by common fire, when suddenly a jet of flame burst out of the Svastica on his breast and reduced his body to ashes. If the above semilegendary account is at all trustworthy, it indicates that S'âkyamuni's mind is supposed to have gradually developed, departing step by step from the popular religions of his time, Brahminism and Shivaism, until, without premeditation, he came to found a new religion, being even pushed to laying a sort of preliminary foundation of an ecclesiastical system. As a teacher, he appears to have been liberal and tolerant, countenancing, rather inconsistently, the worship of those deities which were too popular to be discarded, though he assigned to them a signally inferior position in his own system. Immoral sects, however, whether Brahmanic or Shivaitic, he fought resolutely, conquering generally through magic power rather than by disputations. He remodelled almost every Brahmanic dogma, substituting atheism for pantheism, and ethics for metaphysics. His teachings were in later years further developed by the Mahâyâna, Madhyimâyâna, Yogâtchârya and other Schools. The chronology of Buddhism is not yet sufficiently cleared up. The year when S'âkyamuni entered Nirvâṇa is, according to Chinese accounts, the 53rd year of King Muh of the Chow dynasty, that is to say 949 or about 749 B. C., whilst Southern Buddhist tradition fixed upon the year 543 B. C., but modern excavations, inscriptions and coins indicate the year 275 B.C. as the year of Buddha's Nirvâṇa.

S'ÂKYASIM̃HA (Mong. Shakin un arslan) 釋迦獅子 lit. S'âkya the lion. A title of S'âkyamuni. See also Sim̃hanada.

S'ÂKYA TAṬHÂGATA see Taṭhagata.

S'ÂKYA YAS'AS 釋迦稱 A native of India, author a of the Hastadaṇda s'âstra 手杖論 (translated A. D 711).

SÂLA 娑羅 or 沙羅 explained by 堅固 lit. solid, or by 最勝 lit. most victorious, or by 富貴家 lit. rich and honoured families. (1.) A large timber tree, Shorea robusta, sacred in memory of S'âkyamuni's birth and death. (2.) A bird, s. a. S'ârika.

SALARIBHU 娑羅梨弗 Ancient kingdom of India.

SALA RÂDJA 沙羅王

An epithet of every Buddha, as "most victorious" over vice and passion. See Sâla.

S'ÂLATURA 娑羅覩羅 or 覩羅 Ancient city in Gandhâra, now Lahor near Ohind; birthplace of Pâṇini.

S'ÂLÊNDRA RÂDJA 娑羅樹王 Name of S'ubhavyûha as Buddha. See Sâla râdja.

S'ÂLISAMBHAVA SÛTRA. Title of 5 translations, viz. (1.) 佛說了本生死經 (A. D. 222—280), (2.) 佛說稻稈經 (A. D. 317—420), (3.) 外道問聖大乘法無我義經, (4.) 大乘舍黎娑擔摩經, (5.) 慈氏菩薩所說大乘緣生稻稈喩經.

SAMADATTA MAHÂRÂDJA SÛTRA 衆許摩訶帝經 A history of S'âkyamuni (as a descendant of Mahâ samadatta mahârâdja 大三末多王) from the origin of the world to his visit to his putative father.

SAMÂDHI (Pâli. Samato) 三摩提 or 三摩地 or 三昧 explained by 定 lit. fixity, or by 等特 lit. sam-âdhâ, self-possessed, or by 正定 lit. correct fixity; or 奢摩他 lit. samâdhâ, explained by 止息 lit. stop breathing, or by 寂靜 lit. listless. One of the 7 Bodhyanga (q. v.), the mastery of abstract contemplation and tranquillity (定覺 or 了徹禪定), variously defined, as perfect tranquillity (Hardy), meditative abstraction (Turnour), or self-control (Burnouf). The term Samádhi it sometimes usek ethically, when it designates moral self-deliverance from passion and vice (解脫 Mukti), and sometimes metaphysically, when it is interchanged with Dhyâna (q. v.) and signifies abstract meditation, resulting in physical and mental coma and eventually in Nirvâṇa. "He consumed his body by Agni (the fire of) Samâdhi," is the saint's standing epitaph. This love for quietistic self-annihilation, traced back to Mâudgalyâyana, may have arisen through a natural reaction against the austerities of moral asceticism which characterized primitive Buddhism. The Mahâyâna School invented numberless hair-splitting distinctions of different degrees of Samâdhi. Dhyâna (q.v.) and Samâpatti (q. v.) are practically the preliminary steps leading to Samâdhi.

SÂMADHÎBALA 定力 lit. the power of fixity. The 4th of the 5 Bala, the power of ecstatic meditation (v. Samâdhi).

SAMÂDHÎNDRIYA (Pali.

Samadhi indra) 定根 lit. the root of fixity. The 4th of the 5 Indriya, the organ of ecstatic meditation (v. Samâdhi).

SAMADJÑA SAM̃GHÂRÂMA 娑摩若僧伽藍 or 明賢寺 lit. the monastery (built for) Samadjna (lit. the luminous sage). A vihara, 60 *li* W. of Kustana.

SAMAKAN 颯秣建 or 撒馬兒罕 Ancient province and city of Bokhara, now Samarkand.

SAMANTA BHADRA (Tib. Togmai sangas-rgyas kuntubzangyo) 三曼陀颰陀羅 or 普賢 lit. general sage or 大行 lit. great activity. (1.) One of the 4 Bodhisattvas of the Yogâtchârya School, author of the 受菩提心戒儀 Bodhi hridaya s'ilâdâna sûtra (transtated by Amoghavadjra, A. D. 746—771) and of many dhâraṇî, patron of the Saddharma puṇḍarika. (2.) A fabulous Buddha, residing in the E.

SAMANTA MUKHA DHÂRAÑÎ SÛTRA 普門陀羅尼經 A dhâraṇî delivered by S'âkyamuni at Vais'âli.

SAMANTA PRABHÂSA 普明 lit. general brightness. The name under which each of the 500 Arhats re-appears as Buddha.

SAMÂPATTI (Tib. Snoms par hdjug pa) 三摩鉢底 explained by 欲入定 lit. seeking to enter fixity. The process by which absolute mental indifference (sams) is reached (apatti); a degree of ecstatic meditation, preparatory to Samâdhi (q. v.).

SAMATA or Samatata 三摩呾吒 Ancient kingdom, at the mouth of the Brahmaputra.

SÂMA VÊDA SANHITÂ 娑磨 or 平論 lit. s'âstra of peace, or 歌詠 lit. hymns and chants. The third part of the Vêda, a collection of hymns to be sung at sacrifices.

SAMAYA (Tib. Dous) 三摩耶 explained by 短時 lit. short period. A season of the year.

SAMBHÂVA 好城 lit. good city. The realm of Mahâbhidjñâdjñânâbhibhu Buddha.

SÂMBÎ 商彌 Ancient kingdom (v. S'âkya), S. of the Hindookoosh.

SAMBODHI v. Bodhi.

SAMBODHYANGA v. Bodhyanga.

SAMBHOGA or Sambûtta 三菩伽 An ancient richi of Mathura.

SAMBHOGA KÂYA 三菩伽

迦耶 or 報身 lit. the body of compensation. (1.) The 2nd of the 3 qualities (v. Trikâya) of a Buddha's body, viz. reflected spirituality, corresponding with his merits. (2.) The 3rd of the Buddhakchêtras.

SAMDJAYA or Samdjaya vâiraṭṭi 珊闍邪 or 珊闍夜毗羅胝 or 僧愼彌耶. (1.) A king of Yakchas. (2.) One of 6 Tîrthyas; heretical teacher of Mâudgalyâyana and S'âriputtra.

SAMDJÎVA (Siam. Sanxipa) 等活 or 更活 lit. re-birth. The 1st of the 8 large hot hells (v. Naraka), whence each, after death, is by "re-birth" removed to the 2nd hell (Dâlasûtra).

SAMDJÑA or Samdjñana (Pâli. Sannana. Singh. Sannya. Tib. Du-ses) 想 lit. thought. Consciousness, as the 3rd of the 5 Skandha.

SAMGHA (Burm. Thanga Tib. Dkon-mgoc gsum. Mong Chubarak) 僧伽 or 桑渴耶 (1.) The corporate assembly of (at least four) priests, also called Bhikchu Samgha (比丘僧), under a chairman (Sthavira or Upâdhyâya), empowered to hear confession, to grant absolution, to admit persons into the priesthood, etc. (2.) The third constituent of the Triratna (q.v.), the deification of the church. (3.) Same as Asamgha.

SAMGHA BHADRA 僧伽跋陀羅 or 衆賢 lit. the sage of the priesthood. A S'ramaṇa of Cashmere, follower of the Sarvâstivâdâḥ, author of 2 philosophical works, translator (Canton, 489 A. D.) of the Vibhâcha vinaya.

SAMGHABHEDA 破僧 lit. breaking up the priesthood. One of the Pañtchânantarya.

SAMGHABHEDAKAVASTU 根本說一切有部毗奈耶破僧事 Title of a translation (A.D. 719) of a portion of the Vinaya.

SAMGHA BHÛTI s. a. Samghavars'ana.

SAMGHADÊVA 僧伽提婆 or 衆天 let. dêva of the priesthood (1.) A title of honour. (2.) Same as Gâutama Samghadêva and Samgha vars'ana.

SAMGHÂIS'ÊCHA (Singh. Samghadisêsa) 尸沙 A section of the Vinaya (13 commandments regarding social and sexual relations of priesthood).

SAMGHÂGÂRÂMA s. a. Samghârâma.

SAMGHÂNANDI 僧伽難提 The 17th patriarch, a prince of S'râvastî, who lived as a hermit near the sources of the Hiranjavati, until Rahulata, let there by seeing the shadow of 5 Buddhas, appointed him his successor.

SAMGHAPÂLA 僧伽婆羅 or 僧伽跋摩 (Samgha varman) or 衆鎧 lit. armour of the priesthood. (1.) An Indian S'ramaṇa (of Tibetan descent), translator (under the name 康僧鎧) of 3 works (A. D. 225). (2.) A Burmese S'ramaṇa, who introduced a new alphabet of 50 characters in China and translated 10 works (A. D. 506-520).

SAMGHARAKCHA 僧伽羅刹 A S'ramaṇa of India (700 years after the Nirvâṇa), author of 4 sûtras.

SAMGHÂRÂMA or Samghâgârâma (Burm. Kium. Siam. Vat. Tib Dgon pa Mong. Küt or Ssümä) 僧伽藍(摩) or 僧伽羅摩 or 僧藍 or 伽藍 explained by 衆園 lit. park of the priesthood, or by 僧房 lit. dwelling of priests. (1.) The park of a monastic institution. (2.) A monastery or convent, s. a. vihâra.

SAMGHASÊNA 僧伽斯那 or 僧伽先 A S'ramaṇa of India, author of 3 works.

SAMGHÂTA 僧伽陀 explained by 饒善 lit. abundant goodness; or 衆合 lit. union of the priesthood or 衆磕 lit. clattering of the priesthood. (1.) A S'ramaṇa of the West, translator (A. D. 402-412) of one work. (2.) The 3rd of the 8 large hot hells (v. Naraka), formed by 2 ranges of moveable mountains which compress the criminals into an unshapely mass. Life lasts there 2000 years, but 24 hours, there, are equal to 200 years on earth.

SAMGHÂṬI (Singh. Sangalasivura. Burm. Tingan. Siam. Languti. Mong. Majak) 僧伽胝 or 僧伽梨 (or 黎) explained by 合 lit. united, or by 重 lit. double, or by 重雜衣 lit. a robe made of sundry scraps. The composite priestly robe, reaching from the shoulders to the knees and fastened round the waist. See Kachâya and Uttarasamghâṭi.

SAMGHÂTÎ SÛTRA DHARMA PARYÂYA 僧伽吒經 Title of a translation by Upas'ûnya (A. D. 538).

SAMGHAVARMAN s. a. Samghapâla.

SAMGHAVARS'ANA or Samgha bhûti 僧伽澄 (or 橙) or 衆現 lit. manifestation of the priesthood. A S'ramaṇa of Cabul, translator (A.D. 381-385) of several works. See Samghadêva.

SAMKAKCHIKÂ s. a. Uttarâsamghâti.

SAM̃KÂS'YA (Pâli. Samkassa. Tib. Sgrachen) 僧伽舍 or 僧伽施 or Kapitha. Ancient Kingdom and city in Central India, now Samkassam near Canouge.

SÂM̃KHYA (Pâli. Sañkha) 僧企耶 or 僧佉 or 數論 lit. discoursing on numerical categories, explained by 說二十諦者 lit. those who discourse on the meaning of the 25 tattvas (truths). The heretical atomistic School (v. Kapila), which explains nature by the interaction of 24 elements with purucha, modified by the 3 guṇas, and teaches the eternity of pradhâna (自性) i.e. self-transforming nature and the eternity of human souls (purucha).

SÂM̃KHYÎKA 遍計 lit. general calculations or 數論外道 lit. heretics who discourse on numerical categories. The followers of the Sâm̃khya School.

SÂM̃KHYAKÂRIKÂ v. Kapila.

SAMMATÎYA or Sammatâḥ 三眉底輿部 or 三彌底 or 彌底部 or 彌離底部 or 正量部 or 量弟子部 lit. the School of correct calculators. Three divisions of the Hinâyâna School, viz. Kâurṇkullakâḥ, Avantikâḥ and Vatsiputtrîyâḥ

SAMOTAṬA v. Samataṭa.

SAMPAHA 三波訶 Another name for Malasa.

SAM̃SKÂRA (Tib. Du dyed) 行 lit. action (karma). A metaphysical term, variously defined as illusion (in Nepaul), notion (Tibet), discrimination (Ceylon), action (China).

SAM̃SKṚITA 梵 lit. Brahma or 梵字 lit. Brahmanic (alphabetic) writing, or 天竺語 lit. the Indian language. Sanskrit, the classical Aryan language of India, probably never spoken in its most systematized form, in which it was the accomplishment of the Brahmans, whilst, among the people, it degenerated into Prakrit, a specimen of which is Pâli. The most ancient Chinese texts seem to be translations from Pâli, the more modern texts from Sanskrit. Hiuen-tsang found (about 635 A. D.) in the Pundjab little difference between Sanskrit and Pâli. Various alphabets for the transliteration of Sanskrit characters into Chinese were introduced by Dharmarakcha, Mokchala, Kumâradjîva, Buddhabhadra, Sam̃ghapâla, Mahâyânadêva, Divakara, Sikchanada, Amogha, and other alphabets were sanctioned by Chinese emperors, Yen-tsung (A. D. 1031), Kanghi (A. D. 1662) and Kien-lung (A. D. 1750). The Dêvanagari form of writing Sanskrit was early introduced in China, by way of Tibet, and is still used on charms, amulets, and in sorcery.

SAM̃VADJI v. Vridji.

SAM̃VARA 三跋羅 A deity, worshipped by followers of the Tantra School.

SAM̃VARṬṬAKALPA (Pâli Samvaṭṭa kappa. Mong. Ebderekogalap) 壞刼 or 滅刼 lit. tde kalpa of destruction or annihilation. The Mahâkalpa of the destruction to which every universe is subject, in the course of 64 small kalpas, fire being at work periodically in 56 small kalpas, water during 7 and wind during 1 small kalpa, until the whole, with the exception of the 4th Dhyâna, is annihilated.

SAM̃VARṬṬATTHÂHI KALPA (Pâli. Sanvattatthâhi kappa. Mong. Choghossun galab) 增滅刼 lit. the increasing (period of a small) kalpa of destruction. That period in each of the 64 divisions of a Samvarṭṭa kalpa during which the force of destruction (resp. fire, water, wind) increases in intensity, followed by a period of decrease (滅滅).

SAMYAGÂDJÎVA (Pâli. Sammâdjiva. Singh. Samyaka jiwa) 正業 lit. the correct profession, explained by 乞食 lit. mendicancy. The 4th of the 8 Marga, the vow of poverty, incumbent upon every Arhat or monastic. See Bhikchu.

SAMYAGDRICHṬI (Pâli. Sammâdiṭṭhi. Singh. Samyak drishti) 正見 lit. correct view or ability to discern the truth. The 1st of the 8 Marga, the possession of orthodox views; an attribute of each Arhat.

SAMYAGVÂK (Pâli. Sammâvâtchâ. Singh. Samyak wachana) 正語 lit. correct speech, explained as ability to avoid both nonsense and error in speaking. The 3rd of the 8 Marga, the ability, characteristic of an Arhat, of reproducing exactly any sound uttered in any universe.

SAMYAGVYÂYÂMA (Pâli. Sammâvâyâmo. Singh. Samyakwyagama) 正精進 lit. correct and subtle vîrya or incessant practice of asceticism. The 5th of the 8 Marga, based on the 3rd Pâramitâ; asceticism, as a characteristic of an Arhat.

SAMYAKKARMÂNTA (Pâli. Sammakammanta) 正命 lit. correct life, explained as strict observance of purity. The last of the 8 Marga, honesty and virtue, as a characteristic of an Arhat.

SAMYAKPRAHÂNA (Pâli. Sammapradhana. Singh. Samyakpradhana) 四正勤 lit.

four correct efforts. One of the 37 categories of the Bodhi pakchika dharma, comprehending a fourfold effort, viz. (1.) after the birth of evil to stop its birth for ever, (2.) before the birth of evil to prevent its birth, (3.) before the birth of karma to cause its birth, (4.) after the birth of karma to cause its continuous development.

SAMYAKSAMÂDHI (Pâli. Sammâsamâdhi) 正定 lit. correct samâdhi, or absolute mental coma. The 6th of the 8 Marga, the attainment of Samâdhi (q. v.), as a characteristic of an Arhat.

SAMYAKSAMBODHI v. Anuttara.

SAMYAKSAM̃BUDDHA (Pâli. Sammâsambuddha. Siam. Summasamphutto) 三藐三佛陀 explained by 正偏知 lit. correct and equal knowledge. The 3rd of the 10 titles of S'âkyamuni, an attribute of every Buddha.

SAMYAKSAM̃KALPA (Páli. Sammâsamkappa. Singh. Samyakkalpanâwa) 正思惟 lit. correct thinking, or a mind free from wicked thoughts. The 2nd of the 8 Marga, decision and purity of thought and will, as a characteristic of every Arhat.

SAMYAKSMRITI (Páli. Sammâsati. Singh. Samyak siti) 正念 lit. correct memory, or recollection of the law. The 7th of the 8 Marga, religious recollectedness, as a characteristic of every Arhat.

SAMYUKTÂBHIDHARMA HṚIDAYA S'ÂSTRA 雜阿毗曇心論 A translation (A. D. 434), by Ssm̃ghavarman and others, of a philosophical work by Dharmatrâta.

SAMYUKTÂGAMA v. Agama.

SAMYUKTA PIṬAKA 雜藏 lit. the miscellaneous collection. A supplementary part of the Chinese Tripiṭaka (q. v.), including 西土聖賢撰集 miscellaneous works of Indian authors and 此土著述 doctrinal expositions by native (Chinese) authors, the latter being subdivided into 大明續入藏諸集 miscellaneous collections included in the canon under the Ming dynasty (A. D 1368—1644) and 北藏缺南藏函號附 supplements of the northern canon added, with their case marks, from the southern canon.

SAMYUKTÂVADÂNA SÛTRA. Title of translations of collections of Avadânas (q.v.), viz. (1.) 雜譬喩經 A. D. 25-220, (2.) 雜譬喩經 by Lokarakcha, A. D. 147-186, (3,) 舊雜譬喩經 A.D. 251, (4.) 衆經撰雜譬喩經 by Kumâradjîva, A.D. 405.

S'AṆAKA 商那迦 A plant,

the fibres of which are woven into robes for priests.

S'ÂṆAKAVÂSA or S'aṇavâsa or S'âṇavâsika (Singh. Sambhûta Sânavâsika) 商那迦縛娑 or 商諾縛娑 or 商那和修 explained by 自然服 lit. willing to serve. (1.) A younger brother of Ananda. (2.) The 3rd patriarch, a Vâis'ya of Mathurâ, born 100 years after the Nirvâṇa, identified with Yas'as, the leader at the 2nd synod.

S'ANAIS'TCHARA or Sani 賒乃以室折羅 explained by 土星 lit. Saturn or its regent.

SANDHINIR MOKCHANA SÛTRA. Title of 5 translations, viz. (1.) 深密解脫經 by Bodhirutchi A. D. 386—534, (2.) 相續解脫地婆羅密了義經 by Guṇabhadra A. 420—479, (3.) 相續解脫如來所作隨順處了義經 by the same, (4.) 佛說解節經 by Paramârtha, A.D. 557-589, (5.) 解深蜜經 by Hiuen-tsang, A. D. 645.

SAÑDJAYA v. Saṁdjaya.

SAÑDJÑÂNA v. Saṁdjñâna.

SAÑGA v. Saṁgha.

SAÑGALA v. S'âkala.

SANIRÂDJA 珊尼羅闍 A river of Udyâna.

SAÑKAKCHIKA v. Saṁkakchika.

SAÑKRÂNTIVÂDÂḤ (Singh. Saṁkantikâs) 僧干蘭底婆多部 or 僧迦蘭多部 Another name of the Sâutrântika School.

SAÑSÂRA (Singh. Sangsâra. Tib. Khorba) 輪迴 lit. rotation, explained by 生死大海 lit. the ocean of birth and death. Human existence, as a circle of continuous metempsychosis.

SANYADATTA v. Kanakamuni.

SAÑSKRITA v. Saṁskrita.

SAÑVARṬṬA v. Saṁvarṭṭa.

SAPTA BUDDHA (Tib. Sangs rgyas rabs bdun) 七佛 The seven Buddhas of antiquity, viz. Vipas'yin, S'ikhin, Vis'vabhû, Krakutchanda, Kanakamuni, Kâs'yapa and S'âkyamuni, the latter having rather popularized and systematized pre-existing religious ideas than invented a new religion.

SAPTA BUDDHAKA 佛說七佛經 An account of the Sapta Buddha, taken from the Mahânidâna sûtra.

SAPTA BUDDHAKA SÛTRA. Title of 3 translations, viz., (1.) 虛空藏菩薩問七佛陀羅尼咒經 A. D. 502—557, (2.) 如來方便善

巧咒經 by Guṇabhadra, A.D. 587, (3.) 聖虛空藏菩薩陀羅尼經 by Dharmadêva, A.D. 973—981.

SAPTADAS'A BHÛMI S'ÂSTRA s.a. Yogâtchârva bhûmi s'âstra.

SAPTA RATNA 薩不荅羅的捺 or 七寶 lit. seven treasures. (1.) The insignia of a Tchakravartti, viz. a tchakra of gold, concubines, horses, elephants, guardian spirits, soldiers and servants, the maṇi. (2.) For another series of 7 treasures, not necessarily belonging to a Tchakravartti, see Suvarṇa, Rûpya, Vaidurya, Sphaṭika, Rohitamukti, As'magarbha and Musâragalva.

SAPTA RATNA PADMAVIKRÂMIN 蹈七寶華 The name of Râhula bhadra as Buddha.

SAPTA TATHÂGATA 七如來 The Buddhist substitute for the 7 richis of the Brahmans, an arbitrary series of seven (fictitious) Tathâgatas, viz. (1.) Amitâbha (q. v.), Amritodana râdja (q. v.), Abhayamdada (q. v.), Vyâsa (q.v.), Surupaya (q.v.), Ratnatraya (羅担納担羅耶 or 寶勝 lit. precious conqueror), and Prabhûta ratna (q. v.), which names are inscribed on a heptagonal billar (七如來寶塔) in Buddhist temples.

SAPTATATHÂGATA PÛRVA PRAṆIDHÂNA VIS'ÊCHA VISTARA 藥師瑠璃光七佛本願功德經 A translation (A. D. 707) of a portion of the Mahâpradjñâpâramita.

S'ARADÂ (Tib. Tsa dus) 盛熱 lit. excessive heat. The hot season (16th day of the 3rd moon to 15th day of the 5th moon).

S'ARAKÛPA 箭泉 lit. arrow fountain. An artesian well (near Kapilavastu) opened by an arrow shot by S'âkyamuni.

S'ARAṆA v. Tris'araṇa.

SARASVATI 薩羅娑縛底 or 薩羅酸底 or 大辯才天女 or 大辯天 lit. the dêva of great discrimination. The wife of Brahma, also called S'ri.

S'ARAVATÎ v. S'râvasti.

SARCHAPA or S'ers'apa 薩利刹跛 or 舍利娑婆 or 芥子 lit. mustard seed. (1.) A measure of length, the 10,816000th part of a yodjana, (2.) A weight, the 32nd part of a Raktika.

SARDJARASA 薩闍羅娑 A kind of gum.

S'ARDÛLA KARNA 舍頭諫 explained by 虎耳 lit. tiger's ears. The original name of Ananda.

S'ÂRIKÂ or S'ari or Sala 奢利 or 舍利 or 舍羅 (1.) A long-legged bird. (2.) The wife of Tichya, mother of S'âriputra, famous for her birdlike eyes.

S'ÂRIPUTRA or S'arisuta or S'aradvatiputra (Pali. Sariputta. Singh. Seriyut. Burm. Thariputra. Tib. Sharu by or Saradwatu by or Nid rghial) 奢利弗 (or 富)多羅 or 奢利補担羅 or 舍利弗 or 舍利子 lit. the son of S'ârika, or 身子 lit. the son of S'arîra. One of the principal disciples of S'âkyamuni, whose "right hand attendant" he was; born at Nalandagrama, the son of Tichya (v. Upatichya) and S'ârika, he became famous for his wisdom and learning, composed 2 works on the Abhidharma, died before his master, but is to re-appear as Buddha Padmaprabha in Viradja during the Maharatna pratimandita kalpa.

S'ÂRIPUTRÂBHIDHARMA S'ASTRA 舍列弗阿毗曇論 An reputed work of S'âriputra, translated (A. D. 415) by Dharmagupta and Dharmayas'as.

S'ÂRIPUTRA PARIPRITCHTCHHÂSÛTRA 舍利弗問經 Title of a translation (A. D. 317—420).

S'ARÎRA (Pâli. Sarira. Mong. Shari) 設利羅 or 舍利 or 實利 or 攝哩藍 (s'arîram), explained by 堅固 lit. solids, or 骨分 lit. particles of bones, or 身 lit. body. Bodily relics or ashes (left after cremation) of a Buddha or saint. They are also called Dhâtu or Dharma s'arîra, preserved in Stûpas and worshipped.

SARPAHRIDAYA v. Tchandanêva.

SARPÂUCHADHI 薩褒施殺 or 蛇藥 lit. snake medicine. Name of a saṁghârâma in Udyâna, built on the spot where S'âkyamuni, in a former djâtaka (as Indra), appeared as a snake which sacrificed itself to save starving and sick people. See Sûmasarpa.

SARVÂBHAYA PRADÂNA DHÂRAṆÎ 佛說施一切無畏陀羅尼經 Title of a translation (A. D. 980-1000) by Dânapâla.

SARVA BUDDHA SAṀDARS'ANA 現一切世間 The realm of Mêgha dundubhisvara râdja.

SARVA BUDDHÂṄGAVATÎDHÂRAṆÎ 諸佛集會陀羅尼經 Title of a translation (A. D. 691) by Dêvapradjña and others.

SARVADA 薩縛達 or 一切施 lit. sacrificing all. S'â

kyamuni, who, in a former djâtaka, resigned his kingdom and liberty to save others.

SARVADJÑA 薩婆若 or 一切智 lit. universal intelligence. The mental state in which S'âkyamuni became Buddha.

SARVADJÑA DÊVA 薩婆愼若提婆 or 一切智 lit. dêva of universal intelligence. An epithet of every Buddha.

SARVADURGATI PARIS'ODHANA UCHṆÎCHA VIDJAYA DHÂRAṆI. Title of 6 translations, viz. (1.) 佛頂尊勝陀羅尼經 by Buddhapali (A. D. 676), (2.) 佛說佛頂尊勝陀羅尼經 A. D. 710, (3) 佛頂最勝陀羅尼經 by Divakara, A. D. 618—907, (4.) 最勝佛頂陀羅尼淨除業障經 by the same, (5.) 最勝佛頂陀羅尼經 by Dharmadêva A. D. 973—981, and (6.) 佛說一切如來烏瑟膩沙最勝總持經 by the same.

SARVA LOKA BHAYÂSTAMBHITA VIDHVAM̃SANAKARA 壞一切世間怖畏 A fictitious Buddha in the N. E., an incarnation of the 15th son of Mahâbhidjñadjñanâbhibhu.

SARVA LOKA DHÂTÛPADRA VODVÊGA PRATYUTTÎRṆA 度一切世間苦惱 A fictitious Buddha in the W., an incarnation of the 10th son of Mahâbhidjñadjñânâbhibhu.

SARVA PUṆYA TAMUTCHTCHAYA SAMÂDHI. (1.) A degree of Samâdhi (q. v.), called 集一切功德 the accumulation of all merit and virtue. (2.) Title of 2 translations, viz. (1.) 等集衆德三昧經 by Dharmarakcha (A. D. 265—316), and (2.) 集一切福德三昧經 by Kumâradjîva (A. D. 284—517).

SARVA RUTA KÂUS'ALYA 解一切衆生言語 lit. interpretation of the utterances of of all beings. A degree of Samâdhi.

SARVÂRTTHASIDDHA or Siddhârta or Arthas'iddhî (Pâli. Siddhattu Burm. Thêddhat) 薩婆曷剌他悉陀 or 薩婆悉多 or 悉達 explained by 一切義成 lit the realisation of all auguries. Name given to the newborn S'âkyamuni (with reference to the miracles which happened at his birth).

SARVASATTVA PÂPADJAHANA 一切衆生離諸惡趣 lit. departure of all beings from evil paths (of transmigration). A degree of Samâdhi.

SARVASATTVA PRIYA DAR-

S'ANA 一切衆生喜見佛 lit. the Buddha at whose appearance all beings rejoice. (1.) A Bodhisattva who destroyed himself by fire and, in another djâtaka, burned both his arms to cinders, whereupon he was reborn as Bhêchadjya râdja. (2.) The name under which Mahâprad japati is to be reborn as Buddha.

SARVASATTVA TRÂTÂ 救一切 lit. saviour of all. A fictitious Mahâbrahma.

SARVASATTVÂUDJOHÂRÎ 一切衆生氣精 lit. the subtle vitality of all beings. A certain Rakchasî.

SARVÂSTIVÂDÂḤ 薩婆阿私底婆拖部 or 薩婆多部 or 一切有部 lit. the School of all beings, or 一切語言部 lit. the School which discusses the existence of everything. A philosophical School, a branch of the Vâibhâchika School with which it is generally identified, claiming the sanction of Râhula and teaching the reality of all visible phenomena. It split, 200 years after the Nirvâṇa, into the following Schools, viz. (1.) Dharmaguptâḥ (q.v.), (2.) Mûlasarvâstivâdâḥ 一切有根本, asserting that every form of being has its inherent root and origin. (3.) Kâs'yapîyâḥ (q.v.) (4.) Mahîs'âsakâḥ (q.v.) and (5.) Vâtsiputriyâḥ (q.v.)

SARVA TATHÂGATA 薩哩斡苔塔葛達 Hail, ye Tathagatas all! A sacred phrase, common in litanies.

SARVA TATHÂGATA VICHAYÂVATÂRA 度諸佛境界智光嚴經 A translation, A. D. 350—431.

S'AS'ÂÑKA RÂDJA 設賞迦 or 月王 lit. king of the moon. A king (dethroned by S'îlâditya), who attempted to destroy the Bodhidruma.

S'AS'IKÊTU 名相 Name of Subhûti as Buddha.

S'AS'ORNA 一兎毛塵 lit. an atom of dust on a hare's hair. A measure, the 22,588, 608,000th part of a yodjana.

S'ÂSTÂDÊVA MANUCHYÂNÂM 天人師 lit. teacher of dêvas and men. One of the 10 epithets of a Buddha.

S'ÂSTRAS (Tib. Bstan btchos) 論 lit discourses. A class of Buddhist writings, doctrinal and philosophic disquisitions, in contradistinction from sûtras (經) and works on the vinaya (律).

SAT 妙有 The incomprehensible entity. A metaphysical term. See Asat.

S'ATA BUDDHA NÂMA SÛTRA 百佛名經 A translation (A. D. 581—618) by Narendrayas'as.

S'ATADRU 設多圖盧 (1.) Ancient kingdom of Northern India, noted for its mineral wealth (2.) The river Sutledj.

S'ATAMANYA (Tib. Brgja bjiu) 能作 lit. mighty in deeds. Epithet of Indra.

S'ATAPARṆA (Singh. Sukkattana) 車帝 lit. lord of chariots. A cavern, near Râdjagriha, in which the first synod held its sessions (543 B. C.)

S'ATA S'ÂSTRA 百論 A philosophical work by Dêva Bodhisattva, annotated by Vasubandhu, and translated (A. D. 404) by Kumâradjîva.

S'ATA S'ÂSTRA VAIPULYA 廣百論本 A philosophical work by Dêva Bodhisattva, translated (A. D. 650) by Hiuen-tsang.

SATATASAMITÂBHIYUKTA 常精進 lit constant and subtle energy. A fictitious Bodhisattva, mentioned in the Saddharma puṇḍarika.

SATRUCHNA v. Sutrichna.

SATTÂDHIKARṆA SAMATHA (pâli) 七滅諍法 lit. 7 laws, abolishing disputes. A section of the Vinaya.

SATTVA KÂCHAYA 衆生濁 lit. the corruption of all beings. An epoch in which all beings degenerate.

SATYA SIDDHI v. Harivarman.

S'ÂUTRÂNTIKÂḤ or Sâutrântavâdâḥ or Sañkrântivâdâḥ (Pâli. Sutta vâdâ. Tib. Mdosde dzin) 修丹難多婆拖 or 修多蘭部 or 修妒路句 (Sûtrakâ) or 經部 lit. the Sûtra School, explained by 惟有一經藏 lit. those who recognize but one Piṭaka, viz. Sûtras, or by 說轉部 lit. the school which speaks of (moral) emancipation. An atomistic School founded, 400 years after the Nirvâṇa, by Kumâralabdha. It regarded Purṇamâitrayaṇiputra as its patron saint, and rejected all S'âstras.

SEMENGHÂN v. Hrosminkam.

S'ERS'APA s. a. Sarchapa.

SIDDHA or Siddhârta v. Sarvârthasiddha.

SIDDHA KALPA v. Vivarṭtakalpa.

SIDDHA VASTU 悉曇章 The first chapter of a syllabary (in 12 chapters) attributed to Brahma (梵章).

SIDDHI (Tib Dngos grub) 悉底 Magic powers, obtainable by samâdhi.

S'IGRABUDDHA 明敏 A priest of Nâlanda, famous for his intelligence.

S'IKCHÂNANDA 實义難陀 or 施乞义難陀 or 學喜 lit. joyful student. A S'ramaṇa of Kustana, who (695 A. D) introduced a new alphabet in China and translated 19 works.

S'IKCHÂPADA (Pâli. Sikkhâpada) 十戒 lit. 10 precepts. A series of 10 rules for novices, the transgression of which constitutes the 10 sins (Das'akusala 十惡). Particulars see under (1.) Pânâtipâtâ, (2.) Adinnâdânâ, (3.) Abrahma tchâriyâ, (4.) Musâdâvâ. (5.) Surâmêrêyya madjdjapa mâdaṭṭhânâ, (6.) Vikâlabhodjanâ. (7.) Natchtchagita vâdita visûkadassanâ, (8.) Mâlâghanda vilêpana dhâraṇa maṇḍana vibhûsa naṭṭhânâ (9.) Utchtchasayanâ mahâsayana, and (10.) Djâtarûpa radjatapaṭigghahanâ. See also Pantcha vêramaṇi and Pantchânantarya.

S'IKHÎ 尸棄 or 式棄 explained by 火 lit. flame (s'ikhâ), (1.) A fictitious Mahâbrahma (mentioned in the Saddharma Puṇḍarika). (2.) The 999th Buddha of the last kalpa, being the 2nd of the Sapta Buddha, who was born in Prabhadvadja (光相城) as a Kchattriya, and who converted 250,000 persons, whilst life lasted 70,000 years.

SÎLA 尸羅 or 尸 The 2nd of the 10 pâramitâ; strict osbervance of the Trividha dvâra, resulting in perfect purity.

S'ILÂ (Tib. Chel) 試羅 or 玉 lit. a gem. A precious stone, probably coral.

S'ÎLABHADRA 尸羅跋陀羅 or 戒賢 lit. disciplinary sage. A learned priest of Nâlanda, teacher (A. D. 625) of Hiuentsang.

S'ÎLADITYA 尸羅阿迭多 or 戒日 lit. sun of discipline. A brother of Râdjavardhana, who, under the auspices of Avalokites'vara, became (A. D. 600) king of Kanyâkubdja and conquered India and the Pundjab. He was the most liberal patron of Buddhism, re-established the Mahamokcha parichad, built many stûpas, composed the 八大靈塔梵讚 As'ṭamahâs'rî tchaitya saṁskrita stotra, and specially patronized Hiuentsang and S'îlabhadra.

S'ILPASTHÂNA VIDYÂ S'ÂSTRA 巧明 or 功明 lit. illustration of mechanics, or 功巧論 lit the s'âstra on mechanics, or 術數 lit. mathematics. One of the Pantcha vidyâ s'âstras, a work on arts, mechanics, dual philosophy, and calendaric calculations.

SIṀHA v. Siṁhala and Udâyi.

SIṀHABHIKCHU 師子比丘 The 23rd or 24th patriarch, successor of Haklenayas'as.

SIM̃HADHVADJA 師子相 A fictitious Buddha in the S. E., an incarnation of the 3rd son of Mahâbhidjñadjñânâbhibhu.

SIM̃HAGHOCHA 師子音 A fictitious Buddha in the S. E., an incarnation of tne 4th son of Mahâbhidjñadjñânâbhibhu.

SIMHAHÂNU (Pâli. Siñhahâna kabânâ. Singh. Singhahanu. Tib. Sengghe hgram. Mong. Oghadjitou arsalan) 師子頰王 lit. king with a lion's jaw. The paternal grandfather of S'âkyamuni, a king of Kapilavastu, father of S'uddhodana, S'uklodana, Dronodana, and Amritodana.

SIMHALA 僧伽羅. (1) A son of Sim̃ha (僧訶 or 僧伽 or 獅子 lit. lion), a merchant of India, who, being ship-wrecked on Ceylon, was ensnared by Rakchasîs, but delivered by Avalokitês'vara (appearing as a magic horse). One Rakchasî having followed him to India, and slain the king of his native country, Sim̃hala succeeded to the throne, led an army to Ceylon and destroyed all the Rakchasîs there. (2.) The kingdom 獅子國 lit. the kingdom of Sim̃ha) in Ceylon, founded by Sim̃ha. See Ratnadvîpa.

SIM̃HANÂDA 師子吼 lit. the lion's howl. Buddhist preaching, being equal, in power over demons, heretics and misery, to the power which the lion's voice has over animals. See S'âkyasim̃ha.

SIM̃HANÂDIKA SÛTRA. Title of 2 translations, viz. (1.) 佛說如來師子吼經 by Buddhos'ânta (A. D. 524), (2.) 佛說大方廣師子吼經 by Divâkara (A. D. 680).

SIM̃HAPARIPRITCHTCHHÂ 阿闍世王太子會 Title of a translation (A. D. 618—907) by Bodhirutchi.

SIM̃HAPURA 僧伽補羅 Ancient province and city (now Simla) of Cashmere.

SIM̃HARAS'MI 師子光 lit. lion's light. A learned opponent (A. D. 630) of the Yogâtchârya School.

SIM̃HÂSANA 師子座 (or 牀) lit. lion's throne (or couch). A royal throne, supported by carved lions.

SIM̃HATCHANDRÂ 師子月 lit. lion's moon. A Bhikchunî (converted by Sadâpâribhûta).

SINDHU (Tib. Sindhou. Mong. Sidda or Childa) 信度 or 辛頭 or 信河 explained by 驗河 lit. river of verification. (1.) The Indus (Sanpu) said to rise from lake Anavatapta (or Sirikol), through "the mouth of the golden elephant" in the W., to flow around the lake and then into the S. W. ocean. (2.) Ancient kingdom (Sindh), often visited by S'âkyamuni. See Vitchapura.

SINDHUPARA 辛頭波羅香 Perfume from a plant which grows on the banks (para) of the Indus (Sindhu).

SIRÎSA 尸利沙 The Mimosa siricha (acacia).

S'IS'UMARA 失收摩羅 or 室獸摩羅 explained by 鮮 lit. a crocodile. See Khumbira.

S'ÎTÂ (Tib. Sida, Mong. Chida) 私多 or 私陁 or 悉多 or 徙多 explained by 冷河 lit. cold river. (1.) A river which issues from lake Anavatapta, in the E., through the "diamond lion's mouth," flows round the lake, then loses itself in the ground and reappears on the As'makûṭa mountains as the source of the Hoangho. (2.) The northern outflux of lake Siricol, the modern Yarkand daria, which flows into lake Lop, and thence underneath the desert of Gopi, until it reappears as the source of the Hoangho.

SITÂTAPATRA DHÂRAṆÎ 佛說大白傘蓋總持陀羅尼經 Title of a translation by Amoghavadjra (A. D 746—771).

S'ÎTAVANA 尸多婆那 or 屍陀林 or 男女林 lit. forest of men and women, or 寒林 lit. cold forest. A cemetery. See S'mas'ânam.

S'IVA v. Mahês'vara.

S'IVIKA 尸毗伽 A former djâtaka of S'âkyamuni, when he was a Bodhisattva.

SKANDHA (Pâli. Khanda Tib. Gou lang or Thung po) 塞建陀 or 五蘊 lit. 5 bundles, or 五陰 lit. 5 instincts, or 五衆 lit. 5 aggregates. Five attributes (Pantcha skandha) of every human being, viz. (1.) rûpa, form, (2.) vêdanâ, perception, (3.) saṁdjñâ, consciousness, (4.) karman (or saṁskara), action, and (5.) vidjñâna, knowledge. The union of these 5 attributes dates from the quickening moment of birth and constitutes a personal being. Full maturity of the Pantcha skandha is succeeded by Djarâmarana.

SKANDHARATNA v. Sugandhara.

SKANDHILA 索建地羅 A native of Cashmere, author of tha Vibhâchâ prakarana pâda s'âstra.

S'LOKA or Anus'ṭubh 輸盧迦(波) or 首盧 or 室路迦 The common Sanskrit epic metre, formed by 32 syllables, in 4 half-lines of 8 or in 2 lines of 16 syllables each. Chinese identify it with Gâthâ.

S'MAS'ÂNAM 尸摩舍 (or 賒)那. A burial ground. See S'itavana.

SMRITI (Pâli. Sati. Singh. Smirti) 念 lit. recollection. The power of memory, the 3rd of the 5 Balâ, the 1st of the 7 Bodhyanga.

SMRITÊNDRYA (Pâli. Satîndriya. Singh. Satiindra) 念根 lit. the root of memery. The organ of memory, the 3rd of the 5 Indrya.

SMRITYUPASTHÂNA (Pali. Satara satipatthana. Burm. Thatipathan) 四念處 lit. 4 dwellings of memory. One of the 37 Bodhipakchika dharma, comprehending 4 objects on which memory should dwell. Particulars see under Kâya smrityupasthâna, Vêdanasmrityupasthâna, Tchitta smrityupasthâna, and Dharma smrityupasthâna.

SOMA or Somana (Tib. Snama) 蘇摩(那) or 磨羅 explained by 悅意花 lit. the flower which exhilarates (su) the mind (mana), or by 華鬘 lit. headgear of flowers. (1.) A plant, affected by the moon and sacred to Indra, the juice being used at brahmanic sacrifices; the Asclepia acida or Cynanchum viminale (according to modern Brahmans), or the Ampelus (vine), ar Sarcostema viminalis, or the gogard tree, or Triticum aestivum. (2.) Same as Soma Dêva.

SOMADÊVA 蘇摩提婆 or 月天 lit. the dêva of the moon. The regent of the moon. See Tchandra.

SONAGHIRI v. Suvarṇaghiri.

SPARS'A 觸 lit. contact. The sense of touch, sensatioh, the 7th of the 12 Nidâna. See also Poṭṭabha.

SPHÂṬIKA 塞頗胝迦 or 婆致迦 or 頗胝 (or 黎) explained by 白珠 lit, white pearl, or by 水玉 lit. water crystal. Rock crystal. the 4th of the Sapta ratna.

SPHÎTAVÂRAS or Saptavars'a 霫蔽伐剌祠 A city of Kapis'a, 4o li from Opian.

S'RADDHÂBADA (Pâli. Sadâbala. Singh. Sardhâwa bala) 信力 lit. the power of faith. The 1st of the 5 Bala.

S'RADDHÂRALA DHÂNÂVATÂRA MUDRÂ SÛTRA 信力入印法門經 Title of a translation (A. D. 504) by Dharmarutchi.

S'RADDHÊNDRYA (Pâli Saddindriya. Singh. Sardhâwa indra) 信根 lit. the root of faith. The organ of faith, the 1st of the 5 Indrya.

SRAGHARÂ v. Âryatârâ.

S'RAMAṆA (Pali. Saman. Burm. Phungee. Tib. Dges by ong) 舍羅摩拏 or 室拏 or 沙迦懣囊 or 沙門 or 桑門 explained by 出家人 lit. monastics, or by 勤勞 lit. toiling (from the root sram, to tire), or by 止息 lit stop the breath, or by 息心 lit. restful (from the root sam, to quiet). Ascetics of all denominations, the Sarmanai or Samanaioi or Germanai of the Greeks. (2.) Buddhist monks and priests "who have left their families and quitted the passions."

S'RAMAṆÊRA (Pali. Samanera.
Singh. Samanero ganninanse. Siam. Samanen or Nenor luksit. Burm. Scien. Tib. Bandi. Mong. Schabi or Bandi) 室羅末尼羅 or 沙彌 explained by 策男 lit. a man of zeal, or 室羅摩拏理迦 or 沙尼 explained by 勤策女 lit. a woman of energy and zeal. The religious novice, whether male or female, who has taken the vows of the S'ikchâpada.

S'RÂVAKA (Pali. Savako. Sing. Srawaka. Tib. Nan thos. Mong. Scharwak) 舍羅婆迦 or 聲聞 lit. he who heard the voice (sc. of Buddha). (1.) All personal disciples of S'âkyamuni, the foremost of whom are called Mahâs'râvakas. (2.) The elementary degree of saintship, the first of the Triyâna, the S'râvaka (superficial yet in practice and understanding) being compared with a hare crossing Sañsara by swimming on the surface.

S'RÂVAṆA 室羅伐拏 The hottest month of summer (from the 16th of the 5th moon to the 15th of the 6th moon).

S'RÂVASTÎ or S'arâvatî (Pali. Sâvatthi. Singh. Sewet. Burm. Thawatthi. Tib. Njandu jodpa or Muan yod. Mong. Sonoscho yabui) 室羅筏悉底 or 舍婆提 or 舍衛 explained by 聞物城 lit. the city where one hears things, or 好道 lit. good conduct, or 豐德 lit. prolific virtue, or 仙人住處 lit. the dwelling of the richi (S'ravasta) with the note, "also called Kosala." Ancient kingdom (500 *li* N. W. of Kapilavastu) and city (near a river of the same name), a favourite resort of S'âkyamuni, a deserted ruin in 600 A. D., situated near Sirkhee or near Fuzabad.

S'RÊCHṬHÎ 商主 lit. a merchantprince, or 長者 lit. an elder. A title given to prominent laymen.

S'ṚÎ (Tib Dpal) 尸利 or 室利 or 修利 or 悉利 or 昔哩 explained by 吉祥 lit lucky omen. (1.) An exclamation frequently used in liturgies and sorcery. (2.) A title given to many deities (Sarasvati, etc.), also used as prefix or suffix to names. (3.) An abbreviation for Mandjus'ri.

S'RÎDÊVA 室利提婆 or 吉祥天 A title of Mahês'vara.

S'RÎGARBHA 得藏 A Bodhisattva, also called Vimalanêtra.

S'RÎGUṆARAKTÂMBARA 勝得赤衣 A S'ramaṇa of India, author of the 聖佛母般若波羅蜜多九頌精義論 Ârya buddha mâṭrika pradjñâpâramitâ navagâthâ mahârtha s'âstra, translated (A. D. 1000—1058) by Dharmarakcha.

S'RÎGUPTA 室利毱多 or 勝密 An enemy of S'âkyamuni, whom he sought to kill by fire and poison.

S'RÎGUPTA SÛTRA 佛說德護長者經 Title of a translation (A. D. 583) by Narendrayas'as.

S'RÎKAṆṬHASÛTRA 除恐災患經 Title of a translation, A. D. 385—431.

S'RIKCHÊTRA 室利差呾羅 Ancient kingdom in the delta of the Brahmaputra (near Silhet *i. e.* S'rihatta).

S'RÎKRÎTATI 室利訖栗多底 Ancient name of Kashgar.

S'RÎMÂLÂ DEVÎ SIM̃HANADA. Title of 2 translations, viz. (1.) 勝鬘師子吼一乘大方便方廣經 by Guṇabhadra, A. D. 435. (2.) 勝鬘夫人會 by Bodhirutchi, A. D. 618—907.

S'RÎMATÎ BRAHMAṆÎ PARIPRITCHTCHHÂ. Title of 2 translatios, viz. (1.) 梵女首意經 by Dharmarakcha, A. D. 265—315, (2.) 有德女所問大乘經 by Bodhirutchi, A. D. 618—907.

S'RÎMITRA 室利密多羅 or 尸梨蜜多羅 or 屍黎密 or 吉友 lit. lucky friend A prince of India, who became a priest and translated (in Nanking) 3 works, A. D. 317—322.

S'RÎPÂDA 佛跡 Footprints of Buddha, with tracings of 65 symbolic figures.

S'RÎVASTAYA 室利靺蹉

or 吉祥 lit. lucky omen. A mystic (star-like) diagram of good augury, the favourite symbol of Vishnuites and Jains.

SROTÂPANNA (Pâli. Sotâpan. Singh. Sowan. Tib Gyun du zhug pa) 蘇盧多波那 or 窣路陀阿鉢曩 or 須陀洹 explained by 八流 lit. one who has entered (apatti) the stream (srota) i. e. of holy living. The elementary class of saints, who are not to be reborn in a lower gâti, but to pass, in ascending gradation, through 7 births among men and dêvas, until they reach Nirvâṇa. See Ârya.

S'ROTRA (Pâli. Sota. Singh. Sotan) 耳 lit. the ear. The organ of hearing, one of the Chaḍâyatana.

SRUGHNA 窣祿勤那 Ancient kingdom and city on the upper course of the Yamûna, near Sirinuggur.

S'RUTAVIÑS'ATIKOṬI 室縷多頻設底枸胝 or 億耳 explained by 聞二百億 lit. he (at whose birth his father) heard (of a legacy of) 200 koṭis (of pieces of gold). A worshipper of Sûryadêva, converted by Mâudgalyâyana.

S'RUTI 都致 A measure of length, the 2,214,067,584,000th part of a yodjana.

STHÂNÊS'VARA 薩他泥濕伐羅 Ancient kingdom and city (now Thunesur) in Central India.

STHÂVARA KALPA s. a. Vivarttasiddha.

STHAVIRA (Pâli. Thera. Gnas brtan) 大第子 lit. great disciple (sc. of Ruddha), or 居僧之首 lit. head of the local priesthood i. e. Saṁgha sthavira, or 上坐 lit. chairman i. e. Mahâ sthavira. (1.) Title of the earliest leaders of Buddhist assemblies. (2.) Title of all priests who are licensed to preach and to become abbots.

STHÂVIRÂḤ or Sthavirani-kaya or Sthavirîyas 他毘梨與部 or 他鞞羅部 or 體毗履部 or 上坐部 lit. the School of the chairman. One of the 4 branches of the Vaibhâchika School, founded by Katyayana. About 246 B. C., it sp it into 3 divisions, viz. Mahâvihâra vasinâḥ, Djêtavaniyâḥ, and Abhayagiri vâsinaḥ.

STHIRAMATI 堅慧 lit solid wisdom. A learned priest of Nâlanda

STITHAMATI 安慧 lit. quiet wisdom. The teacher of Djayasêna, author of 3 s'âstras.

STOTRA 讚 or 讚頌 Metrical eulogies.

STRÎVIVARTA VYÂKARAṆA SÛTRA. Title of 5 translations, viz. (1.) 順權方便經 by Dharmarakcha. A.D. 265—316, (2.) 佛說無垢賢女經 by the same, (3.) 佛說腹中女聽經 by the same, (4.) 佛說樂瓔珞莊嚴方便經 by Dharmayas as, A. D. 384—417, (5.) 佛說轉女身經 by Dharmamitra, A. D. 420—479.

STÛPA or Thûpa or Dhâtugopa (Singh. Dhagobah. Burm. Prachadi. Tib. Mtcho rten or Gdung rten. Mong. Ssu wurghan) 窣堵波 or 蘇鍮婆 or 藪斗婆 or 兜婆 or 偷婆 or 塔婆 explained by 寶塔 lit. precious tower or tower for precious (relics), or by 佛舍利處 lit. the place of Buddhist s'ariras, or by 塡陵 lit. orthodox mausoleum (tumulus), or by 廟 lit. a tchaitya. Towers or pyramids of varying shape, originally sepulchres, then cenotaphs, and now mostly mere symbols of Buddhism. The legend says that, as the body consists of 84000 dhâtus, As'oka built 84000 dhâtugopas (of brick and therefore not durable) in different parts of India, to preserve the remains of S'âkyamuni. The ruins of a stûpa at Anurâdhapura (Ceylon) are supposed to date from B. C. 161 to A.D. 137. All ancient stûpas were built in the shape of towers, surmounted by a cupola and one or more tchhatra (parasols). The Chinese stûpas, built since 25-220 A.D., have no cupola but 7-13 tchhatras.

SUBÂHU KUMÂRA SÛTRA Title of two translations, viz. (1.) 蘇婆呼童子經 by S'ubhakarasiṁha, A. D. 724, and (2.) 妙臂菩薩所問經 (lit. Subâhu paripritchtchhă).

SUBÂHU PARIPRITCHTCHHÂ. Title of 3 translations viz. (1.) 太子刷護經 by Dharmarakcha, A. D. 265—316, (2.) 太子和休經 same date and (3.) (2.) 善譬菩薩會 by Kumâradjiva, A.D. 384—417.

SUBANTA or Sumanta 蘇漫多 A grammatical term (of Pāṇini,) designating nouns.

SUBHADRA 蘇(or 須)跋陀 or 須跋 or 善賢 lit. virtuous sage. A Brahman, 120 pears old, who, converted by S'âkyamuni, entered Nirvâṇa a few minutes before him.

S'UBHAKARASIṀHA 輸波迦羅 or 戍婆揭羅僧訶

or 淨師子 lit. pure lion, or (善)無畏 lit. (virtuous and) fearless. A priest of Nâlanda, descendant of Amritodana, who translated (A. D. 716–724) 5 works.

S'UBHAKRITSNAS (Singh. Subhakinho. Tib. Dge rgyas or Ged rgyes) 首阿既那 or 遍淨 lit. general purity. The 9th Brahmaloka, the 3rd region of the 3rd Dhyâna, where the body is 64 yodjanas high and life lasts 64 kalpas.

S'UBHAVASTU 蘇磐伐窣都 or 蘇婆薩都 A river (Soastos, Swat) of Udyâna.

S'UBHAVYÛHA 妙莊嚴王 (1.) A king, during the Priyadars'ana kalpa, of Vairotchana ras'mipratimaṇḍita, who, converted, together with his wife Vimaladatta, by his sons Vimalagarbha and Vimalanetra, was reborn in the time of S'âkyamuni as Padmas'ri Bodhisattva, and is to reappear, during the Abhyudga râdja kalpa, in Vistirṇavati as S'alendra râdja. (2.) The father of Kwanyin. See Avalokites'vara.

SUBÛTI (Tib. Rab hbyor) 蘇部(or 浮)帝(or 底) or 須菩 (or 扶) 提 or 善現 lit. virtuous appearance, or 善實 lit. virtue and truth, or 善吉 lit. virtue and luck, or 空生 lit. birth of emptiness, or 善業 lit. virtuous profession. (1.) A native of S'ravasti, contemporary of S'âkyamuni, a famous dialectician. (2.) A priest of Burmah, translator of the Mahâyânaratnamegha sûtra (lost in A.D. 732).

SUDÂNA or Sudatta 蘇(or 須)達拏 or 善與 lit. virtuous indeed! or 善牙 (or 身) lit. virtuous teeth (or body). S'âkyamuni, in a former djâtaka, as a prince who forfeited the throne by liberal alms-giving.

SUDARS'ANA (Singh. Sudarsana. Siam. Suthat) 修騰娑羅 or 蘇陀沙拏 or 蘇達(梨舍)那 explained by 善 lit. virtuous, or by 好施 lit. benevolent, or by 善見山 lit. mount of virtuous appearance. The 4th of the 7 concentric rocks around Mêru, 5,000 yodjanas high and separated, from 3rd and 5th circles, by oceans.

SUDARS'ANAS (Singh. Sudassa. Tib. Chintu mthong ba) 達須 or 善見 lit. virtuous appearance. The 16th Brahmaloka, the 7th region of the 4th Dhyâna, where life lasts 4,000 great kalpas and the body is 4,000 yodjanas high.

SUDATTA 蘇達多 or 須達 or 善施 lit, virtuous donor, or 樂施 lit, cheerful giver. Original name of Anâthapiṇḍika, sometimes confounded with Sudâna.

S'UDDHAMATI 淨意 Author of the Pratîtya samutpâda s'âstra, translated by Bodhirutchi (A.D. 508—534).

SUDDHAVÂSADÊVA (Singh. Ghatikara. Tib. Gnas gtsang mahi lha) 淨居天 lit. the dêva of the pure dwelling, or 澡缾天子 lit. the dêva with the clean vase. The guardian angel of S'âkyamuni, who brought about his conversion.

SUDDHARMA 大法王 A king of Kinnaras.

S'UDDHODANA RÂDJA (Singh. Sudhodana. Burm. Thoodaudana. Tib. Zas gtsang ma. Mong. Arighon idegethu) 首圖馱那羅闍 or 閱頭檀 or 淨飯王 lit. king of pure rice, or 淨梵 lit. pure Brahman. A S'âkya king of Kapilavastu, son of Siṁhahanu, husband of Mahâmâyâ, putative father of S'âkyamuni. See Djatiṁdhara.

S'ÛDRA (Tib. Dmang rigs) 輸(or 戍)達羅 or 首陀 explained by 農夫 lit. husbandmen. The caste of farmers (in India).

SUDRIS'AS (Singh. Sudassi. Tib. Gyr nom suang ba) 須達黎舍那 or 須達天 or 善現色 lit. (form of) virtuous appearance. The 7th Brahmaloka, the 8th region of the 4th Dhyâna, where the body is 8000 yodjanas high, and life lasts 8000 great kalpas.

SUGANDHARA or Skandharatna 塞建地羅 Author of the Abhidharmâvatâra (q. v.), translated (A.D. 658) by Hiuentsang.

SUGATA v. Svagata.

SUGATAMITRA 蘇伽多密多羅 or 如來友 lit. the friend of Tathâgata. A learned priest of the Sarvastivâdâḥ (A.D. 640) in Cashmere.

SUGATA TCHÊTANÂ 尼思佛 lit. a novice who thought of Buddha. An Upâsaka, who, having slighted Sadâparibhûta (q. v.) in a former birth, was converted through the same (then S'âkyamuni) and became a Buddha.

SUGHOCHA (Tib. Sgra snan). (1.) 妙音 A sister of Kwanyin. See Avalokitês'vara. (2.) 水天德佛 The 743rd Buddha of the present kalpa.

SUKHÂVATÎ (Tib. Gtsangris) 西方極樂世界 lit. the paradise in the West, or 淨土 lit. the pure land. A land, in some universe in the West, the Nirvâṇa of the common people, where the saints revel in physical bliss for aeons, until they re-enter the circle of transmigration. See under Amitâbha.

SUKHÂVATÎ VYÛHA. Title of many translations, e. g. 佛說阿彌陀經 by Kumâradjîva, A.D. 402, and 稱讚淨土佛攝受經 by Hiuen-tsang, A.D. 950.

S'UKLAPAKCHA 白分 Half a month. See Kris'napakcha.

S'UKLODANA RÂDJA (Tib. Zas dkar) 白飯王 lit. king of white rice. A prince of Kapilavastu, 2nd son of Simhanu, father of Tichya, Dêvadatta and 難提伽 Nandika.

S'UKRA 戍羯羅 or 金星 The planet Venus.

SUMAN or Chuman 愉漫 Ancient kingdom (between Chagaman and Sayad) in Transoxania.

SUMANTA v. Subanta.

SÛMASARPA 蘇摩蛇 lit. the sûma (water) serpent. A former djâtaka of S'âkyamuni, when, as a water serpent, he sacrificed his life to provide medicine. See Sarpâuchadhi.

SUMATI (Tib. Blo gros bzang) 須摩提 or 善意 The 2nd son of Tchandra sûrya pradîpa.

SUMATI DÂRIKÂ PARIPRITCHTCHHÂ. Title of 3 translations, viz. (1.) 佛說須摩提經 by Dharmarakcha, A.D. 265—316, (2.) 佛說須摩提菩薩經 by Kumâradjîva, A. D. 384—417 (3.) 妙慧童女會 by Bodhirutchi, A.D. 618—907.

SUMATIKRITI (Tib. Tsong khapa) 宗客巴 The reformer of the Tibetan church, founder of the 黃帽敎 Yellow Sect (A. D. 450), worshipped as an incarnation of Amitabha, now incarnate in every Bokdo gegen Chutuktu reigning in Mongolia. He received (A.D. 1426) the title 大寶法王 Mahâratna dharma râdja.

SUMÊRU or Mêru (Burm. Miem mo. Tib. Rirab Chunpo. Mong. Sûmmer Sola) 蘇迷盧 or 須彌樓 or 須彌妙高山 lit. mountain of wonderful height, or 好光 lit. good light. The central mountain or axis of every universe, the support of the tiers of heaven, surrounded by 7 concentric circles of rocks 金七山 and forming the centre round which all heavenly bodies revolve. It rises out of the ocean to a height of 84,000 yodjanas, but its total height is 168,000 yodjanas, as it rests immediately on the circular layer of earth, which, with its lower strata (a layer of water and a layer of wind), forms the foundation of every world. Its diameter is greatest where it emerges from the ocean, and at the top, but smallest in the middle. One side of it is formed of gold, the 2nd of silver, the 3rd of Lapis lazuli, the 4th of glass. It is covered with fragrant shrubs.

SUMÊRUGARBHA 大集須彌藏經 Title of a translation (A.D. 558) by Narendrayas'as.

SUMUNI 善寂 Author of the Sarvadharma ratnottara saṃgîtis'âstra 集諸法寶最上義論 translated (A. D. 980—1000) by Dânapâla.

SUNANDA or Sundarananda 孫陀羅(難陀) or 好愛 lit. lovely. Nanda, the husband of Sundara, so called in contradistinction from Ânanda.

SUNDARA 孫陀羅 (or 利) (1.) A Brahman who called S'âkyamuni a murderer. (2.) A king of Yakchas. (3.) The wife of Sunanda.

SÛNURIS'VARA 窣菟黎濕伐羅 The ancient capital of Lañgala.

S'ÛNYA or S'ûnyata (Pâli. Sunna. Tib. Stong panyid) 順牙 or 舜若多 or 空 lit. emptiness. The illusoriness and unreality of all phenomena, all existence being but like a dream, phantom, bubble, shadow, dew or lightning.

S'ÛNYAPURUCHPAS 空花 A heretical branch of the Mahâyâna School.

SUPANTA or Subanta s. a. Sumanta.

SUPRA BUDDHA (Singh. Supraboddha. Tib. Chin tu par legs rtogs pa) 善覺長者 lit. the virtuous and intelligent s'rêchṭhin. The father of Mahâmâyâ.

SUPRATICHṬHITA TCHÂRITRA 安立行 A Bodhisattva who rose out of the earth to salute S'âkyamuni.

SURÂ (Tib. Khambu) 窣羅 Rice brandy, as distinguished from Madja 末陀, wine of grapes.

SURÂCHṬRA 蘇剌咤 Ancient kingdom (Syrastrene) in Gujerat, now Surat.

SURÂMERÊYYA MADJDJA PAMÂDAṬṬHÂNÂ 不飲酒

Drink no wine. The 5th of the Pantcha veramaṇî and of the S'ikchapâda.

SÛRAÑGAMA SAMÂDHI 佛說首楞嚴三昧經 Title (sûrañ 健 lit. heroic, gana 相 lit. like) of a translatian (A.D. 384—417) by Kumâradjîva.

SURASKANDHA 修羅騫駄 or 廣肩 A king of Asuras.

SURATA PARIPRITCHTCHHÂ. Title of 2 translations, viz. (1.) 佛說須賴經 A.D. 220—265, and (2.) 善順菩薩會 by Bodhirutchi, A. D. 618—907.

SURES'VARA 自在王 A fabulous king contemporary of S'ikhin Buddha.

SURI 窣利 Ancient kingdom, W. of Kashgar, peopled (A. D. 600) by Turks.

SURUKÂYA 妙色身 A fictitious person; one of the Sapta Tathâgata.

SÛRYA (Pali. Suriya. Siam. Phra atithi. Tib. Nima) 蘇利耶 or 斯哩牙 or 蘇利耶提婆 (Sûryadêva) or 日天 lit. dêva of the sun. (1.) The sun (circumference 135 yodjanas, diameter 51 yodjanas), moving at the rate of 48,080 yodjanas a day, for 6 months in a more northerly and for 6 months in a more southerly direction. (2.) The regent of the sun "worshipped by heretics." (3.) The dêvas inhabiting the sun, where life lasts 500 years. (4.) A learned priest (A. D. 640) of the Mahâsaṃghikâḥ in Dhanakatchêka. (5.) Colocynth.

SÛRYAGARBHA SÛTRA 大乘大方等日藏經 Title of a translation (A. D. 565) by Narendrayas'as.

SÛRYARAS'MI 妙光佛 The 930th Buddha of the present kalpa.

SÛRYÂVARTA 日旋 A degree of Samâdhi.

SUSAṂBHAVA 善生 A former djâtaka of S'âkyamuni, as a king in the time of S'ikhin Buddha.

SUSIDDHIKÂRA SÛTRA 蘇悉地羯羅 A text book of the Tantra School, translated by S'ubhakarasiṃha, A. D. 724.

SUTCHINTI DÊVAPUTRA SÛTRA 須眞天子經 Title of a translation (A. D. 265—316) by Dharmarakcha.

SÛTRA (Pâli. Sûtta. Burm. Thoot. Tib. Mdo) 素怛纜 or 修多羅 or 修妒路 explained by 綫 lit. strung together (sûtra), or 籙書 lit. tablets, or 契書 lit. documents. Canonical writings (v. Sûtrapiṭaka), originally aphoristic, expanded in later years (v. Vaipulya sûtra), containing words of S'âkyamuni and generally begining with 如是我聞 lit. this is what I heard (Etanmayâ srutam).

SÛTRÂLAÑKÂRA S'ÂSTRA 大莊嚴經 A philosophical work by As'vaghocha, translated (A. D. 405) by Kumâradjîva.

SÛTRÂLAÑKÂRA ṬÎKÂ 大乘莊嚴經論 An exposition of the teachings of the Tantra School, by Asaṁgha, translated (A. D. 630—633) by Prabhâkaramitra.

SÛTRAPIṬAKA 素怛覽藏 or 藏經 lit. collection of sûtras. One of the Tripiṭaka (q. v.), the collection of all Sûtras (q. v.), forming the first division of the Chinese canon, andsdivided into Mahâyâna sûtras (大乘經), Hinâyâna sûtras (小乘經) and Sung or Yuen dynasty sûtras (宋元入藏諸大小乘經).

UTRICHNA or Satruchna or Osruchna or Uratippa 窣都利瑟那 Ancient city, between Kojend and Samarcand.

SUVARCHAKÂḤ 蘇跋梨柯部 or 遊梨沙部 or 蘇跋梨沙部 or 善歲部 lit. School of the good year. Another name for the Kâs'yapîyâḥ.

SUVARṆA (Pâli. Suvanna. Tib. Gser) 蘇伐剌 or 金 lit. gold. One of the Sapta ratna.

SUVARṆA BHUDJÊNDRA 金龍尊 A king; patron of the Suvarṇaprabhâsa.

SUVARṆA DHÂRAṆÎ 金總持 A (foreign?) S'ramaṇa, translator of several works.

SUVARṆAGOTRA 蘇伐剌拏瞿咀羅 or 金氏 lit. the golden family, or 女國 lit. kingdom of women. A kingdom, famous for minerals and for its throne succession confined to women (W. of Tibet. S. of Kustana. E. of Sampah),

S'UVARṆA PRABHÂSA. Title of 3 editions of a textbook of the Tantra School, viz. (1.) 金光明經 translated (A. D. 397—439) by Dharmarakcha, (2.) 金光明最勝王經 A. D. 703, (3.) 合部金光明經 a compilation of 3 incomplete translations, by Djñanagupta and others A.D. 597, by Paramârtha A. D. 552 and by Yas'ogupta A.D. 557—581.

SUVARṆA RAS'MI KUMÂRA SÛTRA 佛說金耀童子經 Title of a translation, A.D. 980—1301.

SUVARṆA SAPTATI S'ÂSTRA 金七十論 A (heretical) work by Kapila, explaining the 25 tattvas (v. Sâṁkhya); translated (A. D. 557—569) by Paramârtha.

SUVARṆA TCHAKRA 金輪 A golden disk which falls from heaven at the investiture of a Tchakravartti (q.v.) of the highest rank, who thereby becomes a 金輪王 Suvarṇa tchakra râdja.

SUVIKRÂNTA VIKRAMI SÛTRA 勝天王般若波羅蜜經 Translation (A. D. 565), by Upas'ûnya, of a portion of the Mahâpradjñâpâramitâ.

SUVIS'UDDHA 善淨 The future realm of Dharmaprabhâsa.

SVABHÂVAḤ 莎發斡 or 自性 lit. self existent nature. The original nature of beings, as the source of their existence. See Purucha.

SVABHAKÂYA s.a. Dharmakâya.

SVÂGATA or Sugata (Siam. Sukhato. Tib. Legs hongs) 沙婆揭多 or 莎(or 修)伽多 (or 度) or 修 (or 蘇 or 騷) 伽 (or 揭) 陁 (or 多) explained by 善來 lit. well come, or 善逝 lit. well departed. (1.) An unfortunate Arhat, "born on the road side," who had his name changed, by S'âkyamuni, to Durâgata, and is to re-appear as Samantaprabhâsa Buddha. (2.) A title of every Buddha, in the sense 讚歎 lit. one whose every sigh is praise, or 不迴 lit. one who is exempt (from transmigration), or 圓滿 lit. absolutely complete, or 圓事已畢 lit. one who has accomplished every good thing.

SVÂHÂ or Svadhâ (Tib. Gji srung) 娑訶 or 莎訶 or 莎曷 or 宿哈 or 娑縛賀 An exclamation, "may the race be perpetuated," used at ancestral (Brahmanic and Buddhist) sacrifices.

SVAPNA NIRDÊS'A 淨居天子會 Title of a translation (A.D. 265—316) by Dharmarakcha.

SVÂS'AYA 善樂 Name of a s'rêchṭhin, a contemporary of S'âkyamuni.

SVASTIKÂ (Pâli. Sotthika or Suvathika. Tib. Gyung drung or Gzagsang) 卐 or 塞縛悉底迦 or 穢佉阿悉底迦 or 寶悉底迦 explained by 吉祥萬德之所集 lit. accumulation of innumerable virtues in one lucky sign, or by 佛心印 lit. the symbol stamped on Buddha's heart.

(1.) A mystic diagram (the cross cramponee) of great antiquity, mentioned in the Ramâyaṇa, found in (rock temples of) India, in all Buddhist countries, among Bonpos and Buddhists in Tibet and China, and even among Teutonic nations (as the emblem of Thor) (2.) One of the 65 figures of the S'ripâda. (3.) The symbol of esoteric Buddhism. (4.) The special mark of all deities worshipped by the 蓮宗 Lotus School of China.

SVAYAMBHÛ 自然 lit. spontaneity. A philosophical term; the self-existent being.

SVAYAMBHÛ S'ÛNYATÂ 空自然 lit. emptiness and spontaneity. A philosophic term; the self-existence of the unreal.

SVAYAMBHUVAḤ (Tib. Rang byung) 自然成佛道 lit. the Mârga of automatic Buddhaship. The method of attaining independently to Buddhaship, without being taught.

S'VETAPURA 濕吠多補羅 A monastery near Vâis'âli.

S'VETAVARAS v. Aruna.

T.

TADJIKS 條支 An ancient tribe, once settled near lake Sirikol.

TÂGARA (Tib. Rgya spos) 多伽 (or 揭) 羅 explained by 根香 lit. root perfume, or by 木香 lit. putchuck. A tree, indigenous in Aṭali, from the wood of which incense is made; Vangueria spinosa or Tabernae montana coronaria.

TÂILA PARNIKA s. a. Tchanda nêva.

TAKCHAKA 德义迦 or 現毒 A king of Nâgas.

TAKCHAṆA 呾刹那 The 2,250th part of an hour.

TAKCHAS'ILÂ or Takcha sîra 呾义始羅 or Tchutya sîra 竺刹尸羅 or 家世國 Ancient kingdom and city (Taxila, now Sirkap near Shah dheri), where Buddha made an almsgift of his head.

TÂLA or Talavrikcha 多羅(樹). (1.) The fan palm, Borassus flabelliformis, or Lontarus domestica. (2.) A measure of length (70 feet).

TALAS or Taras 呾羅斯 (1.) Ancient city, 150 li W. of Mingbulak, in Turkestan. (2.) A river, issuing from lake Issikol and flowing N. W. into another lake.

TALEKÂN 呾刺健 Ancient kingdom and city (now Talekan, in Ghardjistan).

TALILA 達麗羅 or 陀歷 Ancient capital of Udyâna, (in the Dârel valley, occupied by Dards), famous for its statue of Maitreya.

TAMÂLA 多摩羅 An odoriferous shrub, Xanthochymus pictorius.

TAMÂLA PATRA 多摩羅跋 explained by 賢無垢 lit. sage-like and stainless, or by 藿葉香 Betonica officinalis. The leaf of the Laurus cassia, from which an ointment (malabathrum) was made.

TAMÂLA PATRA TCHAṆḌANA GANDHA 多摩羅跋旃檀香 explained by 性無垢 lit. stainless nature. (1.) A Buddha, residing N.W. of our universe, an incarnation of the 11th son of Mahâbhidjñadjñânâbhibhu. (2.) The name under which Mahâmâudgalyâyana is to reappear as Buddha in Manobhirâma during the kalpa Ratipûrṇa.

TÂMALIPTA or Tâmaliptî (Pâli. Tâmalitti) 多摩梨帝 or 呾(or 耽) 摩栗底 Ancient kingdom, and city (now Tamlook, at the mouth of the Hoogly), a centre of trade with Ceylon and China.

TAMAS 陰 (1.) The principle of darkness, the opposite of radjas 陽. (2.) Stupidity, the lowest of the 3 guna.

TÂMASAVANA 荅秣蘇伐那 or 闇林 lit. dark forest. A monastery, 50 li S E. of Tchînapati, at the junction of the Vipâs'a and S'atadru, perhaps identic with the Djâlandhara monastery in which the 4th synod (B. C. 153) was held.

TAMASTHITI 達摩悉鐵帝 Ancient province of Tukhâra (inhabited by ferocious tribes). See Kandat.

TÂMRÂPA 銅水 The 7th part of a S'as'orna.

TANMÂTRA 五行 Five elements, taught by the later Mahâyâna philosophy, viz., earth, water, fire, air and ether.

TANTRA 神變 Supernatural formulae, of mystic or magic efficacy, and necromantic books, taught by the Yogâtchârya School. See Upadês'a.

TANTRAYÂNA (Tib. Snags kyi theg pa) 大教 The Mahâtantra School, s. a. Yogâtchârya.

TAPANA (Siam. Dapha) 炎熱 or 燒炙獄 lit. the hell of burning or roasting. The 6th of the 8 large hot hells (v. Nâraka), where 24 hours are equal to 2600 years on earth, life lasting 16000 years.

TÂPASU TARU 道樹 The

tree of the ancient anchorites (Ingudî), or Sesamum orientale.

TAPASVÎ (Tib. Skah thub) 道師 Ascetics (Tauist or Buddhist) of all denominations.

TARA or Tair 多羅 S'âkyamuni, in a former djâtaka as a Bodhisattva.

TÂRÂ 陁羅 (Tib. Sgrol ma). (1.) Parvati, wife of Mahês'vara. (2.) Name of 2 goddesses of the Tantra School, known in the history of Tibet as the white and green Tara, incarnate in the 2 wives of Srongtsangampo. (3.) The planet Venus.

TARABHADRA v. Ârya, Târâbhadra.

TARAS v. Talas.

TARKA S'ÂSTRA 如實論 A work on dialectics by Vasubandhu, translated (A. D. 550) by Paramãrtha.

TATHÂGATA (Tib. De bjin gshegs ba. Mong. Toguntchilen ireksen) 怛他揭 (or 孽) 多 or 多陁阿伽度 or 怛闥阿竭 or 苔塔葛達 or 怛佗議多 or 如來 lit. one who (in coming into the world) is like the coming (of his predecessors). (1.) The highest epithet of a Buddha. See also Sapta Tathâgata. (2.) Abbreviation for Tathâgatagupta.

TATHÂGATA DJÑÂNA MUDRÂ SÛTRA. Title of 3 translations, viz., (1.) 佛說慧印三昧經 A .D. 222—280, (2.) 佛說如來智印經 A. D. 420—479, (3.) 佛說大乘智印經 by Djñânas'rî, A.D. 1053.

TATHÂGATA GARBHA SÛTRA Title of 2 translations, viz., (1.) 大方廣如來秘密藏經 A. D. 350—431, (2) 大方等如來藏經 by Buddha bhadra, A. D. 317—420.

TATHÂGATA GUṆA DJNÂÑÂTCHINTYA VICHAYÂVATARA NIRDÊS'A. Title of 2 translations, viz., (1.) 佛說嚴入如來德智不思議境界經 by Djñânagupta, A. D. 589—618, and (2.) 大方廣入如來智德不思議經 by S'ikchânanda, A.D. 618—907.

TATHÂGATAGUPTA 怛他揭多毱多 or 如來護 lit. the guardina Tathâgata. (1.) A king of Magadha, son of Buddhagupta, grandson of S'akráditya. (2.) A learned priest (A. D. 640) of the Sarvâstivâdâḥ, in Hiranyaparvata.

TATHÂGATA MAHÂKÂRUNIKA NIRDÊS'A 大哀經 Translation (A. D. 291) by Dharmarakcha of the first two chapters of the 大方等

大集經 Mahâvaipulya mahâsannipâta sûtra, translated (A.D. 397—439) by the same.

TATHÂGATA SYÂNTIKE DUCHṬATCHITTA RUDHI ROTPÂDANA 瀉佛血 lit. shedding the blood of a Buddha. The 5th of the Pantchânantarya.

TATHÂGATA TCHINTYA GUHYA NIRDÊS'A. Title of 2 translations, viz., (1.) 密跡金剛力士會 by Dharmarakcha, A.D. 280, and (2.) 佛說如來不思議秘密大乘經, another Dharmarakcha, A.D. 1004—1058.

TATTVA SATYA S'ÂSTRA 怛埵三第鑠論 or 辯論 A philosophical work by Guṇaprabha.

TCHADJ 赭時 or 石國 Ancient city (now Tashkend) in Turkestan.

TCHAGAYANA 赤鄂衍那 Ancient province and city (now Chaganian) in Tukhâra.

TCHÂITRA 制呾羅 First month in spring.

TCHAITYA (Pâli. Tchetiya. Burm. Dzedi. Tib. Mchod rten) 脂帝浮圖 or 支提 or 支帝 or 制多 or 刹 or 塔 or 廟 (1.) A place (with or without some monument) sacred as the scene of some event in the life of Buddha. Eight such Tchaityas existed, viz. at Lumbinî, Buddha-gayâ-Vârânas'i, Djetavana, Kaṇyakubdja, Râdjagriha, Vais'ali; and the Sâla grove in Kus'inagara. (2.) All places and objects of worship.

TCHAITYA PRADAKCHINA GÂTHÂ 佛說右繞佛塔功德經 Title of a translation (A.D. 618-907) by S'ikchânanda.

TCHAKAS 赭羯 A warlike tribe near Samarkand.

TCHAKCHUR (Pâli. Tchakkhun) 眼 lit. the eye. The first Chaḍâyatana, the eye as an organ of sensation; hence Tchakchur dhâtu, 眼界, the faculty of sight, and Tchakchur vidjñâna dhâtu, 眼識界, perception by sight, the first Vidjñâna.

TCHAKCHUR VIS'ODHANA VIDYÂ 佛說咒目經 Title of a translation (A. D. 317—420) by Dharmarakcha.

TCHAKRA (Tib. Khor lo 撌祴羅 or 斫迦羅 or 輪 lit. a wheel. (1.) The symbol of a Tchakravartti, a disk (according to his rank) either of gold or copper or iron, which falls from heaven on his investiture; originally a symbol of destruction; later a symbol of divine authority. (2.) One of the figures of the S'rîpâda.

TCHAKRAVÂLA (Singh. Sakwalagala. Siam. Chakravan Tib. Hkor yug) 斫迦羅 or 拘羯羅 or 鐵圍山 or 輪圍山 A double circle of mountains (one higher than the other) forming the outer periphery of every universe and running concentric with the 7 circles (see under Mêru) between which and the Tchakravâla the 4 continents are situated.

TCHAKRA VARTTI RÂDJA (Burm. Tsekia wade. Tib. Hkor los sgyur bai) 斫 (or 遮) 迦羅伐辣底羯羅闍 or 遮迦越羅 explained by 輪王 lit. Tchakra râdja, or by 轉輪聖王 lit. the holy king who turns the wheel (Tchakra.) A military conqueror of the whole or a portion of a universe, whose symbol is the Tchakra (q. v.), and who is inferior to Buddha who, as a Dharma tchakra vartti, uses the Dharma tchakra (q. v.) to convert the world.

TCHAKUKA 所 (or 折) 句迦 Ancient kingdom and city (now Yerkiang) in Bokhara.

TCHAMADHANA 拆摩馱那 or 涅末 (Nimat). Ancient kingdom and city, on S. E. border of Gobi desert.

TCHÂMARA 苫末羅 A tree "which grows on the sea-shore in the West, the resort of birds with gold-coloured wings and spotted yellow plumage."

TCHAMPÂ 瞻波 Ancient kingdom and city (now Champanagur, near Boglipoor) in Central India.

TCHAMPAKA 旃簸迦 or 瞻蔔 (加) or 瞻博 (or 波) (1.) A tree with fragrant flowers, Michelia champaca. (2.) A district in the upper Pundjab.

TCHAṆḌANA (Tib. Tsandan) 旃檀 General appellation for sandal wood (used for incense, etc.) and divided into Rakta tchaṇḍana 赤檀 lit. red sandal wood. or Pterocarpus santolinus, Tchaṇḍanêva (q.v.) and Gos'ircha (q.v.).

TCHAṆḌANÊVA or Sarpa hridaya tchaṇḍana or Uragasâra 旃檀你婆. White sandal wood or Sandalum album.

TCHANDRA or Tchandradêva (Siam. Phra chan. Tib. Zlava) 旃 (or 戰) 達羅 or 旃達提婆 or 月天 lit. dêva of the moon. (1.) Soma dêva, the regent of the moon which is said to be 50 yodjanas in diameter and 132 in circumference. (2.) The dêvas inhabiting the moon, where life lasts 500 years.

TCHANDRA BHÂGÂ 旃達羅婆伽 or 月分 The river

Chenab (Acesines) in the Pundjab.

TCHANDRA DÎPA SAMÂDHI SÛTRA 月燈三昧經 Title of a translation (A. D. 557) by Narendrayas'as.

TCHANDRA GARBHA VAIPULYA SÛTRA 大方等大集月藏經 Title of a translation (A. D. 566) by Narendrayas'as.

TCHANDRAKÂNTA 月愛珠 A pearl which sheds tears in the moonlight.

TCHANDRAKÎRTI see under Dêva.

TCHANDRAPÂLA 護月 A learned priest of Nâlanda.

TCHANDRA PRABHA 戰達羅鉢刺婆 or 月光 lit. moonlight. S'âkyamuni, in a former djâtaka, when he cut off his head (at Tackchas'ilâ) as an alms offering to Brahmans.

TCHANDRA PRABHA BODHISATTVÂVADANA SÛTRA 佛說月光菩薩經 Title of a translation (A. D. 973–981 by Dharmadêva.

TCHANDRA PRABHASVARA RÂDJA 月明燈明 The name under which 20,000 koṭis of beings attained to Buddhaship.

TCHANDRA SIM̃HA 旃陀羅僧訶 or 月獅子 lit. lunar lion. A native of Central India, school fellow of Sim̃haras'mi.

TCHANDRA SURYA PRADIPA or Tchandrárkadipa 日月燈明 A name given to several Buddhas, one of whom was the father of Mati, Sumati, Autanamati, Ratnamati, Vis'êchamati, Vimatisamudghâtin, Ghochamati and Dharmamati.

TCHANDRAVARMA 旃達羅伐摩 or 月胃 A learned priest of Nâgarandhana.

TCHANDRA VIMALASÛRYA PRABHÂSACHI 日月淨明德 A Buddha whose realm resembles Sukhavatî.

TCHANDROTTARÂ DÂRIKÂ VYÂKARAṆA SÛTRA 月上女經 Title of a translation (A. D. 591) by Djñâna gupta.

TCHANGKRAMANA or Tchangkramasthâna (Pâli. Tchankama. Burm. Yatana zengyan) 經行禪窟 Raised platforms or corridors for peripatetic meditation, sometimes built of costly stones (Ratna tchangkrama) after the model of the Bodhimaṇḍa.

TCHAÑS'TCHA (Pâli. Tchintchi) 戰庶摩那 or 戰庶 A Brahman girl who, calumniating Buddha at the instigation of Tirthyas, was swallowed up by hell.

TCHAÑS'UṆA 占戍挐 The ancient capital of Vridji.

TCHARITRA 拆利怛羅 or 發行城 lit. city of departure. A port, on S.E. frontier of Uḍa, for trade with Ceylon.

TCHARYÂMÂRGABHÛMI SÛTRA 修行道地經 A work by Saṁgharakcha, translated (A. D. 284) by Dharmarakcha.

TCHATURABHIDJÑAS 四神足 Four of the 6 Abhidjñas (q. v.).

TCHATURAÑGA BALA KÂYA 四兵 The 4 divisions of an Indian army, viz. Hastikâya, elephant corps; As'vakâya, cavalry; Rathakâya, chariots; Pattikâya, infantry.

TCHATUR ARÛPA BRAHMA LOKA or Arûpa dhâtu 四空天 lit. 4 heavens of unreality. The 4 heavens of the Arûpa dhâtu (above the 18 Brahmalokas), viz, (1.) Akâs'ânantâyatana (Singh. Akasananchayatana) 空(無邊)處 lit. dwelling in (unlimited) unreality; (2.) Vidjñânânantâyatana (Sing. Winyananchayatana) 識(無邊)處 lit. dwelling in (unlimited) knowledge; (3.) Akintchanyâyatana (Singh. Akinchannyayatana) 無(所有)處 lit. dwelling in (absolute) non-existence; (4.) Naivasañdjñana sañdjñâyatana (Singh. Newasannya nasannyayatana) 非想非非想處 lit. a dwelling (or state of mind) where there is neither consciousness nor unconsciousness. Life lasts 20,000 great kalpas in the 1st, 40,000 in the 2nd, 60,000 in the 3rd and 80,000 in the 4th of these heavens. See also under Vimokcha.

ACHATURDVÎPA 四洲 The 4 continents of every universe, situated between As'vakarna (q. v.) and the Tchakravâlas, and facing each a different side of the Mêru. Two small islands are attached to each continent. Particulars see under Pûrvavidêha, Djambudvîpa, Godhanya, and Uttarakusu.

TCHATUR LABHA SÛTRA 四不可得經 Title of a translation (A. D. 265—316) by Dharmarakcha.

TCHATURMAHÂRÂDJAS (Pâli. Tchatur Maharajika. Tib. Rgya tschen bjihi rigs. Mong. Macharansa) 四大(天)王 Four demon kings, who guard the world (v. Lokapâla) against Asuras; placed each on one side of the Mêru and watching each one quarter of the heavens. Amogha introduced their worship in China, where their images adorn the temple gates. Particulars see under Dhritarâchṭra, Virûḍhaka, Virûpâkcha and Dhanada.

TCHATUR MAHÂRÂDJA KÂYIKAS 四王天 lit. the dêvas of the Tchatur Mahârâdjas. The inhabitants of the 1st Dêvaloka, situated on the 4 sides of the Mêru. They form the retinue of the Tchatur Mahârâdjas, each of whom has 91 sons and is attended by 8 generals and 28 classes of demons. Life lasts there 500 years, but 24 hours, there, equal 50 years on earth.

TCHATUR SATYA S'ÂSTRA 四諦論 A philosophical work by Vasuvarman, translated (A. D. 557—569) by Paramârtha.

TCHATURYONI or Karmaya (Singh. Karmaja. Tib. Skye ba bzi) 四生 lit. 4 (modes of) birth. Four modes of entering the course of transmigration, viz., (1.) 胎生 (Tib. Mnal las) from an uterus, as mammalia, (2.) 卵生 (Tib. Sgo na las) from an egg, as birds, (3.) (濕生 Tib. Drod gser las) from moisture, as fish and insects, (4.) (化生 Tib. Rdzus to) by transformation, as Bodhisattvas. See also Anupapâdaka.

TCHATUS SATYA SÛTRA 佛說四諦經 Translation (A.D. 25—220) of a portion of the Madhyamâgama.

TCHATVARA SÛRYAS 四日 lit. the 4 suns. The 4 luminaries of the ancient Buddhist church, viz. As'vaghocha, Dêva, Nâgârdjuna and Kumâralabdha.

TCHATVARI SAÑGRAHA VASTUNI 四攝法 lit. 4 methods of pacification. Four social virtues, viz. (1.) Dâna 布施 almsgiving, (2.) Priyavatchana 愛語 loving speech, (3.) Arthakriya 利行 conduct which benefits (others), and (4.) Samanarthata 同事 co-operation (with and for others).

TCHHANḌAKA (Singh. Channa. Burm. Tsanda. Tib. Hdun pa tchan). 闡擇 (or 鐸 or 釋)迦 or 車匿 S'âkyamuni's coachman.

TCHHANḌÂLA (Tib. Gdol pa) 旃陀(or 荼)羅 explained by 屠刹者 lit. butchers, or by 惡人 lit. wicked people, or by 嚴幟 lit. (those who have to carry) a warning flag. The lowest, most despised, caste of India, but admitted to the priesthood in the Buddhist church.

TCHHANDA RIDDHI PÂDA (Singh. Tchandidhi pada) 欲足 lit. the step of desire. Renunciation of all desire, as the 1st condition of supernatural power. See Riddhipâda.

TCHHATRA PATI v. Djambudvîpa.

TCHÊKA 磔迦 Ancient kingdom (near Umritsir) in the Pundjab.

TCHIKDHA 擲枳多 Ancient kingdom and city (now Chittore) in Central India.

TCHIKITSA VIDYÂ S'ÂSTRA 醫方明 lit. illustration of medicine. A treatise on magic prescriptions, one of the Pañtcha Vidya s'âstras.

TCHÎNA or Mahâ tchîna (Tib. Rgya nag) 支那 or 指那 or 震旦 or 眞丹 explained by 思惟 lit. reflection. The name by which China is referred to in Buddhist books, since the Ts'in (秦) dynasty (B. C. 349—202).

TCHÎNADÊVAGOTRA 指那提婆瞿怛羅 or 漢日天種 lit. the solar deva of Han descent. The first king of Khavanda, born, through the influence of the solar genius, of a princess of the Han dynasty (B.C. 206—A.D. 220) on the way, as bride elect, to Persia.

TCHÎNÂNI 至那你 explained by 漢持來 lit. brought from China. The Indian name for the peach tree.

TCHÎNAPATI 至那僕底 Ancient kingdom (near Lahore), whose first kings were said (A.D. 640) to have come from China.

TCHÎNARÂDJAPUTRA 至那羅闍弗怛羅 or 漢王子 lit. prince of the Han (dynasty). Indian name for the pear tree (as imported from China).

TCHITRASÊNA 質怛羅細那 A king of Yakchas.

TCHITTA RIDDHI PÂDA (Singh. Tchittipada) 念足 lit. the step of memory. Renunciation of memory, as the 3rd condition of supernatural power. See Riddhipâda.

TCHITTA SMRITY UPASTHÂNA (Singh. Tchittanupada) 念心生滅無常 lit. keeping in mind that birth and death continue incessantly. One of the 4 objects of Smrity upasthâna, recollection of the transitory character of existence.

TCHÎVARA 支伐羅 A dyed, red garment; s. a. Kachâya.

TCHULYA or Tchaula 珠利耶 Ancient kingdom (N.E. of Madras), peopled (A. D. 640) by semi-savage heretics.

TCHUNDA (1.) 周陀 or 大路邊生 lit. born on the road

side. One of the earliest disciples of S'âkyamuni, to be reborn as Buddha Samanta prabhâsa. (2.) 準(or 純)陀 A native of Kus'inagara from whom S'âkyamuni accepted his last meal.

TCHUNDI 準提 (1.) In Brahmanic mythology, a vindictive form of Durga or Parvarti. (2.) Among Chinese Buddhists identified with Mârîtchi.

TCHUNDÎ DEVÎ DHÂRAṆÎ. Title of 3 translations, viz., (1.) 佛說七俱胝佛母心大準提陀羅尼經 by Divâkara, A. D. 685, (2.) 佛說七俱胝佛母準提大明陀羅尼經 by Vadjrabodhi, A. D. 720, (3.) 七俱胝佛母所說準提陀羅尼經 by Amoghavadjra, A. D. 618—907.

TEMURTU or Issikol 清池 or 熱海 Mongol name of a lake (400 li N. of Lingshan).

TERMED or Tirmez 咀蜜 Ancient kingdom and city on the Oxus.

TICHYA (Singh. Tissa. Tib. Pd ldan) 至沙 or 帝沙 (1.) An ancient Buddha. (2.) A native of Nâlanda, father of S'âriputra. (3.) A son of S'uklodana.

TICHYA RAKCHITÂ 帝失羅叉 A concubine of As'oka, the rejected lover and therefore enemy of Kuṇâla.

TILADHÂKA or Tilas'âkya 低羅擇(or 釋)迦 A monastery (now Thelari, near Gayâ), W. of Nâlanda.

TIÑANTA or Tryanta 底彥多 Verbs (according to Pâṇini).

TÎRTHAKAS or Tirthyas (Tib. Mustegs tchah) 外道師 lit. heretical teachers. (1.) General designation of Brahmanic and other non-Buddhist ascetics. (2.) Brahmanic enemies of S'âkyamuni, and especially the following six (外道六師), Puraṇa Kâs'yapa, Maskarin, Saṁdjayin, Adjita Kes'akambala, Kakuda Kâtyâyana, and Nirgrantha. Hiuentsang met (A. D. 640) a sect of Tirthyas, who practised austere asceticism, worshiped Kchuṇa and used magic spells for healing the sick.

TOKSUN 篤進 A city in Mongolia.

TRAIDHATUKÊ 三界第一 The circumference of the Trâiloka.

TRAILOKYA or Trilokya (Siam. Traiphum. Tib. Khams gsum) 得羅盧迦 or 三界 lit. 3 regions, or 三有 lit. 3 classes of beings. In imitation of the Brahmanic Bhuvanatraya (4 worlds), the Buddhists divide every universe into 3 regions, but substitute for the physical categories (Bhur or earth, Bhuvah or heaven, and Svar or atmosphere) of the Brahmans, the ethical categories of desire, form and formlessness. Particulars see under Kâmadhâtu, Rûpadhâtu, and Arûpadhâtu.

TRAILOKYA VIKRAMIN 越三界菩薩 Name of a fictitious Bodhisattva.

TRAIYASTRIMS'AS (Pâli. Tavatinsa. Singh. Tavutisa. Siam. Davadung. Tib. Sum tchu rtas gsum) 多羅夜登陵舍 or 怛利夜登陵奢 or 怛利耶怛利奢 or 怛利天 or 三十三天 lit. 33 dêvas, or the heaven of 33 (cities or beings). (1.) The 33 ancient gods of the Vêdas, viz. 8 Vasus, 11 Rudras, 12 Âdityas and 2 As'vins. (2.) Indra with 32 worthies who were his friends in a former djâtaka, when he was 憍尸迦 Kaus'ika all having been reborn on the summit of Mêru. (3.) The heaven of Indra (s. a. the Svarga of Brahmanism), situated between the 4 peaks of Mêru. It consists of 32 cities of dêvas, (8 of which are located on each of the 4 corners of Mêru) and of the capital 善見城 (Sudassana or Umravati), where, in the palace Vaiayanta 禪延 or 毗闍(or 禪)延 Indra (having 1000 heads, 1000 eyes and 4 arms grasping the Vadjra) revels with Sakchi and 119,000 concubines, and receives monthly the reports of the Tchatur Mahârâdjas. Chinese books frequently identify or confound this heaven with Tuchita (q.v.).

TRICHNÂ (Singh. Trisnâwa. Tib. Sredma) 愛 lit. love Pure love; the 4th Nidâna.

TRIDJÑÂNA 三慧 Three modes of knowledge, viz. belief, hearing and practice.

TRIDJÑÂNA SÛTRA 三慧經 Title of a translation, A. D. 397—439.

TRIKÂYA Tib. Skugsum) 三身 lit. 3 bodies, or threefold embodiment. (1.) Three representations of Buddha, viz. his statue, his teachings, and his stûpa (q. v.) (2.) The historical Buddha, as uniting in himself 3 bodily qualities, see Dharmakâya, Sambhogakâya and Nirmanakâya. (3.) Buddha, as having passed through, and still existing in, 3 forms or persons, viz. (a.) as 釋迦牟尼千百億化身 "S'âkyamuni (or earthly Buddha, endowed with the) Nirmanakâya (which passed through) 100,000 koṭis of transformations" (on earth);

(b.) as 盧舍那圓滿報身 "Lochana (or heavenly Dhyâni Bodhisattva, endowed with the) Sambhoga kâya of absolute completeness" (in Dhyâna); (c.) as 毗盧蔗那清淨法身 "Vairotchana (or Dhyâni Buddha, endowel with the) Dharmakâya of absolute purity" (in Nirvâṇa). In speaking of Buddha as now combining the foregoing (historically arranged) persons or forms of existence, the order here given is, of course, reversed. As to how this doctrine arose, we can only guess. Primitive Buddhism (in China) distinguished a material, visible and perishable body (色身 or rûpa kâya) and an immaterial, invisible and immortal body (法身 or dharma kâya), as attributes of human existence. This dichotomism—probably taught by S'âkyamuni himself—was even afterwards retained in characterizing the nature of ordinary human beings. But in later ages, when the combined influence of Shivaism, which ascribed to Shiva a threefold body (Dharmakâya, Sambhogakâya and Nirmana kâya) and Brahminism, with its Trimurti (of Brahma, Vishnu and Shiva), gave rise to the Buddhist dogma of a Triratna (Buddha, Dharma and Saṅgha), trichotomism was taught with regard to the nature of all Buddhas. Bodhi 覺 being the characteristic of a Buddha, a distinction was now made of "essential Bodhi" 覺性 as the attribute of the Dharmakâya, "reflected Bodhi" 覺相 as the attribute of the Sambhoga kâya, and "practical Bodhi" 覺用 as the attribute of the Nirmana kâya; and Buddha, combining in himself these 3 conditions of existence, was said to be living, at the same time, in 3 different spheres, viz. (1.) as "having essentially entered Nirvâṇa," being as such a Dhyâni Buddha, living in Arûpadhâtu in the Dharmakâya state of essential Bodhi, (2.) as "living in reflex in Rûpa dhâtu" and being, as such, in the intermediate degree of a Dhyâni Bodhisattva in the Sambhoga kâya state of reflected Bodhi, and (3.) as "living practically in Kâmadhâtu," in the elementary degree of a Manuchi Buddha in the Nirmana kâya state of practical Bodhi. In each of these 3 forms of existence, Buddha has a peculiar mode of existence, viz., (1.) absolute purity as Dhyâni Buddha, (2.) absolute completeness as Dhyâni Bodhisattva, and (3.) numberless transformations as Manuchi Buddha. Likewise also Buddha's influence has a different sphere in each of these 3 forms of existence, viz., (1.) as Dhyâni Buddha he rules in the "domain of the spiritual" (4th Buddha kchêtra), (2.) as Dhyâni Bodhisattva he rules in the "domain of success" (3rd Buddha kchêtra), and (3.) as "Manuchi Buddha he rules in the domain of mixed qualities" (1st and 2 d Buddhakchêtra). There is clearly the idea of a unity in trinity underlying these distinctions and thus the dogmas of the Trailokya, Trikâya and the Triratna (q. v.) are interlinked, as the subjoined synoptic table shews in detail.

TRIPIṬAKA (Pâli. Pitakattaya. Singh. Tunpitaka. Tib. Sde snod gsum. Mong. Gourban aimak saba) 三藏 lit. 3 collections. The three divisions (in imitation of the Brahmanic distinction of Mantras, Brahmanas and Sûtras) of the Buddhist canon, viz., (1.) doctrinal books, v. Sûtras, (2.) works on ecclesiastical discipline, v. Vinaya, and (3.) philosophical works, v. Abhidharma. Chinese Buddhists added a fourth class of miscellaneous, canonical works (v. Samyukta piṭaka). The principal Chinese editions of the complete Buddhist canon are the 南藏 Southern collection, Nanking, A. D. 1368—1398, and the 北藏 Northern collection, Peking, A. D. 1403—1424.

Synoptical Scheme of the Triratna, Trikâya and Trailokya.

Dharma	Samgha	Buddha
Essential Bodhi	Reflected Bodhi	Practical Bodhi
Vairotchana	Lochanâ	S'âkyamuni
Dhyâni Buddha	Dhyâni Bodhisattva	Manuchi Buddha
Dharmakâya	Sambhogakâya	Nirmanakâya
Purity	Completeness	Transformations
4th Buddha-kchêtra	3rd Buddha-kchêtra	1st and 2nd Buddha-kchêtra
Ârûpadhâtu	Rûpadhâtu	Kâmadhâtu

TRIRATNA or Ratnatraya (Siam. Ratanatrai. Tib. Dkon mtchog gsum) 三寶 lit. the 3 precious ones, explained by 佛寶法寶僧寶 lit. the preciousness of Buddha, the law and the priest-hood, or by 佛陀 or 勃塔耶 Buddha, 達摩 or 達而麻耶 Dharma, and 僧伽 or 桑渴耶 Saṁgha. Triratna signifies the doctrine of a trinity, which, peculiar to Northern Buddhism, has its root in the Tris'araṇa (q. v.), common among Southern and Northern Buddhists. Under the combined influence of Brahmanism which taught a Trimurti (Brahma, Vishnu and Shiva) and of the later Mahâyâna philosophy which taught the doctrine of the Trikâya (q.v.), Northern Buddhists in Tibet and China ascribed to one living personality the attributes of the three constituents (Tris'araṇa) of their faith, viz. Buddha, Dharma and Saṁgha, considering "Bodhi" as the common characteristic of the historic Buddha, of the law which he taught and of the corporate priesthood which now represents both. Accordingly they viewed S'âkyamuni Buddha as personified Bodhi (覺性), Dharma as reflected Bodhi (覺相), and Saṁgha as practical Bodhi (覺用). The Tantra School (A. D. 500) then spoke of these three as united in one (the Dhyâni or Nirvâṇa form of S'âkyamuni). This School was particularly influenced by Nepaulese Buddhism and by its doctrine of a triple existence of each Buddha as Nirvâṇa Buddha, Dhyâni Buddha and Manuchi Buddha. Accordingly S'âkyamuni was now simply spoken of as personified Bodhi, i. e. as "Buddha," but as one, who in passing from this world, left behind him the reflex of his Bodhi in "Saṁgha" i. e. in the corporate existence of the Buddhist church as represented by the priesthood whilst he is now living in Nirvâṇa as the perpetual fountain source of "Dharma" i. e. the doctrines of Buddhism. Thus Buddha, Saṁgha and Dharma were viewed synthetically as three progressive stages in the development of Bodhi through the person of Buddha, to whom separate names were given corresponding to these stages, viz. S'âkyamuni corresponding with Buddha, Lochana corresponding with Saṁgha, and Vairotchana corresponding with Dharma (see under Trikâya). Next came atheistic philosophy which dealt with this dogma of a Triratna analytically, placing Dharma in the first rank as the first element in the trinity from which the others proceeded by evolution.

According to these philosophical Schools, "Dharma" is not a person, but an unconditioned and underived entity, combining in itself the spiritual and material principles of the universe, whilst from Dharma proceeded, by emanation, "Buddha" as the creative energy which produced, in conjunction with Dharma, the third factor in the trinity, viz. "Saṁgha," which is the comprehensive sum total of all real life. Thus the dogma of a Triratna, originating from three primitive articles of faith, and at one time culminating in the conception of three persons, a trinity in unity, has degenerated into a metaphysical theory of the evolution of three abstract principles. The common people, however, know nothing of this philosophical Triratna, but worship a triad of statues, representing either Amitabha with Avalokitês'vara and Mahasthama, or S'âkyamuni with Avalokites'vara and Maitreya, and calling the latter triad, "the Buddha of the past, present and future."

TRIRATNÂRYA 三寶尊 An Indian Bodhisattva, author of a commentary on the 佛母般若波羅蜜多圓集要義論 Buddha mâtrika pradjñâpâramitâ mahârtha saṁghiti s'âstra by Mahâdignâga.

TRIS'AMBARA NIRDÊS'A 三律儀會 The first sûtra of the Mahâratnakûṭa collection; a translation (A.D. 618—907) by Bodhirutchi.

TRIS'ARAṆA (Pâli. Saranagamana. Burm. Tharanagon. Tib. Mtchio gsum) 三歸 lit. 3 ret fuges. The ancient Buddhisformula fidei, viz. (1.) 歸依佛 lit. I take refuge in Buddha, (2.) 歸依法 I take refuge in Dharma, and (3.) 歸依僧 I take refuge in Saṁgha. Out of these articles of faith, the dogma of the Triratna (q. v.) may have arisen.

TRIVIDHA DVÂRA 三門 or 三業 lit. 3 gates professions (sc. body, mouth and mind). Purity of body, of speech and of thought. See S'îla.

TRIVIDYÂ 三明(智) lit. 3 clear (conceptions). Three elementary axioms, viz. (1.) Anitya 無常 lit. impermanency (of all existence), (2.) Dukha, 苦 lit. misery (as the lot of all beings), (3.) Anâtmâ 身如泡沫 lit. bodily existence as unreal as a bubble.

TRIYÂNA (Siam. Trai pidok) 三乘 or 三車之教 or 三乘法門 (1.) Three vehicles (sc. across Saṅsâra into Nirvâṇa), (a.) sheep, i.e. S'ravakas (b.) deer, i.e. Pratyêka

Buddhas, (c.) oxen, i. e. Bodhisattvas; salvation by three successive degrees of saintship. (2.) The three principal Schools of Buddhism, viz. the Mahâyâna, Hinâyâna and Madhyimâyâna Schools.

TSÂUKÛTA 漕矩吒 Ancient (Arachotos) kingdom in N.W. India (near Ghuznee).

TUCHITA (Singh. Tusita. Burm. Toocita. Siam. Dusit. Tib. Dga ldan. Mong. Tegiis bajasseno laugtu) 兜率陀 or 兜術(陀) or 兜師(or 駛 or 史)多 or 覩史多 (or 陀) explained by 喜樂 lit. joyful, or by 聚集 lit. assembly. The 4th Devaloka, where all Bodhisattvas are reborn before finally appearing on earth as Buddha. Maitreya resides there, but is, like all other Bodhisattvas, now in Tuchita, already engaged in promoting Buddhism, and occasionally appears on earth by the Anupapadaka birth. Life lasts in Tuchita, 400 years, 24 hours being equal to 400 years on earth.

TUKHARA 兜佉勒 or 覩貨羅 or 月支國 lit. the kingdom of the Yueh-chi (Getae). (1.) The region around Badakchan. (2.) The Tochari Tartars. See Kanichka.

TYÂGÎHRADA or Djivakahrada 烈士池 lit. the heroe's lake. A lake near Mrigadava.

U.

UCHṆÎCHA (Tib. Gtsug tor or Thor tchog) 烏 (or 鬱) 失 (or 瑟)尼沙 or 烏瑟膩沙 explained by 肉髻 lit. a coiffure of flesh or by 佛頂骨 lit. Buddhôchṇicha (q. v.), with the note "a fleshy protuberance on Buddha's cranium, forming a natural hairtuft." Originally a conical or flame-shaped hairtuft on the crown of a Buddha, in later ages represented as a fleshy excrescence on the skull itself; one of the 23 Lakchaṇas. See Sarvadurgati, etc.

UḌA or Utkala or Udradesa 烏茶 Ancient kingdom (now Orissa) in India.

UDAGAYANA 北行 lit. (the sun) moving northwards. See under Sûrya.

UḌAKHÂṆḌA 烏鐸迦漢茶 Ancient capital (Embolina, now Ohind N. E. of Attok) of Gandhâra.

UDÂNA 鬱(or 優)陀那 or 烏枕南 explained by 無問自說 lit. (unasked) impromptue discourses. Sûtras, differing in form from ordinary Sûtras (in which the subject matter is introduced by a question addressed to Buddha).

UDAYANA RÂDJA (Tib. Htch

arpo) 烏陀衍那 or 優塡 or 出愛王 A king of Kâu-s'ambi, entitled 弗少王 Vatsarâdja, said to have had the first statue of Buddha made. But see under Prasenadjit and S'âkyamuni.

UDAYANA VATSARÂDJA PARIPRITCHTCHHÂ. Title of 3 translations, viz. (1.) 佛說優塡王經 A. D. 265—316, (2.) 優陀延王會 by Bodhirutchi, A. D. 618—907, and (3.) 佛說大乘日子王所問經.

UDÂYI or Udayibhadra 優陀夷 or 出現 lit. (born when) the sun shone forth. (1.) A disciple of S'âkyamuni, to be reborn as Buddha Samantaprabhâsa. (2,) A son of Adjâtas'atru, also called Siṁha.

UDITA 烏地多 A king in N. India, who patronized Hiuen-tsang (A.D. 640).

UDJDJAYANA. or Udjdjayini 優禪尼 or 烏闍衍那 Ancient kingdom and city (Ozene, now Oujein) in W. India.

UDJDJAYANTA 有善多 A mountain (with a monastery) in Surâchṭra.

UDJIKAN v. Hudjikan.

UDYÂNA or Udjiyâna 烏耆延那 or 烏杖烏 or 烏(孫)場 or 烏萇(or 長) explained by 苑 lit. (a country of) parks. Ancient kingdom (Suastene) in N. W. India, along the S'ubhavastu. Some identify it with Urdhastâna.

UDRA RÂMA PUTRA or Udraka or Rudraka (Tib. Rangs byed kyi bu Lhag spyod) 鬱陀羅摩子 or 鬱頭藍子 lit. Udra the son of Rama. A Brahman, for a time teacher of S'âkyamuni.

UDUMBARA 優曇鉢羅 or Nila udumbara 尼羅優曇鉢羅 explained by 靈瑞 lit. a supernatural omen. (1.) The Ficus glomerata, symbol of Buddha because "it flowers but once in 3000 years," sometimes confounded with Panasa. (2.) A lotus of fabulous size.

UIGURS 偽彝 or 偽胡 The Turkish tribe of 高車 or 高昌 Kao-chang, settled (A. D. 649) near Turfan, then (A. D. 750) divided into 2 branches (Abhulgasi and Tokus Uigurs) which (A. D. 1000) invaded Tangut but were driven westward by Chinghis Khan. He adopted their alphabet (probably of Nestorian origin), which was even tually used to translate (A.D. 1294) the whole Buddhist canon from Sanskrit and Tibetan texts.

ULAG 烏落 A Tibetan (or Uigur) term for compulsory post (socage) service, supply of porters and beasts of burden for travelling officials and priests (in Mongolia and Tibet).

ULLAMBANA 烏藍婆(拏) explained by 倒懸 lit. hung up by the heels (?), or 盂蘭 or 盂蘭盆 explained by 貯食之器 lit. a utensil to pile up (offerings of) food. The festival of all souls (醮) as now held in China annually during the 7th moon, when Buddhist (and Tauist) priests read masses to release the souls of those who died on land or sea from purgatory, scatter rice to feed Prêtas, consecrate domestic ancestral shrines, burn paper clothes, on the beach or in boats, for the benefit of those who were drowned (燒衣節), and recite Yoga Tantras (such as are collected in the 瑜伽集要燄口食儀 translated by Amoghavadjra, (A. D. 746—771) accompanied by magic fingerplay (Mudrâ) to comfort ancestral spirits of seven generations in purgatory Nâraka), in temporary sheds in which statues of the popular Buddhist deities, groups of statuettes representing scenes from Chinese history, dwarf plants, silk festoons, chandeliers and lamps are brought together in a sort of annual religious exhibition, enlivened by music and fire works, the principal ceremonies being performed at midnight (especially on the 15th day of the 7th moon). The expenses of the priests and the exhibition are defrayed by local associations (盂蘭勝會) levying contributions on every shopland household, the whole performance being supposed to exorcize the evil spirits which otherwise would work financial and sanitary ruin in the neighbourhood, besides giving every individual an opportunity of obtaining the intercessory prayers of the priests for the benefit of his own deceased ancestors or relatives. The similarity which exists between these ceremonies and the ancient (and modern) Gtorma "strewing oblations" of Tibet is so great, that it is probable that the Chinese ceremonial is the Tibetan Gtorma ritual engrafted upon Confucian ancestral worship. This agrees with the known fact that a native of Tukhâra, Dharmarakcha (A. D. 265—316), introduced in China and translated the Ullambana Sûtra 佛說盂蘭盆經 which gives to the whole ceremonial the (forged) authority of S'âkyamuni, and supports it by the alleged experiences of his principal disciples, Ananda being said to have appeased Prêtas by food offerings presented to Buddha and Saṁgha, and Mâudgalyâyana to have brought back his mother who had been reborn in hell as a Prêta. Although introduced in China in the 3rd century, this ceremonial was popularized only through Amoghavadjra (A.D. 732) and the popular influence of the Yogâtchârya School. The whole theory, with its ideas of intercessory prayers, priestly litanies and requiems, and ancestral worship, is entirely foreign to ancient and Southern Buddhism.

ULLAṀGHA 鬱楞迦 or 鬱伽 A native of India, author of 2 philosophical works, viz. 緣生論 Nidâna s'âstra, translated (A. D. 607) by Dharmagupta, and 大乘緣生論 Mahâyâna nidâna s'âstra, translated (A. D. 746—771) by Amoghavadjra.

UMA s. a. Durga.

UṆÂDI 嗢(or 温)那地 A class of poems composed of 2500 s'lokas.

UPÂDÂNA 取 lit. grasp. Clinging to life as long as possible; the 4th of the 12 Nidânas.

UPADÊS'A 烏(or 鄔)波第(or 提)鑠 or 優波提舍 or 論議 lit. s'âstras and discussions. (1.) Dogmatic treatises (s'âstras), a section of the canon, s. a. Abhidharma piṭaka. (2.) Another name for Tantras, as text books of the Yogâtchârya.

UPADHYÂYA 烏波陀耶 or 有波第耶夜 or 和闍 or 和闍, or 和尙 explained by 親教師 lit. selftaught teacher, or by 知有罪無罪 lit. one who knows sinfulness from sinlessness, or by 近誦 lit. one who reads (the canon) near (to his superior), with the note, "in India the vernacular term for Upadhyâya is 殞社 (Munshee?), in Kustana and Kashgar they say 鶻社 (hwah-she) and from the latter term are derived the Chinese synonymes 和闍 (hwo-she) and 和尙 (hwo-shang)." Upadhyâya was originally the designation, in India, of those who teach only a part of the Vedas, the Vedangas. Adopted by Buddhists of Central Asia, the term Upadhyâya signified the ecclesiastics of the older ritual, in distinction from both Lamas and Bou-po or Bonzes (adherents of the indigenous religion of Tibet, corresponding with the Tauists 道師 of China). In China, the term 和尙 was first used as a synonyme for 法師 i.e. Buddhist (not

Tauist) ecclesiastics, engaged in popular teaching (whether belonging to the Lotus School 蓮宗, or to the Tient'ai School 天台八教, or to the Avatamsaka School 華嚴部), in distinction from ecclesiatics of the Vinaya School 律師 and of the Dhyâna School 禪師. The term Upa'dhâya (Tib. Mkhan po) is now-a-days, and specially in Tibet, also a designation of the abbot of a monastery, but in popular parlance it signifies in China simply a Buddhist ecclesiastic (of any rank whatsoever) as distinguished from a Tauist priest or from a Confucian scholar.

UPADJITA v. Upas'ânta.

UPAGARUḌA 優波迦婁荼 A fabulous bird. See Garuḍa.

UPAGUPTA (Tib. Oye sbas) 烏(or 鄔)波毱多 or 優波掘多 explained by 近護 lit. near protection. The fourth patriarch, a native of 吒利 (Pâṭaliputtra?), a S'ûdra by birth, personal conqueror of Mara; laboured at Mathura; died B. C. 741 (or 335).

UPÂLI (Tib. Nye var khor. Mong. Tchikola Aktchi) 優波離 A disciple of S'âkyamuni, a S'ûdra by birth, a barber, to whom Buddha gave the title 持戒 "supporter of the Vinaya," one of the 3 Sthaviras of the 1st synod (B.C. 543), one of the reputed compilers of the Vinaya.

UPÂNANDA (Tib. Nye dgah vo) 烏波難陀 or 跋難陀 (1.) An Arhat, disciple of S'âkyamuni. (2.) A Nâga king.

UPÂSAKA (Singh. Upasika. Tib. Dge snen. Ming. Ubaschi) 烏波索(or 娑)迦 or 烏婆塞 or 近侍 lit. close attendant, or 信事男 or 近事男 lit. male devotees. Lay-members of the Buddhist church who, without entering upon monastic life, vow to keep the principal commandments. If females, they are called Upâsikâ (Singh. Upasikawa. Tib. Dge snen ma. Mang. Ubaschanza) 烏波斯(or 賜)迦 or 優波夷 explained by 近事女 or 近善女 lit. female devotees.

UPAS'ÂNTA or Upadjita 優波扇多 or 法勝 (Dharmadjina?). A native of India, authore of the Abhidharma hridaya s'âstra (q. v.), translated (A. D. 391) by Saṁghadêva, with a commentary 法勝阿毗曇心論, translated (A.D. 563) by Narendrayas'as.

UPASÊNA 頞鞞 A military title, like As'vadjit.

UPASTHÂNA (Pâli. Patthâna, Singh. Passana) 處 lit. condition, dwelling See Smrity upasthâna.

UPAS'ÛNYA 月婆首那 or 高空 A prince of Udjdjayana. who came to China A.D. 538—541, and translated several works.

UPATICHYA (Pâli. Upatissa. Tib. Nergyal) 優婆室 (or 底)沙 (1.) Another name for S'âriputra. (2.) A native of India, author of the Vimokchamarga s'âstra 解脫道論, translated (A. D. 505) by Saṁghapâla.

UPÂYA or Upâya kâus'alya 方便度 lit. salvation by (proper) means. The knowledge and use of the proper means of salvation; the 7th of the 10 Pâramitâs.

UPECKCHÂ 優畢乂 or 捨 lit. renunciation. A state of absolute indifference, attained by renouncing any exercise of mental faculties.

UPOCHAṆA v. Pochadha.

URAGASARA s.a. Tchandanêva.

URAS'I 烏剌尸 Ancient province (Ouastene) of Cashmere (the modern district of Rash, W. of Muzafarabad).

URDDHASTHÂNA or Vardhasthâna 佛栗持薩儻那 Ancient kingdom (Ortospana) and city (now the Bala Hisar of Cabul).

URṆA (Tib. Mdzod spu) 眉間白毛 lit. white hair between the eye brows. A circle of hair (issuing rays of light illumining every universe) between the eye-brows of a Buddha; one of the 32 Lakchaṇas.

URUVILVÂ (Singh. Uruwelaya) 苦行林 lit. forest of painful practices, or 木瓜林 lit. papaya forest. A place near, Gayâ where S'âkyamuni practised austeie asceticism for years.

URUVILVÂ KÂS'YAPA 優樓(or 盧)頻螺迦葉波 One of the principal disciples of S'âkyamuni, so called either because he practised asceticism in Uruvilvâ or because he had on his breast a mark resembling the papaya (v. Uruvilvâ) fruit. He is to re-appear as Buddha Samantaprabhâsa.

UTCHTCHASAYANÂ MAHÂSAYANÂ 不坐高廣大牀 lit. not to sit on a high, broad and large couch. The 9th of the S'ikchâpada.

UTKALA s. a. Uḍa.

UTKAṬUKÂSANA (Tib. Skyil mo krung) 結跏趺坐 lit. sitting cross-legged (on the hams), with the note "so that body and soul remain motionless." The orthodox posture of ascetics, best adapted for meditation, viz. sitting one's hams so that the feet are not seen, or so that the soles are turned upwards.

UTPALA 鬱(or 優)鉢羅 or 嗢鉢 or Nila utpala 尼羅烏(or 漚)鉢羅 explained by 青蓮花 lit. blue lotus, or 黛花 lit. dark (blue) flower. (1.) One of the 8 large cold hells (Nâraka), where the cold causes the skin to burst, till it seems covered as with lotus buds. (2.) One of the 10 hot Lokantarika hells (Nâraka), where the flames resemble numberless lotus flowers.

UTTARA 嗢呾羅 or 上 lit. superior. An Arhat of Tchulya, a disciple of Dêva.

UTTARÂCHÂDHA 嗢呾羅頞沙荼 The month of S'âkyamuni's conception (14th day of 4th moon to 15th day of 5th moon).

UTTARAKURU or Kurudvîpa (Singh.) Uturakura. Siam. Udorakaro thavib. Tib. Byang gyi sgra mi snan. Mong Moh dohtou) 鬱怛(or 多)羅拘(or 究)樓(or 瑠) or 鬱怛羅越 or 鬱單越 or 殟怛羅句(or 拘)盧(or 羅) or 烏荅羅孤羅尼 or 俱盧州 explained by 高上 lit. higher than any (other continent), or 勝州 lit. the superior continent. (1.) The northern of the 4 continents around the Mêru, square in shape, inhabited by square-faced people. (2.) The dwelling of gods and saints in Brahmanic cosmology.

UTTARÂSAṂGHÂṬI 鬱(or 郁)多羅僧伽 or 漚(or 郁)多羅僧 explained by 衣著上 lit. overcoat, or by 覆左肩衣 lit. a robe flung over the left shoulder (sc. leaving right arm and breast free). Part of a priest's ornate, also called Saṁkakchika (Mong. jeke majak) 僧脚崎 or 僧祇支 or 僧脚差 or 僧瓶. See also Kachâya and Saṁghâṭi.

UTTARAS'ÂILÂḤ 鬱多世羅部 or 北山部 The so-called School of the northern mountain.

UTTARASÊNA 嗢怛羅犀那 or 上軍 lit. superior army. A king of Udyâna, who obtained some of Buddha's s'arirâs.

V.

VÂCHPA (Pâli. Wappa. Tib. Rlangs pa) 婆沙波 or 婆敷 or Das'abala kâs'yapa 十九迦葉 One of the first 5 disciples of S'âkyamuni.

VADI or Vati 伐地 Ancient kingdom and city (now Betik) on the Oxus.

VADJRA (Tib. Rdo rje. Mong. Ortschir) 伐 (or 跋) 闍 羅 or 跋折羅 or 金剛杵 lit. the diamond club. (1.) The sceptre of Indra, as god of thunder and lightning, with which he slays the enemies of Buddhism. (3.) The ritual sceptre of priests, exorcists and sorcerers, held and moved about in different directions during prayer, as the symbol of supernatural power. (4.) The emblem of Buddha's power over evil (金剛喻佛性). (5.) A Nirgrantha, who foretold Hiuentsang's return to China.

VADJRA BHAIRAVA TANTRA KROTA TATTVARÂDJA 佛說妙吉祥瑜伽大敎金剛陪囉縛輪觀想成就儀軌經 Title of a Yoga Tantra, translated A. D. 982—1,001.

VADJRA BODHI 跋日羅菩提 or 金剛智 lit. wisdom of the Vadjra. A Brahman of Malaya (A. D. 719).

VADJRA GANDHA 金剛香 A fictitious Bodhisattva.

VADJRA GARBHA RATNA RADJATANTRA 最上大乘金剛大敎寶王經 Title of a translation (A. D. 746—771) by Dharmadêva.

VADJRA KUMÂRA TANTRA 聖迦柅忿怒金剛童子菩薩成就儀軌經 Title of a translation (A. D. 746—771) by Amogha vadjra.

VADJRA MAṆḌA DHÂRAṆÎ. Title of 2 translations, viz. (1.) 金剛上味陀羅尼經 by Buddhas'ânta, A.D. 386—534, and (2.) 金剛場陀羅尼經 by Djñânagapta, A.D. 487.

VADJRAPÂṆI or Vadjradhara (Tib. Lag na rdo rje, or Phyag rdor. Mong. Utschir bani) 斡資羅巴尼 or 跋闍羅波膩 or 和夷羅洹閱叉 explained by 手執金剛杵 lit. the holder of the vadjra, or by 密跡金剛菩薩 lit. guhyapada bodhisattva (a noted wrestler). (1.) Indra (q.v.), who, in a former djâtaka, as a son of a Tchakravartti, took an oath to defend Buddhism, and was then reborn as king of the Yakchas, in which capacity he holds the vadjra ready to crush every enemy of Buddhism. (2.) Mandjus'ri, as the Dhyâni Bodhisattva (i. e. the spiritual son, or reflex existing in the world of forms), of the Dharma kâya form of existence (see under Trikâya) of the Dhyâni Buddha Akchobhya. (3). A popular deity, the terror of all enemies of Buddhist believers, specially worshipped in exorcisms and sorcery, by followers of the Yogâtchârya School.

VADJRA SAMÂDHI 金剛三昧 A degree of Samâdhi.

VADJRA SAMBHAVE 斡資羅三葩微 or Vadjra dbhave 斡資魯忒葩微 Thou who art originated in (or hast existence from) the vadjra An exclamation, addressed to Buddhas in prayer.

VADJRÂSANA s.a. Budhimaṇḍa.

VADJRASATTVA (Tib. Bhardje sems dpar snang) 斡資羅薩埵 A fictitious Bodhisattva, who became the 6th Dhyâni Buddha of the Yogâtchârya School.

VADJRAS'EKHARA VIMÂNA SARVA YOGAYOGI SÛTRA 金剛峰樓閣一切瑜伽瑜祇經 Title of translation (A.D 723—730) by Vadjra bodhi.

VADJRASÛKI S'ÂSTRA 金乘針論 Title of a translation (A. D. 973—981) by Dharmadêva.

VADJRÂTCHÂRYA 金剛上師 lit. superior master of the vadjra. Epithet of leaders of the Yogâtchârya School.

VADJRA TCHTCHHEDIKÂ PRADJÑÂPÂRAMITÂ. Title of 3 translations (of a portion of the Mahâpradjñâpâramitâ), viz. (1.) 金剛般若波羅蜜經 by Kumâradjîva, A. D. 384—417, also by Bodhirutchi, A.D. 509, and by Paramârtha, A.D. 592, (2.) 能斷金剛般若波羅蜜經 by Hiuentsang, A.D. 648, and again A. D. 603 by another, (3.) 金剛能斷般若波羅蜜經 by Dharmagupta, A.D. 589—918,

VADJRODBHAVE v. Vadjra sambhave.

VAIBHÂCHIKAS 毗婆沙論師 lit. masters of the Vibhâcha s'âstra. A School of philosophers who held that mental concepts are formed through direct contact (denied by the Sâutrântikas) between the mind and the external objects. See Sarvâstivâdâḥa.

VÂIDÊHÎ (Tib. Lus hphags) 實提希 or 提希 or 思惟 lit. thought. The wife of Bimbisâra, mother of Adjâtas'atru, also called S'ribhadrâ.

VÂIDURYA (Tib. Dkarpo or Shgon po) 毗頭利 or 鞞稠利夜 or 吠瑠璃耶 or (毗)瑠璃 (1.) Lapis lazuli, described as a green, incombustible, gem. (2.) A mountain near Vârâṇas'i.

VAIHARA (Pâli. Vibharo) 賓波羅窟 A cavern temple (Baibhargiri) near Râdjagriha, where Buddha engaged in meditation.

VAIPULYA 毗富羅 one of the 10 fabulous mountains.

VAIPULYA or Mahâvaipulya sûtras 毗佛略 or 方等 or 廣方 or 無量義經 lit. sûtras of unlimited meaning. A class of sûtras, viz. amplified and diffuse editions (of later date), first introduced in China (A. D. 266—317) by Dharmarakcha.

VAIRÂTA 般里夜多羅 Ancient kingdom and city (now Beerat) in India.

VAIROTCHANA (Tib. Rnam par snang mdzad) 毗盧遮(or 折)那 explained by 遍照 lit. all illumining. (1.) The highest of the Trikâya (q. v.), corresponding with Dharma in the Triratna (q. v.), the personification of essential bodhi and absolute purity, who lives in the 4th Buddhakchetra or Ârupa dhâtu as the first of the 5 Dhyâni Buddhas, having for his Dhyâni Bodhisattva (or reflex in the world of form) Samantabhadra. (2.) A S'ramaṇa of Cashmere (contemporary of Padma sambhava) who introduced Buddhism in Kustana and laboured in Tibet as one of the great translators (Lo tsa ba tchen po) of the canon.

VAIROTCHANA RAS'MI PRATIMAṆḌITA 淨光莊嚴 (1.) A fabulous universe (v. Kamaladala). (2.) The fabulous realm of S'ubhavyuha and Djaladhara gardjita.

VAIROTCHANA RAS'MI PRATIMAṆḌITA DHVADJA 光照莊嚴相 A Bodhisattva, disciple of S'âkyamuni. See a so Vimaladattâ.

VAIS'AKA 鞞索迦 Ancient kingdom in India, probably the region near Biswah in Oude.

VAIS'ÂKHA or Vis'âkha matri (Pâli. Wisâkhâ matawi. Singh. Wisakha) 鞞索迦 or 鼻奢佉 or 毗舍佉母 The wife of Anathapiṇḍika, so called because born in the month Vâis'âkha 吠舍佉 (2nd month in spring, 15th day of 2nd moon to 16th day of 3rd moon). She built a vihâra for Sâ'kyamuni, and became "mother" superioress of a number of Upâsikâs.

VAIS'ÂKHYA 毗舍佉 A S'ramaṇa of India, author of a work on the (Mûlasarvâstivâda) vinaya.

VAIS'ÂLÎ (Pali. Vesaliya Singh. Wisala. Tib. Spong byed Mong. Utu) 毗舍離 or 吠舍釐 or 維耶離 or 鞞奢隸夜

Ancient republic (v. Litchhavis) and city (near Bassahar, N. of patna), where the 2nd synod (B. C. 443) was held.

VAIS'ECHIKA (Tib. Bye brag pa) 鞞思迦 or 衞世師 or 勝宗 lit. School of conquerors, explained by 勝論外道 lit. heretics who defeated the (adherents of the) s'âstras. An atomistic School (founded by Kanâda). It taught, like the Saṁkhya philosophy, a dualism of an endless number of souls and a fixed number of material principles, by the interaction of which, without a directing unity, cosmic evolution proceeds and it occupied itself, like the orthodox Nyâya philosophy, chiefly with the theory of knowledge, but it differed from both by distinguishing 6 categories or objects of cognition, 六諦, viz. substance, quality, activity, species, distinction and correlation, and 9 substances (possessed of qualities), 九陰, viz. the 5 elements, time and space, spirit (manas) and soul (atma).

VAIS'RAMAṆA or Vais'ravaṇa or Dhanada (Singh. Wesamuna. Siam. Vetsuvan. Tib. Rnam thos kyi bu. Mong. Bisman tegri) 鞞舍羅婆拏 or 鞞室羅懣囊 or 毗沙門 or 毗捨明 explained by 遍聞 or 普聞 or 多聞 lit. universal (or varied) hearing; or Kuvêra 俱乞羅 explained by 財神 lit. the god of riches. (1.) The god of riches (Kuvêra) of ancient Brahmanism, who was reborn as such, because he was, when a man, specially attached to Brahmanic students of the Vedas. (2.) Kuvêra, as a god of modern Brahmanism, one of the 8 Lokapâlas (regent of the North) and guardian of the mineral treasures (of Kailâsa), with 3 heads, 3 legs, 8 teeth, 1 ear-ring, green eyes and leprous body, who is moved by magic incantations to grant wealth. (3.) One of the Tchatur Mahârâdja (q. v.), guardian of the North and king of Yakchas, reborn as such because he was converted by S'âkyamuni who admitted him to the priesthood, whereupon all other disciples, affrighted, exclaimed, 伊是沙門 "Why? He a S'ramaṇa!" Hence his name Vais'ramaṇa. He is also styled "regent of the stars," and worshipped as the god of wealth, since the emperor Hiuen-tsung (A. D. 753) canonized him as such. He plays an important part in the Tantras, in sorcery and exorcism.

VAIS'RAMAṆA DIVYARÂDJA SÛTRA 佛說毗沙門

天王經 Title of a translation (A. D. 973—981) by Dharmadêva.

VAIS'YA (Tib. Rdje hu rigs) 毗舍多(or 羅) or 吠奢 or 吠舍 explained by 居士 lit. burghers, or 商賈 lit. merchants. The Indian caste of traders.

VAKCHU v. Vanksu.

VAKHAN v. Invakan.

VAKULA 薄句(or 枸)羅 or 善容 (1.) An intelligent disciple of S'âkyamuni, to be reborn as Buddha Samantaprabhâsa. (2.) A demon.

VALLABHÎ 伐臘毗 Ancient kingdom and city on E. coast of Gujerat. See Lâra.

VANA 越鞋 (1.) A s'rêchṭhin of the time of S'âkyamuni. (2.) Another name for Varaṇa.

VANKSU or Vakchu (Tib. Pak tchhu. Mong. Amudena) 縛芻 or 博义 or 薄义 or 婆义 explained by 清河 lit. blue river, or 淸河 lit. pure river The Oxus, said to issue from lake Anavatapta (or Sirikol), through "the horse's mouth (of lapis lazwli)," to flow once round the lake, and then W. (or N. W.), until it falls into "the northern ocean" (Caspian).

VARAHAMULA v. Paramalagiri.

VARAṆA 伐刺拏 or Vana 跋那 Ancient province and city (Banagara) of Kapis'a, now Banu on the lower Kuram.

VÂRÂṆAS'Î (Burm. Baranathee. Tib. Waranasse) 波刺那斯 or 波羅奈(斯) or 波羅痆(or 捺)斯(or 寫) explained by 江遶城 lit. a city surrounded by rivers. Ancient kingdom and city, the headquarters of Shivaism, now Benares.

VARANGALA v. Viñgila.

VARAPRABHA 妙光 Maitrêya, in a former djâtaka, when he was a Bodhisattva, with 800 disciples.

VARASÊNA 婆羅犀那 A pass (the Paresh or Aparasvin of the Zendavesta) on the Paropamisus, now called Khawak, S. of Inderaub.

VARAVALÎN s. a. Alni.

VARCHA VASANA (Pâli. Vassa) 跋利沙 or 婆利師 or 雨時 lit. rainy season, or 雨安居 lit. rest during rains, or 坐臘 lit. retreat during the month Nabhas. or 夏坐 lit. summer retreat, The ancient duty of spending the rainy season in devotional exercises in a monastery, in China either from the 16th day of 5th moon to the 15th day of 9th moon or during one month in each season.

VARCHIKA (Pâli. Varcha) 婆(利)師(or 使)迦 or 婆師波利 or 雨時生花 lit. a flower which grows in the rainy season, or 夏生花 lit. flower which grows in summer. A kind of perfume, perhaps Lignum aloes.

VARDASTHÂNA v. Urddhasthâna.

VARDDHANA v. Puṇḍravarddhana.

VARIKATCHA or Varukatchêva s. a. Barukatchêva.

VARMA VYÛHA NIRDÊS'A 被甲莊嚴會 Title of a translation (A. D. 618—907) by Bodhirutchi.

VARUCHA 跋盧沙 Ancient town (now Palodheri or Pelley) in Gânbhâra.

VARUNA (Tib. Tchu lha) 婆樓那 or 水天 lit. the dêva of waters. The Brahmanic god of heaven, regent of the sea, and, as one of the 8 Lokapâlas, guardian of the West.

VAS'AVARTI s.a. Paranirmita Vas'avarti.

VAS'IBHA 婆私瑟侘 or 大仙 lit. the great richi. One of the 7 Brahmanic richis, a patron of Buddhist priests, now worshipped as regent of a star.

VASUBANDHU 伐蘇盤度 or 婆藪槃豆 or 婆修盤頭 or 世親 or 天親 A native of Râdjagriha, descendant of Vais'akha, younger brother of Asaṁgha, twin brother of Kchuni (蒭尼), a disciple of Nâgârdjuna and, like the latter, teacher of the Amitâbha doctrine; laboured (until 117 A.D.) in Ayodhyâ, as the 21st (or 22nd) patriarch; author of some 36 works; now revered as a Bodhisattva residing in Tuchita.

VASUBHADRA 婆素跋陀 or Giribhadra 山賢 A S'ramaṇa of India, author of the 三法度論 Tridharmaka s'âstra, commented on by Saṁghasêna, and translated (A.D. 391) by Saṁghadêva.

VASUDÊVA 婆藪天 In Brahmanic mythology, the father of Krishna.

VASUDHARA SÛTRA 持世經 Title of a translation (A. D. 384—417) by Kumâradjîva, s.a. Dharma mudrâ sûtra 佛說法印經 translated (A. D. 980—1000) by Dânapâla.

VÂSUKI 和修吉 or 多頭 lit. many-headed. A king of Nâgas.

VASUMITRA 伐(or 婆)蘇蜜多(or 呾)羅 or 和須蜜多羅 or 婆須蜜 or 世友 lit. friend of the world. (1.)

A native of N. India, converted by Mikkaka; one of the 500 Arhats; a follower of the Sarvastivâdâḥ and author of many philosophical works; sometimes counted as successor to Mikkaka and therefore 7th patriarch (in which case Buddhanandi is counted 8th, Buddhamitra 9th, and so on); died B. C. 590. (2.) Name of the president of the 3rd or 4th synod (B. C. 153).

VASUVARMAN 婆蘇跋摩 An adherent of the Hinayâna, author of the Tchatur satya s'âstra.

VATAYANA RÂDJA 隙塵 The atom of dust that lodges in the tiniest crack; the 7th part of a Sas'arâdja.

VATI v. Vadi.

VATSARÂDJA v. Udâyanarâdja.

VATSAPATTANA v. Kaus'âmbî.

VATSARA 歲 The solar year. See Ayana, Udagâyana, Dakchiṇâyana and Sûrya.

VATSA SÛTRA. Title of 2 tranlations, viz. 佛說犢子經 A. D. 220—280, and 佛說乳光佛經 by Dharmarackcha A. D. 265—316.

VATSU or Vasu 跋私 An ancient richi.

VATSIPUTRÎYÂḤ or Vâsaputriyâḥ 跋私弗多羅部 or 跋私弗底與部 or 婆蹉富羅部 or 佛婆羅部 or 婆雌子部 or 犢子部 lit. the School of Vatsa, or 可住子部 lit. the School of Vâsa. A philosophical School "the Vinaya texts of which never reached China;" a sub-division of the Sarvâstivâdâḥ (or Sammatâḥ), founded by Vatsa, a descendant of Vatsu (or by Vâsa):

VÂYU 止息 lit. stop breathing. Holding one's breath, as a preliminary condition of entering samâdhi (and obtaining magic power).

VÊDA (Tib. Rig byed) 吠陀 or 韓陀 or 韋陀 or 馱 or 毗陀 explained by 知 lit. knowledge. (1.) The Vêda (never translated into Chinese), viewed by Chinese Buddhists as a heretical work, compiled by Brahma and subsequently by Vyâsa (q. v.), first in one book, then in 4 books (see Ayurvêda, Radjurvêda, Sâmavêda and Atharvavêda) and finally in 25 books. (2.) A Bodhisattva, general (天將) of the Tchatur Mahârâdjas, worshipped as a Vihârapâla.

VÊDANÂ 受 lit. sensation The second of the 5 Skandha perception (by the senses) the 6th Nidâna.

VÊDANÂ SMRITY UPASTHÂNA (Pâli. Wêdanânu

pasâna) 念受苦處 lit. remember that the dwelling of sensations is misery. One of the 37 Bodhipakchika. dharma; one of the 4 Smrity upasthâna, viz. the recognition that all forms of sensation are but so many forms of misery.

VÊMATCHITRA 毗摩質多羅 or 海水波音 A king of Asuras, residing at the bottom of the sea; father of Indra's wife.

VEṆUVANA (Tib. Od ma) 竹林 or 竹苑 lit. bamboo park. The Karaṇda vêṇuvana (q.v.) with a vihâra (竹林精寺 or 竹苑寺), the favourite resort of S'âkyamuni.

VÊTÂLA SIDDHI 毗陀羅悉底 The art of obtaining siddhi (q. v.) by means of incantations and sacrifices performed over a corpse.

VÊRAMAṆÎ v. Pantcha vêramaṇî.

VÊTÂLA 毗陀羅 or 韋陀羅 or 赤色鬼 lit. red demon, or 厭禱鬼 lit. a demon who loathes prayer. A class of demons dwelling in, and able to quicken, dead bodies.

VIBHÂCHA S'ÂSTRA 鞞婆沙論 A philosophical work by Kâtyâyanî putra, translated (A.D. 383) by Saṁghabhûti.

VIBHÂCHA VINAYA 善見毗婆沙律. A work on ecclesiastical discipline by Manura, translated (A. D. 489) by Saṁghabhadra.

VIBHÂDJYA VÂDINÂḤ 分別說部 lit. a School which discusses distinctions. A subdivision of the Sarvâstivâdâḥ.

AICHÂṆA 毗沙拏 or 角 lit. horn (sc. of the Khadga). Epithet of every Pratyêka Buddha, as he lives lonely (khadga) like the one-horned rhinoceros.

VIDÊHA (Tib. Lus hphags) 毗提訶 or 佛提婆 or 弗于建 (1.) Abbreviation for Purvavidêha. (2.) Another name for Vais'âlî and the region near Mâthava.

VIDHI 術 The methods employed in magic performances.

VIDJAYA 月桜耶 or 最勝 lit. most victorious. An epithet of all Buddhas.

VIDJÑA S'ÂSTRAS 因明論 Works on the Nyâya (orthodox) philosophy, on logic and dialectics.

VIDJÑÂNA (Pâli. Vinnana. Singh. Winyâna. Burm. Wignian. Tib. Rnam shes) 識 lit. knowledge. (1.) The 10th of the 12 Nidânas, viz. perfect knowledge of the various organs, objects and forms of knowledge, in their concatenation and unity. (2.) General designation of each of the Chaḍâyatana or 六處 i.e. the 6 organs of knowledge, viz. Tchakchur, S'rotra, Ghrâṇa, Djihvâ, Kâya and Manas. (3.) General designation of each of the Chaḍbâhya âyatana or 六塵 i.e. the 6 objects of knowledge, viz. Rûpa, S'abda, Gandha, Rasa (精神 lit. subtle spiritual vitality), Poṭṭabha and Dharma. (4.) General designation of each of the Achṭa vidjñâna 八識 lit. the 8 forms of knowledge, viz. the above Chaḍâyatana with the addition of Klichṭa manas 訖利瑟吒耶末那識 or 染汗意識 lit. a knowledge of what defiles the mind, and Âlaya 阿賴耶藏識 lit. a knowledge of the written canon (Tripiṭaka).

VIDYÂ or Vidyâ mantra 禁咒 lit. spells (mantras) for exorcizing, or 明咒 lit. mantras of (mystic) knowledge. Mystic formulae, said to be derived each from a separate deity (of the Yoga School) and consisting of translations or, more frequently, of transliterations from Sanskrit (now not understood in China), sometimes also of syllables which give no meaning at all.

VIDYÂ DHARA PIṬAKA or Mantra piṭaka ar Dhâraṇi piṭaka 禁咒藏 lit. collection of mantras for (purposes of) exorcism. A class of books, some of which are included in the Samyukta piṭaka, and consisting of dhâraṇîs, mantras, vidyâ mantras, tantras, yoga tantras, and other formularies of supposed mystic, magic and exorcistic efficacy.

VIDYÂ MÂTRA S'ÂSTRA. Title of 3 treatises by Vasubandhu (on the Lankâvatâra sûtra), viz. (1.) 大乘楞伽經唯識論 translated (A. D. 508--535) by Bodhirutchi, (2.) 大乘唯識論 translated (A. D. 557—569) by Paramârtha, and (3.) 唯識二十論 translated (A.D. 661) by Hiuen-tsang.

VIDYÂ MATRA SIDDHI RATNA DJÂTI S'ÂSTRA 成唯識寶生論 A commentary (on the Vidyâ mâtra s'âstra) by Dharmapâla, translated (A. D. 710) by Chang Wen-ming (Itsing).

VIDYA MÂTRA SIDDHI TRIDAS'A S'ÂSTRA KÂRIKA 唯識三十論 A philosophical work by Vasubandhu, translated (A. D. 648) by Hiuen-tsang, with a commentary called 成唯識論 Vidyâ mâtra s'âstra by Dharmapâla, translated (A. D. 659) by Hiuen-tsang.

VIDYÂ NIRDÊSA S'ÂSTRA 顯識論 Title of a translation (A. D. 557—569) by Paramârtha.

VIDYÂ PRAVARTANA S'ÂSTRA 轉識論 Title of a translation (A. D. 557—569) by Paramârtha.

VIDYA S'ÂSTRAS v. Pañtcha vidyâ s'âstra.

VIGATABHAYA 最清淨 The 730th Buddha of the present kalpa.

VIGHNA 維祇難 or 障礙 A S'ramaṇa of India (originally a fire worshipper), who brought to China and translated the 曇鉢經 lit. Dharma pada sûtra.

VIHÂRA (Siam. Pihan or Vat. Tib. Gtsug lag. Mong. Küt or Saüma) 毗訶羅 or 鼻訶羅 explained by 僧坊 lit. dwelling of the Saṁgha, or by 僧遊履處 lit. place for the peripatetics of priests, or by 精舍 or 精廬 lit. cottage of purity, or by 佛寺 lit. Buddhist temple. (1.) Any place (academy, school or temple) used for regular study (or practice) of Buddhism. (2.) The temple within a monastery, as the principal meeting place. (3.) A monastery or nunnery, which "ought to be built of red sandal wood (tchaṇḍana), with 32 chambers (each 8 tâla trees high), with garden, park, bathing tank and tchang kramana, and to be richly furnished with stores of clothes, food, bedsteads, mattresses, and all creature comforts" Vihâras are now built in town and out of town, but solitude and mountain scenery are the favourite surroundings. See also Sâmghârâma.

VIHÂRAPÂLA 毗訶羅波羅 or 護寺 Title given to patrons and tutelary deities of Buddhist monasticism.

VIHÂRASVÂMIN (Tib. Mkhan po) 毗訶莎弭 or 寺主 lit. superior of a vihâra. Abbot (or abbess). See also Karmadana.

VIKÂLABHODJANÂ 不非時食 lit. eat not at improper hours, or 不食肉 lit. eat no flesh. The 6th rule for novices. See S'ikchâpada.

VIKAUTUKA 毗俱胝 A fabulous Bodhisattva, possessed of 108 different names.

VIKRAMÂDITYA 馝柯羅摩阿佚多 or 毗訖羅摩阿迭多 or 馝柯 explained by 超日 lit. surpassing the sun. A king of S'râvastî (1000 years after the Nirvâṇa), a lavish patron of Buddhism.

VIKRÎTAVANA 買林 lit. the bought park. A vihâra, 200 *li* N. W. of the capital of Cashmere.

VIMALA (Tib. Drima med) 無垢 or 淨 lit. undefiled. (1.) The universe of a Buddha (daughter of Sâgara). (2.) A degree of samâdhi.

VIMALADATTÂ 淨德(or 得) lit. undefiled virtue (orgift). (1.) The wife of S'ubhavyûha. (2.) A degree of samâdhi.

VIMALA DATTÂ PARIPRITCHTCHHÂ Title of 3 translations, viz. (1.) 無垢施菩薩應辯會 A. D. 265—316, (2.) 佛說離垢施女經 by Dharmarakcha (A. D. 282), and (3.) 得無垢女經 by Pradjñârutchi (A.D. 541).

VIMALAGARBHA 淨藏 lit. undefiled receptacle. (1.) The eldest son of S'ubhavyûha, reborn as Bhechadjya râdja. (2.) A degree of samâdhi.

VIMALÂGRANÊTRA s. a. Vimalanêtra.

VIMALÂKCHAS 毘摩羅叉 or 無垢眼 lit. undefiled eye. A S'ramaṇa of Cabul, expositor of the Sarvâstivâda vinaya and teacher of Kumâradjîva at Kharachar; came to China (A. D. 406) and translated 2 works.

VIMALAKÎRTTI 毘摩羅詰 or 維摩詰 or 維磨羅鷄利帝 explained by 無垢稱 lit. undefiled reputation. A native of Vais'âlî, contemporary of S'âkyamuni, said to have visited China.

VIMALAKÎRTTI NIRDÊS'A SÛTRA. Title of 6 translations, viz. (1.) 維摩詰經, A.D. 222—280, (2.) 大方等頂王經 by Dharmarakcha, A.D. 265—316, (3.) 維摩詰所說經 by Kumâradjîva, A.D. 384—417, (4.) 大乘頂王經 by Upas'ûnya, A. D. 502—557, (5.) 說無垢稱經 by Hiuen-tsang, A. D. 650, and (6.) 善思童子經 by Djñânagupta, A.D. 591.

VIMALAMITRA 毗末羅蜜多羅 or 無垢友 lit. undefiled friend. A S'ramaṇa of Kas'mîra (a follower of Saṁghabhadra), who fell down dead whilst vowing to write against the Mahâyâna School.

VIMALANÊTRA or Vimalagranêtra 淨眼 lit. pure eye. (1.) Second son of S'ubhavyûha, reborn as Bhechadjyasamudgata. (2.) A title given to S'rîgarbha.

VIMALANIRBHÂSA 淨光 lit. pure light. A degree of Samâdhi.

VIMALAPRABHA 淨光明 lit. pure light and brightness (1.) A degree of samâdhi. (2.) A fabulous Buddha (Tib. Dri med pahi od).

VIMATI SAMUDGHÂTIN 除欵意 The 6th son of Tchandra.

VIMBASARA or Vimbisâra or Bimbisâra.

VIMOKCHA or Mokcha or Vimukti or Mukti (Pâli. Vimokha or Vimutti. Tib. Grol pa) 解脫 lit. liberation (as an act), or 解脫處 lit. the âyatana (conception of, or dwelling in) liberty. [1.] Moral liberation (from vice and passion), by means of observing the 8 sections of the Pratimokcha sûtra (containing 250 ascetic and monastic precepts). [2.] Mental liberation, or liberty gained gradually by 8 successive intel ectual operations, 八解脫 lit. Achṭa vimokcha, viz. (a.) 觀內有色外亦觀色解脫 lit. liberation from (the conception that) notions have both subjective and objective realities corresponding to them, (b.) 觀內無色外亦觀色解脫 lit. liberation from (the conception that) notions have indeed no subjective, but have objective, realities corresponding to them, (c.) 內外諸色解脫 lit. liberation from (the conception of) any realities whatsoever, whether subjective or objective, (d.) 空無邊處解脫 lit. liberation by the recognition (âyatana) that unreality (âkâs'a) is unlimited (ananta), (e.) 識無邊處解脫 lit. liberation by the recognition (âyatana) that knowledge (vidjñâna) is unlimited (ananta), (f.) 無所有處解脫 lit. liberation by the recognition (âyatana) of absolute non-existence (akintchanya), (g.) 非想非非想處解脫 lit. liberation by a state of mind (âyatana) in which there is neither consciousness nor unconsciousness (nâivasamdjñanâsamdjña), and (h.) 滅受想處解脫 lit. liberation by means of a state of mind (âyatana) in which there is final extinction (nirvâṇa) of both sensation (vêdanâ) and consciousness (samdjña). [3.] Mystic liberty (vimukti) or a dwelling of the mind successively in 8 different localities, corresponding with the above 8 intellectual operations, viz. the 1st, 2nd and 3rd Dhyâna (q. v.) corresponding with (a.), (b.) and (c.) above; the Tchaturarûpa brahmalokas (q. v.) corresponding with (d.), (e.), (f.) and (g.) above; and finally Nirvâṇa (q. v.) corresponding with (h.) above. The foregoing Chinese account of Vimokcha differs from that which Burnouf extracted from records of Southern Buddhism

VIMOKCHA MÂRGA. See under Upatichya.

VIMOKCHA PRADJÑÂ RICHI or Vimokchasena 毗目智仙 A S'ramaṇa of Udyâna, a descendant of the S'âkya family, translator (A. D. 541) of 5 or 6 works.

VIṆA (Tib. Pibang) 批那 or 空篌 The Indian or Tibetan guitar.

VINATAKA (Siam. Vinatok) 毗泥怛迦那 or 毗那怛迦 (Vinayaka) explained by 象鼻 lit. elephant's trunk. (1.) A demon (with a proboscis like an elephant's trunk), who stops wayfarers; probably confounded with Vinâyaka. (2.) A mountain, the peak of which resembles that demon; the 6th of the gold mountains which encircle the Meru, 1,250 yodjanas high.

VINAYA (Burm. Wini. Tib. Dul bai) 毗奈耶 or 毗那耶 or 鼻那夜 or 鞞尼迦 or 毗尼 explained by 聿 lit. statutes, or by 離行 lit. walk in isolation, or by 滅 lit. extinction (vinâs'a), or by 調伏 lit. to tame. The precepts of moral asceticism and monastic discipline. See Vinaya piṭaka.

VINÂYAKA 頻那夜迦 (1.) The brahmanic deity Ganês'a (with the head of an elephant), son of Shiva, god of prudence, remover of obstacles. (2.) An evil spirit, often confounded with Vinataka.

VINAYAKAMÂTRIKA 毗尼摩得勒伽 The Vinaya of the Sarvâstivâdâḥ, translated (A. D. 445) by Saṁghavarman.

VINAYA NIDÂNA SÛTRA 戒因緣經 Title of a translation, A. D. 378.

VINAYA PIṬAKA 毗奈(or 那)耶藏 or 毗尼藏 explained by 律藏 lit. collection of statutes. One of the 3 divisions of the Buddhist canon (v. Tripiṭaka), consisting of works on ascetic morality and monastic discipline, supposed to have been compiled under the auspices of Upâli. This section of the Chinese canon is now subdivided into Mahâyâna vinaya 大乘律 and Hinayana vinaya 小乘律. See also under Pratimokcha and Vimokcha.

VINAYA VIBHÂCHÂ S'ÁSTRA 毗奈耶毗婆沙論 A commentary to the Vinayapiṭaka (in 100,000 s'lokas), sanctioned by the 4th synod (B.C. 153).

VINAYA VINIS'TCHAYA UPÂLI PARIPRITCHTCHHÂ. Title of 2 translations, viz. 佛說決定毗尼經 A. D. 371—420, and 優波離會 by Bodhirutchi, A. D. 618—907.

VIÑGILA or Vinkila or Varangala 瓶耆羅 Ancient capital of Andhra.

VINIRBHOGA 離衰 The kalpa of Bhichmagardjita ghochasvara râdja.

VINÎTA PRABHA 毗膩多鉢臘婆 or 調伏光 lit. taming the light. A learned priest of Dûchasana; author of several s'âstras.

VINÎTA RUTCHI 毗尼多流支 or 滅喜 lit. extinction of joy. A S'ramaṇa of Udyâna, translator (A. D. 582) of 2 works.

VIPASÂ 毗播奢 The river Hyphasis (now Beas) in the Pundjab.

VIPAS'YI or Vipasvi or Djinendra (Tib. Rnam par gzigs) 毘鉢尸 or 毗婆尸 or 重重見 lit. manifold views. The first of the Sapta Buddha, the 998th Buddha of the last kalpa, a Kchattriya by birth, son of Paṇḍu (槃頭), a native of Paṇḍupati (槃頭婆提), who lived under an As'oka tree, converted on 3 occasions 348,000 persons, whilst life lasted 80,000 years.

VIPAS'YI BUDDHA SÛTRA 毗婆尸佛經 Title of a translation of part of the Mahânidâna Sûtra.

VIPULA (Pâli. Veputto) 毗布羅 A mountain near Kus'âgârapura.

VIPULA PRADJÑÂ or Vipulamati 廣慧 lit. vast wisdom. An epithet of every Buddha.

VÎRADATTA 無畏授 or 勤授 lit. bold giver. Name of a s'rechṭhin, a contemporary of S'âkyamuni.

VÎRA 力士 A strong man heroe, demigod.

VIRASANA 毗羅删拏 Ancient kingdom and city (now Karsanah) between Ganges and Yamuna.

VIRÛḌHAKA (Siam. Virulahok. Tib. Hphags skyes po. Mong. Ulumtschi tereltu) 毗盧擇(or 釋)迦 or 毗留勤叉 or 毗樓勤迦 or 鼻溜茶迦 or (incorrectly) 毗流離 (Vaidurya), explained by 增長 lit. increase of growth. (1.) A name of Iksvaku, the cruel father of the 4 founders of Kapilavastu. (2.) A king of Kosala (son of Prasenadjit), the cruel destroyer of Kapilavastu. (3.)

One of the Tchatur Mahârâdjas, guardian of the South, king of Kumbhaṇḍas, worshipped in China as one of the 24 Dêva Ârya (天尊). His favourite colour is blue.

VIRUPAKCHA (Siam. Virupak. Tib. Migmibzang. Mong. Sain bussu nidüdü) 毗流波义 or 毗留博义 or 毘樓博义 or 鼻路波阿义 or 髀路波阿迄 explained by 惡眼 or 醜眼 lit. wicked or vile eye, or by 雜語 lit. mixed talk, or by 重重色根 lit. roots of sundry colours (rûpa). (1.) One of the Tchatur Mahârâdjas, guardian of the West, king of Nâgas. His colour is red. He is worshipped in China as one of the 24 Dêva Ârya (天尊). (2.) Another name for Mahês'vara or Rudra (Shiva).

VÎRYA (Pali. Wiraya. Singh. Wirya) 毗利耶 or 毘黎耶 or 精進 lit. zealous advance. Energy, as the 3rd of the 7 Bodhyanga, the 4th of the 10 Paramita, the 3rd (Viryâbala) of the 5 Bala, and the 2nd (Vîryêndriya) of the 5 Indriya.

VÎRYARDDHIPÂDA (Singh. Wiriyidhipâda) 精進力 lit. the step of energy. Energy the 2nd of the 4 Riddhipada, as a means of obtaining magic power.

VÎRYASÊNA 毗離耶犀那 A priest of Bhadravihâra, who taught Hiuen-tsang (about A.D. 640).

VÎRYÊNDRIYA v. Vîrya.

VIS'ÂKHÂ v. Vais'âkha.

VIS'ÊCHAMATI 增意 The 5th son of Tchandra sûrya pradîpa.

VIS'ÊCHATCHINTA BRAHMA PARIPRITCHTCHHÂ. Title of 3 translations, viz. (1.) 持心梵天所問經 by Dharmarakcha, A.D. 286, (2.) 思益梵天所問經 by Kumâradjîva, A. D. 402, (3.) 勝思惟梵天所問經 by Bodhirutchi, A. D. 517, and of a commentary 勝思惟梵天所問經論 by Vasubandhu, translated (A. D. 531) by Bodhirutchi.

VIS'ICHṬA TCHÂRITRA 上行(意) A Bodhisattva who rose out of the earth before S'âkyamuni.

VISTÎRNAVARTÎ 大光國 The realm of S'ubhavyûha as Buddha.

VIS'UDDHASIM̃HA 毗戍陀僧訶 or 淨師子 A follower (A. D. 740) of the Mahâyâna School.

VIS'UDDHA TCHÂRITRA 淨行 The companion of Vis'ichṭa tchâritra.

VIS'VABHÛ 毗舍浮 or 毗攝羅 or 毗濕婆部 or 隨葉佛 explained by 重重變現 lit. apparition of various transformations, or by 遍一切自在 lit. all beings everywhere independent, or by 一切有 lit. all beings. The last of the 1000 Buddhas of last kalpa. The 3rd of the Sapta Buddha, born a Kchâttriya, who converted 130,000 persons, when life lasted 10,000 years.

VIS'VAKARMAN (Singh. Wiswakarmma) 毗濕縛羯磨 or 毗首羯摩 explained by 重重功業 lit. all sorts of handicraft. The creator (in Brahmanic cosmogony) who, transformed as an artist, went with Mâudgalyâyana to Traiyastrims'as to take a likeness of Buddha and then carved the first statue.

VIS'VAMITRA or Kaus'ika (Tib. Kun gyi bches) 毗奢蜜多羅 An ancient richi, teacher of the infant S'âkyamuni.

VITASTI 搩手 lit. a span. The 32,000th part of a yodjana.

VITCHAVAPURA 毗苫婆補羅 The ancient capital of Sindh.

VIVÂDAS'AMANA S'ÂSTRA 囘諍論 A philosophical work by Nâgârdjuna, translated (A. D. 541) by Vimokchapradjña.

VIVARA (Tib. Dkhrigs pa) 頻婆羅 One quadrillion.

VIVARṬṬA KALPA (Vivatta kappa. Mong. Toktachoi galab) 成刧 lit. the kalpa of formation. The period of 20 small kalpas, during which, after the evolution of rain clouds, floods, lotus flowers, there arise worlds, one out of each flower, and in each world successively evolve the rûpadhâtu, kamadhâtu, human beings, all other sentient beings, the tchakravâlas, mêru, the 10 highest mountains, the regions of demons, the oceans, all jewels and magic trees. See Kalpa.

VIVARṬṬA SIDDHA KALPA (Pali. Vivattatthahi kappa. Mong. Oroschichoi galab) 住刧 lit. the stationary kalpa. A period of 20 kalpas (succeeding a Vivarṭṭa kalpa), when sun and moon rise out of the water, whereupon, in consequence of the food eaten by human beings, the difference of sex arises, then heroes (beginning with Sammata) arise, the 4 castes are formed, social life evolves, Tchakravarttis and finally Buddhas rule. See Kalpa.

VRIDJI (Pali. Vaddji) 弗栗持 or Samvadji 三伐恃 Ancient kingdom, N. of the Ganges, S.E. of Nepaul.

VRIDJISTHÂNA v. Urrdhasthana.

VRIHASPATI (Tib. Gza phur bu) 勿哩訶娑跋底 or 木星 The planet Jupiter.

VRIHATPALAS (Singh. Wehappala. Tib. Hbras bu tchhe) 惟于頗羅 or 廣果 lit. vast merit. The 12th Brahmaloka; the 3rd region of the 4th Dhyâna, where life lasts 500 great kalpas.

VYÂKARAṆA (Tib. Lund du ston pa) 毗耶羯剌諵 or 毗伽羅 or 和伽羅 (1.) Works which contain prophecies (授記) regarding the destiny of saints. (2.) A grammar (聲明記論 or 記論) of Sanskrit by Paṇini, traced back to Indra and Brahma.

VYÂKARAṆA KÂUṆḌINYA 授記憍陳如 lit. that Kâuṇḍinya who received the instruction (from Buddha viz. that a Buddha is too spiritual to leave any material relics behind). An Arhat, to be reborn as Samanta prabhâsa. See under Kâuṇḍinya.

VYÂSA 毘耶娑 or 廣博仙人 lit. the richi who expanded (the Veda). One of the Sapta Tathâgata, grandson of Brahma, compiler of the Veda.

VYÛHA RÂDJA 莊嚴王 (1.) A Bodhisattva of the retinue of S'âkyamuni. (2.) A degree of samâdhi.

Y.

YACHṬIVANA 洩瑟知林 or 杖林 lit. the forest of the staff, sc. where the (bamboo) staff took root, with which a Brahman in vain endeavoured to measure the constantly increasing height of S'âkyamuni. A forest near Râdjagriha, on (mount) Yachtivanagiri (杖林山), the abode of Djayasêna.

YADJUR VÊDA 夜殊 or 祭祀 or 祭祠論 A part of the Vêda, a liturgy for sacrifices.

YADJÑA 演若 or 祠 Brahmanic sacrifices, for which Buddhism substituted oblations (pudjâ).

YAKCHA (Singh. Yaka. Siam. Jak. Tib. Gnod sbyin) 夜叉 or 藥叉 or 閱叉 explained by 傷 lit. hurtful, or by 能敢 lit. daring, or by 勇健 lit. valorous. A class of demons (the retinue of Kuvêra or Vais'ravana), who devour men, and, when moving fast, resemble shooting stars or comets.

YAKCHA KRITYA 夜叉吉蔗 A class of demons, who

have the appearance of Yakchas and the power of Krityas.

YAMA (Siam. Phaja jam. Tib. Gchinrdje. Mong. ErlikKhan) 閻摩羅 or 夜摩盧迦 (or 閻 or 剡 or 琰) 魔 or 閻羅 explained by 時分 lit. a division of time, or by 雙王 lit. the twin rulers (Yama and Yamî) or the twofold ruler (being both judge and criminal), or by 遮止 lit. restraining (evil doers). (1.) The Aryan lord of the day, his twin-sister Yamî (queen of night) who opens to mortals the path to the West. (2.) In later Brahmanic mythology, one of the 8 Lokapâla, guardian of the South and ruler of the Yama dêvaloka (q. v.), also judge of the dead. (3.) In Buddhist mythology, the regent of the Nârakas, residing South (yamas) of Djambudvîpa, outside the Tchakravâlas, in a palace of copper and iron. He was originally a king of Vais'alî, who, when engaged in a bloody war, wished he were master of hell, and was accordingly reborn as Yama in hell, together with his 18 generals and his army of 80,000 men, who now serve him in hell as assistant judges, jailors and executioners. His sister (Yamî) deals with female culprits. But three times (三時 yama) in every 24 hours a demon pours into Yama's mouth boiling copper (by way of punishment), his subordinates receiving the same dose at the same time, until their sins are expiated, when he will be reborn as Samantarâdja (普王).

YAMADAGNI 焰摩火大山 One of the 7 ancient richi.

YAMA DÊVALOKA 夜摩天 or 焰摩天 explained by 時 lit. time, or by 善時天 lit. the heaven of good time (where there is no change of day and night). The 3rd Dêvaloka, above Traiyastrims'as, 160,000 yodjanas above Mêru, with a circumference of 80,000 yodjanas. Life lasts there 2,000 years, but 24 hours on earth are equal to 200 years there. See Yama.

YAMÂNTAKA (Tib. Gchin rjei gched) 閻曼德迦 An epithet of Shiva (s.a. Mahês'vara or Rudra), as "destroyer of Yama."

YAMUNÂ 閻牟那 or 琰毋那 A tributary of the Ganges; the Jumna.

YAS'ADA or Yas'as or Yads'aputra (Tib. Ja shei ka) 邪舍陀 A native of Kos'ala, disciple of Ananda, a leader at the 2nd synod (A. D. 443).

YAS'ASKAMA 求名 lit. seeker of fame (yas'as). An ambitious,

but thoughtless, disciple of Varaprabha.

YAS'ODHARA (Singh. Yasodhara dêwi. Siam. Phimpa. Burm. Yathandara. Tib. Grags dzin ma) or Yas'ovati 耶輸陀羅 or 耶輸 explained by 華色 lit. variegated, or by "the mother of Rahula, also called Gopa." The (second name of the) legitimate wife of S'âkyamuni, who, after giving birth to Râhula, entered monastic life and is to re-appear as Buddha Ras'mi s'ata sahasra pari purṇa dhvadja.

YAS'OGUPTA 耶舍崛多 or 稱藏 A foreign Sramaṇa, translator (A. D. 561—578), with Djñânagupta, of some 4 works.

YAVA 耶婆 or 麥 lit. (a grain of) barley. The 2,688,000th part of a yodjana.

YAVANA or Yamana dvîpapura or Yavadvîpa (Pali. Yawana or Yona) 閻摩那洲國 lit. the island kingdom of Yamana, or 野寐尼 (Yamani) or 耶婆提 (Yava dvîpa). The island of Java, deseribed (by Fah-hien and Hiuentsang) as peopled by Brahmans and other heretics.

YODHAPATIPURA or Yuddharâdjapura 戰主(or王)國 lit. the State of the combatant lord (or king). Ancient kingdom and city near the Ganges, 150 *li.* S. W. of Vais'ali.

YODJANA (Burm. Yudzana. Singh. Yosjana) 踰繕那 or 踰延那 or 由旬 A measure of distance, variously computed, as equal to a day's march [4,650 feet], or 40 or 30 or 16 *li* [i.e. 33½ or 10 or 5½ English miles].

YOGA (Tib. Thig le or Rnal byor) 瑜伽 or 遊迦 explained by 觀 lit. contemplation or by 境行果相應 lit, mutual relation of sphere, practice and results, with the note "the first of this trio refers to the heart, the 2nd to [doctrinal] principles, the 3rd to the 3 degrees of saintship," or by 手口意相應 lit. mutual relation of hand [mudrâ], mouth [tantra] and mind [yoga]. The ancient practice of ecstatic meditation [as a means of obtaining spiritual or magic power], revived by the Yogâtchârya (q. v.) School, and vulgarly abused for purposes of exorcism, sorcery and jugglery.

YOGAS'ÂSTRA s. a. Yogâtchârya bhumi s'astra.

YOGÂTCHÂRYA (Tib. Rnal pa). [1.] 瑜伽師 A Yogi (q. v.) who has mastered the theory and practice of ecstatic meditation (v. Yoga). [2.] 瑜伽部 or 遊迦部 or 大敎 [lit. Mahâ tantra). The Yoga or

Yogâtchârya or Tantra or Mahâtantra School, which claims Samantabhadra for its founder. The teaching of this School is derived from the Yoga system (a deistic branch of the Saṁkhya) of Patandjali [B. C. 200—150], who taught abstract meditation to be reached by means of moral consecration to Is'vara and mental concentration upon one point with a view to annihilate thought, whence would result the Achṭa Mahasiddhi (8 great powers of Siddhi), viz. the ability. [1.] to make one's body lighter (laghiman) or [2.] heavier (gariman), or [3.] smaller (animan) or [4.] larger (mahiman) than anything in the world, and [5.] to reach any place (prapti) or [6.] to assume any shape (prakamya), also [7.] to control all natural laws (is'atva) and [8.] to make everything depend upon oneself (vas'itva), all at pleasure of will (v. Riddhi). On this basis, but in harmony with the leading ideas of the Mahâyâna School, Asaṁgha compiled (A.D. 550) the mystic doctrines of his Yoga School, which taught that by means of mystic formularies (tantras) or litanies (dharaṇis) or spells (mantras), the reciting of which should be accompanied by music and certain distortions of the fingers (mudrâ), a state of mental fixity (samadhi) might be reached, characterized by there being neither thought nor annihilation of thoughts and consisting of sixfold bodily and mental happiness (yogi), whence would result endowment with supernatural miracle-working power. This Yoga (or Tantra or Mantra) system was made known in China (A.D. 647) by Hiuen-tsang's translation of the Yogâtchârya bhumi s'âstra (q.v.), on which basis Amoghavadjra (A.D. 720) established the Chinese branch of the Yoga School which was popularized chiefly by the labours of Vadjrabodhi (A.D. 732).

YOGÂTCHÂRYA BHÛMI S'ÂSTRA 瑜伽師地論 A work by Asaṁgha (derived from Maitreya), the textbook of the Yogâtchârya School, translated (A. D. 647) by Hiuen-tsang with a commentary by Djinaputra.

YOGI 瑜祇 (1.) A state of sixfold bodily and mental happiness as the result of fixity of ecstatic meditation. (2.) The devotee (s.a. Yogâtchârya) who has attained to that state and has therefore magic power.

YUGA (Tib. Dus) 世 lit. an age. The 1000th part of a Kalpa.

YUGAṀDHARA. (1.) 踰健達羅 or 踰(or 由)乾陀

or 陁羅 explained by 持雙山 lit. a mountain resting on a pair (yuga) sc. on Mêru and Tchakravâla, with the note, "its peak is perforated in two places." The 1st of the 7 concentric mountains which surround the Mêru (q. v.), 40,000 yodjanas high. (2.) 加持 lit. adding and holding, Name of a magic formula (tantra) of the Yoga School.

YÛKA 蝨 lit. a louse. The 7th part of a Yava.

END OF PART I.

PART II.

—:o:—

A PALI VOCABULARY.

[Note.—Those Pâli terms which coincide with their equivalents in Sanskrit are here, as in the whole work, omitted.]

END OF PART II.

PART III.

—:o:—

A SINGHALESE VOCABULARY.

[Note.—Those Singhalese terms which coincide with their equivalents in Pâli or Sanskrit are here, as in the whole work, omitted.]

END OF PART III.

PART IV.

—:o:—

A SIAMESE VOCABULARY.

END OF PART IV.

PART V.

—:o:—

A BURMESE VOCABULARY.

END OF PART V.

PART VI.

—:o:—

A TIBETAN VOCABULARY.

END OF PART VI.

PART VII.

—:o:—

A MONGOLIAN VOCABULARY.

END OF PART VII.

PART VII.

—:o:—

A JAPANESE VOCABULARY.

[Note.—The figures in the subjoined Vocabulary designate respectively the page, column, and paragraph to be found above. For instance, "Abadana, 23, a, 3" signifies that the Sanskrit and Chinese equivalents, for the Japanese term Abadana will be found explained above, on page 23, in the first column, in the 3rd paragraph, undor the heading Avadana.]

END OF PART VIII.

PART IX.

—:o:—

A CHINISE INDEX.

ARRANGED ACCORDING TO THE RADICALS.

A.

A KEY TO THE INDEX.

[NOTE.—THE FIGURES IN PARENTHESES REFER TO THE NUMBER OF THE STROKES OF EACH CHARACTER EXCEPT ITS RADICAL.]

RAD.

1 STR.

1. [一] 一 (1) 七, (2) 三 上下, (3) 不, (4) 世.

2. [丨] (3) 中.

3. [丶] (4) 主.

5. [乙] (1) 九, (2) 乞, (10) 乾.

6. [亅] (1) 了.

2 STR.

7. [二] (1) 于, (2) 互五, (6) 亞.

RAD.

9. [人 亻] 人 (2) 仁, (3) 他 仙, (4) 伊伏伐, (5) 伽低住佉何 佛作, (6) 侍供 依, (7) 信, (8) 修 俱倒, (9) 偈健 偷, (10)傿, (11)傳 傷, (12) 像僕僧, (13) 億, (15) 優.

10. [儿] (2) 元, (4) 光, (9) 兜.

11. [入] 入 (2) 內.

RAD.

12. 〔八〕八, (2) 六, (6) 具,
14. 〔冖〕(8) 冥.
15. 〔冫〕(9) 減.
17. 〔凵〕(3) 出.
18. 〔刀 刂〕(2) 分切, (5) 初刪別刼利, (6) 到制剎, (7) 前, (8) 剩.
19. 〔力〕力 (3) 功加, (5) 劬, (7) 勃勇, (8) 勒, (10) 勝, (11) 勤, (18) 勸.
20. 〔勹〕(2) 勿.
21. 〔匕〕(2) 化, (3) 北.
24. 〔十〕十 (1) 千, (3) 半, (4) 卍, (6) 卑, (7) 南, (10) 博.
25. 〔卜〕(3) 占.
26. 〔卩〕(4) 印.
27. 〔厂〕(12) 厭.
28. 〔厶〕(3) 去.
29. 〔又〕(6) 取受.

3 STR.

30. 〔口〕(2) 只叫可右, (3) 合吉名向, (4) 吠, (5) 周呪咽呵命呾和, (6) 哈, (8) 唯唵商啞, (9) 善喜喝喬, (10) 嗅嗔嗢, (11) 嘔, (12) 噌.

RAD.

31. 〔囗〕(2) 囘, (3) 回 (因) 四, (10) 圓.
32. 〔土〕土 (3) 地, (4) 坐, (8) 堅執堂, (9) 堪報, (10) 塔塗塡, (11) 塵, (12) 增隨壁, (16) 壤.
33. 〔士〕士 (11) 壽.
34. 〔夊〕(7) 夏.
36. 〔夕〕(2) 外, (3) 多, (5) 夜, (11) 夢.
37. 〔大〕大 (1) 天太, (2) 失, (5) 奇奈. (6) 契奔, (9) 奢.
38. 〔女〕女 (3) 好如, (4) 妙, (5) 姓, (6) 姞威, (7) 娑, (8) 婆, (10) 嫓嬰嫣.
39. 〔子〕子 (1) 孔, (4) 孛, (5) 孤, (7) 孫, (13)

RAD.

學.

40. [宀] (3) 守安宋, (5) 宗定, (6) 室, (7) 宮家, (8) 宿寂密富, (9) 寒, (10)
(19) 囊.
塞, (11) 實寠, (16) 寶.

41. [寸] (3) 寺, (9) 尊, (11) 對.

42. [小] 小 (1) 少.

43. [尸] 尸 (2) 尼, (5) 居屈, (6) 屍屏, (9) 屠.

45. [山] 山 (9) 嵐.

48. [工] (3) 巧, (7) 差.

49. [己] (1) 巴.

50. [巾] (2) 市布, (4) 希, (5) 帕, (6) 帝, (7) 師, (8) 常.

51. [干] (2) 平年.

52. [幺] (1) 幻, (2) 幼.

53. [广] (6) 度, (7) 庫, (8) 庶康, (12) 廟廣, (16) 廬.

54. [廴] (6) 建.

RAD.

56. [弋] (3) 式.

57. [弓] 弓 (1) 引, (2) 弗弘, (6) 弭, (7) 弱. (9) 强, (12) 彈, (13) 彊, (14) 彌.

59. [彡] (11) 彰, (12) 影.

60. [彳] (6) 律後, (7) 徒, (8) 得, (9) 循, (12) 德.

4 STR.

61. [心 忄] (2) 忉, (3) 忍志. (4) 念, (5) 怖怛思性, (6) 恒恭息, (7) 悅悉, (8) 悲惟惡, (9) 想愉意愛, (10) 愼慈, (11) 慢慕慧, (12) 憍憚, (13) 應, (16) 懿.

62. [戈] 戈 (2) 戍成, (3) 我戒, (13) 戰.

63. [戶] (4) 房所, (6) 扇,

64. [手 扌] 手 (4) 扭扶批抖, (5) 拆拔拘, (6) 持指, (7) 捕,

RAD.

(8) 捨捫捺授, (9) 提揭, (10) 搩. (11) 摩, (12) 撒撰, (13) 擇擔, (15) 擲攞, (17) 攘, (18) 攝.

65. [支] 支.

66. [攴] (4) 放, (7) 敎救, (11) 數.

67. [文] 文.

68. [斗] 斗 (7) 斛, (10) 斡.

69. [斤] (5) 斫, (8) 斯, (14) 斷.

70. [方] (4) 於, (5) 施, (6) 旆.

72. [日] 日 (4) 明昏昔, (5) 星昧, (6) 時, (8) 普智, (12) 曇.

73. [曰] (2) 曲, (3) 更, (5) 曷, (7) 曼, (8) 最, (10) 朅.

74. [月] 月 (2) 有.

75. [木] 木 (1) 未末本, (3) 李杖杜, (4) 東林, (5) 枸柔染柯柰, (6) 栗

RAD.

根案桑, (7) 梅條梨梵, (8) 棓棍, (9) 楞業極, (10) 槃, (11) 樂, (12) 樹橙, (13) 檀櫓, (14) 檳.

76. [欠] (7) 欲, (10) 歌, (18) 歡.

77. [止] 止 (1) 正, (2) 此, (3) 步, (9) 歲, (14) 歸.

78. [歹] (6) 殊, (7) 殑, (10) 殞殟.

79. [殳] (6) 殺.

80. [毋] 毋.

81. [比] 比 (5) 毗.

82. [毛] 毛.

85. [水] 氵 水 (2) 求, (3) 江, (4) 沉沒沙, (5) 河法波泥, (6) 洛洩洲活流, (7) 浮海涅, (8) 涷深清添, (9) 渴, (10) 準溼滅, (11) 滿漏演漕漚漢漸, (12) 澳, (13)

RAD.

5 STR.

RAD.

RAD.

6 STR.

118. 〔竹〕竹 (2) 竺, (5) 第筊, (6) 等答, (8) 箋, (9) 箭, (10) 篤, (13) 簸 簿.

119. 〔米〕(8) 精.

120. 〔糸〕(3) 紇, (4) 納 素索, (5) 細紺, (6) 結絡給, (7) 經, (8) 綫維緊, (9) 緣練, (10) 縛.

122. 〔罒〕(12) 罽, (14) 羅.

123. 〔羊〕羊 (3) 美, (7) 義, (9) 羯, (14) 羼.

124. 〔羽〕(11) 翳.

125. 〔老〕老 (4) 耆.

126. 〔而〕(3) 耐.

127. 〔耒〕(10) 耨.

128. 〔耳〕(3) 耶 (7) 聖, (8) 聚聞, (11) 聲.

129. 〔聿〕聿.

130. 〔肉〕肉 (5) 胎胡, (6) 能脂脅, (13) 臂, (15) 臘.

132. 〔自〕自.

RAD.

133. 〔至〕至.

134. 〔臼〕(9) 與, (12) 舊.

135. 〔舌〕舌 (2) 舍.

136. 〔舛〕(6) 舜.

137. 〔舟〕(4) 般, (5) 船.

139. 〔色〕色.

140. 〔艸〕艹 (4) 芥芬花芳, (5) 苑若苦英苫 茲茂茆, (6) 荅草, (7) 莊莎莫, (8) 菩萃菴, (9) 落葉葛, (10) 蒻, (11) 蓮蔣蔑, (13) 薄薛薩, (14) 藍藏, (15) 藥藪, (16) 藿蘇, (17) 蘭.

141. 〔虍〕虍 (5) 處虛, (7) 號.

142. 〔虫〕(4) 蚊, (5) 蛇, (8) 蜜, (9) 蝨, (12) 蟒蟣.

143. 〔血〕血 (6) 衆.

144. 〔行〕行 (5) 術, (10) 衞衡.

145. 〔衣〕衤 (5) 袈被, (7) 裙補, (9) 褐, (17)

RAD.

襪.

146. 〔西〕西 (12) 覆,

7 STR.

147. 〔見〕見 (5) 視, (9) 覩親, (13) 覺, (18) 觀.

148. 〔角〕角 (6) 解, (13) 觸.

149. 〔言〕(3) 訖記, (4) 設, (5) 訶詞, (6) 試, (7) 說, (8) 調論, (9) 諸諾, (11) 謨, (12) 識, (13) 譫譬, (14) 護, (19) 讚.

150. 〔谷〕(10) 豁.

151. 〔豆〕豆 (11) 豐.

152. 〔豕〕(5) 象.

154. 〔貝〕(3) 財, (4) 貨貪, (5) 貯買, (7) 賒, (8) 賢質, (9) 賴, (13) 贍.

155. 〔赤〕赤 (9) 赭.

156. 〔走〕(5) 超越.

157. 〔足〕(5) 跋跏, (6) 路, (9) 踰, (10) 蹈.

RAD.

158. 〔身〕身.

159. 〔車〕車 (2) 軌軍, (8) 輪, (9) 輸, (11) 轉.

160. 〔辛〕(6) 辟, (9) 辨, (14) 辯.

161. 〔辰〕辰 (3) 辱, (6) 農.

162. 〔辵 ⻌〕(4) 近, (5) 迦, (6) 逆, (7) 途通連逝, (9) 遊遍道達, (11) 遮遷, (14) 邊.

163. 〔邑 阝〕(4) 邠那邪, (8) 部, (9) 都, (12) 鄧,

164. 〔酉〕(10) 醜, (11) 醫. (12) 醮醯.

165. 〔釆〕(13) 釋.

166. 〔里〕(2) 重, (4) 野, (5) 量.

8 STR.

167. 〔金〕金 (5) 鉢, (6) 銀銅銖, (7) 鋪, (8) 錫, (14) 鑊, (15) 鑠.

RAD.

168. 〔長〕長.

166. 〔門〕門 (3) 閉, (7) 閱, (8) 閻, (9) 闊闍, (12) 闡, (13) 闢.

170. 〔阜 阝〕(5) 阿陀陁, (7) 除, (8) 陰陳, (9) 陽, (10) 隙, (11) 障, (13) 隨.

172. 〔隹〕(4) 集, (10) 雙 雜, (11) 離難.

173. 〔雨〕雨 (3) 雪, (4) 雲, (7) 震, (8) 霍, (11) 霫, (12) 露, (16) 靈.

174. 〔靑〕靑.

175. 〔非〕非.

9 STR.

177. 〔革〕(8) 鞞鞠, (9) 鞫.

178. 〔韋〕韋 (8) 韓.

180. 〔音〕音 (13) 響.

181. 〔頁〕(2) 頂, (3) 順須, (4) 煩, (5) 頗, (6) 頞頡, (7) 頭頻, (10) 願, (13) 纇, (14) 顯.

RAD.

182. 〔風〕(5) 颯颰.

184. 〔食〕食 (4) 飲, (7) 餓, (12) 饒.

185. 〔首〕首.

186. 〔香〕香 (5) 馝.

10 STR.

187. 〔馬〕馬 (4) 馱, (13) 驗, (16) 驢.

188. 〔骨〕骨 (8) 髀, (11) 髏, (13) 體.

189. 〔高〕高.

191. 〔鬥〕(10) 鬪.

192. 〔鬯〕(19) 鬱.

194. 〔鬼〕鬼 (10) 魔.

11 STR.

195. 〔魚〕魚 (9) 鰐, (12) 鱓.

196. 〔鳥〕(2) 鳩, (4) 鳫, (5) 鴦, (6) 鴿, (11) 鶴鵑雞, (12) 鷲, (17) 鸚.

198. 〔鹿〕鹿.

199. 〔麥〕麥.

RAD.

12 STR.

201. 〔黃〕黃.
202. 〔黍〕(3) 黎.
203. 〔黑〕黑 (5) 黛.

14-17 STR.

209. 〔鼻〕鼻.

RAD.

211. 〔齒〕齒.
212. 〔龍〕龍.
213. 〔龜〕龜.

B.

INDEX.

[NOTE.—EACH CHINESE WORD OR PHRASE IS TO BE LOOKED FOR UNDER THE RADICAL TO WHICH ITS *FIRST* CHARACTER BELONGS. THE NUMBERS REFER TO THE NUMBER OF EACH PAGE. *a*, SIGNIFYING THE FIRST, *b* THE SECOND COLUMN.]

一 RAD. 1.

丨 RAD. 2.

丶 RAD. 3.

乙 RAD. 5.

亅 RAD. 6.

二 RAD. 7.

人 RAD. 9.

儿 RAD. 10.

入 RAD. 11.

八 RAD. 12.

—

冖 RAD. 14.

—

冫 RAD. 15.

凵 RAD. 17.

—

刀(刂) RAD. 18.

力 RAD. 19.

勹 RAD. 20.

匕 RAD. 21.

十 RAD. 24.

卜 RAD. 25.

卩 RAD. 26.

厂 RAD. 27.

厶 RAD. 28.

又 RAD. 29.

口 RAD. 30.

囗 RAD. 31.

土 RAD. 32.

—

士 RAD. 33.

—

夊 RAD. 34.

—

夕 RAD. 36.

—

大 RAD. 37.

女 RAD. 38.

—

子 RAD. 39.

—

宀 RAD. 40.

寸 RAD. 41.

小 RAD. 42.

尸 RAD. 43.

山 RAD. 45.

工 RAD. 48.

己 RAD. 49.

—

巾 RAD. 50.

—

干 RAD. 51.

—

幺 RAD. 52.

—

广 RAD. 53.

廴 RAD. 54.

弋 RAD. 56.

弓 RAD. 57.

彡 RAD. 59.

彳 RAD. 60.

心 忄 RAD. 61.

戈 RAD. 62.

戸 RAD. 63.

手 RAD. 64.

—

支 RAD. 65.

—

攴 RAD. 66.

文 RAD. 67.

斗 RAD. 68.

斤 RAD. 69.

方 RAD. 70.

日 RAD. 72.

日 RAD. 73.

—

月 RAD. 74.

—

木 RAD. 75.

欠 RAD. 76.

止 RAD. 77.

—

歹 RAD. 78.

—

殳 RAD. 79.

—

毋 RAD. 80.

—

比 RAD. 81.

毛 RAD. 82.

水 RAD. 85.

火 RAD. 86.

牛 RAD. 93.
牜

犬 RAD. 94.
犭

玄 RAD. 95.

玉(王) RAD. 97.

瓦 RAD. 98.

甘 RAD. 99.

生 RAD. 100.

田 RAD. 102.

疋 RAD. 103.

疒 RAD. 104.

癶 RAD. 105.

白 RAD. 106.

皿 RAD. 108.

目 RAD. 109.

矢 RAD. 111.

石 RAD. 112.

—

示 RAD. 113.

礻

—

禾 RAD. 115.

—

穴 RAD. 116.

——

立 RAD. 117.

——

竹 RAD. 118.

网(罒) RAD. 122.

羊 RAD. 123.

羽 RAD. 124.

肉 RAD. 130.

自 RAD. 132.

至 RAD. 133.

臼 RAD. 134.

舌 RAD. 135.

—

舛 RAD. 136.

—

舟 RAD. 137.

—

色 RAD. 139.

—

艸 RAD. 140.

——

虍 RAD. 141.

——

虫 RAD. 142.

——

血 RAD. 143.

角 RAD. 148.

言 RAD. 149.

谷 RAD. 150.

豆 RAD. 151.

—

豕 RAD. 152.

—

貝 RAD. 154.

—

赤 RAD. 155.

—

走 RAD. 156.

足 RAD. 157.

身 RAD. 158.

車 RAD. 159.

辛 RAD. 160.

辰 RAD. 161.

辵 ⻍ RAD. 162.

邑 ⻏ RAD. 163.

酉 RAD. 164.

釆 RAD. 165.

里 RAD. 166.

金 RAD. 167.

長 RAD. 168.

門 RAD. 169.

阜 阝 RAD. 170.

隹 RAD. 172.

雨 RAD. 173.

青 RAD. 174.

非 RAD. 175.

—

革 RAD. 177.

—

韋 RAD. 178.

—

音 RAD. 180.

—

頁 RAD. 181.

風 RAD. 182.

食 RAD. 184.

首 RAD. 185.

香 RAD. 186.

馬 RAD. 187.

骨 RAD. 188.

高 RAD. 189.

鬥 RAD. 191.

鬯 RAD. 192.

鬼 RAD. 194.

魚 RAD. 195.

鳥 RAD. 196.

鹿 RAD. 198.

麥 RAD. 199.

黃 RAD. 201.

黍 RAD. 202.

黑 RAD. 203.

鼻 RAD. 209.

齒 RAD. 211.

龍 RAD. 212.

龜 RAD. 213.